PLANTING DESIGN FOR DRY GARDENS

Among all those who helped me with this book I should like to express particular thanks to the following:

James Aronson and Jacques Tassin for their contribution to the reflections on invasive plants;

Aïté Bresson whose criticisms and suggestions were of great value during the writing of this book;

And Clara, who was not only the first person to read through the various different versions of the manuscript but who above all shared in the research and the botanical expeditions that inspired this book.

All the photographs and illustrations are by the author with the exception of: page 16 (left) © RMN (Domaine de Chantilly)/René-Gabriel Ojéda; page 16 (right) © RMN/ Franck Raux.

NOTE: Throughout the text "Mediterranean" with a capital M refers to the Mediterranean Sea, the countries around it and their plants, while "mediterranean" with a lower case m refers to the climate, other parts of the world that share this climate, and their plants. Thus "mediterranean gardens/gardeners" refers not only to those in the Mediterranean Basin but also to those in, for example, California or southern Australia.

Copyright © 2011 Actes Sud
Olivier Filippi: Alternatives au Gazon

© Actes Sud, Le Mejan, place Nina-Berberova, 13200 Arles

English language edition copyright © 2016 by Filbert Press.
All rights reserved.

Published in 2016 by Filbert Press

filbertpress.com

Printed in China

ISBN 978-0-99338-920-7

A catalogue record for this book is available from the British Library.

Cover photograph
In our experimental garden, cushion-shaped plants, carpeting plants and gravel paths offer a lawn alternative which is tolerant of drought and easy to maintain.

PLANTING DESIGN FOR DRY GARDENS

Beautiful, resilient groundcovers for terraces,
paved areas, gravel and other alternatives to the lawn

Olivier Filippi

Translated by
Caroline Harbouri

filbert press

CONTENTS

PREFACE

Many gardeners dream of the perfect lawn. This is understandable because lawns are so easy to establish and within weeks transform a nondescript piece of land into an oasis of green. But maintaining a beautiful lawn in a dry-climate region demands an inordinate amount of maintenance in return for what is often a disappointing result.

So what alternatives are there for gardens where lawns struggle to survive? My wife Clara and I have been researching lawn alternatives for over 20 years and during the course of our botanical travels, we have studied natural or semi-natural groundcovers throughout the mediterranean regions of the world. In our own experimental garden we have then observed how these groundcovers perform as lawn alternatives. In this book, we share our experiences in the hope that gardeners will give up their lawns in favour of other solutions that are better adapted to their local climate conditions.

This book is divided into four sections. In the first section, I suggest groundcovers as a new approach to managing space in gardens and public spaces. In the second section, I look closely at the various lawn alternatives that we have been able to test, noting their pros and cons. The third part of the book deals with all the practical aspects of creating a groundcover garden: preparing the ground, planting, watering and maintenance. Finally, in the fourth section, I describe a wide range of plants which can be used in the different areas of a groundcover garden, specifying where and how to use them in order to reduce both watering and maintenance.

This book is addressed primarily to gardeners in mediterranean climates but also to gardeners in other climates who wish to reduce the maintenance demands of a lawn. Some of the groundcover plants are adapted only to gardens in summer-dry climates, but others are suited to all regions. In the pages that follow I shall clarify whether or not the plants and techniques I discuss are suitable for different climates and soil conditions.

Lawns are now so ubiquitous that they run the risk of making our gardens bland and monotonous. Finding ways to replace them with something else, wherever you live, is a decisive move against this dreary uniformity. I hope that by showing the huge range of lawn alternatives, I shall encourage gardeners to broaden their horizons and, freed from the constraints of the lawn, create gardens that are open to possibility.

LAWNS AND GROUNDCOVER PLANTS

THE HISTORY OF LAWNS AND RISE OF ALTERNATIVES

During the last few decades lawns have invaded Mediterranean gardens. They have spread over green spaces in the South of France, Italy, Greece and Spain. They surround swimming pools in new garden plots and insinuate themselves into the patios of old houses. The ubiquitous green carpet is to be found in front of the Acropolis Museum in Athens and on the promenade of the Prado in Madrid. Palm trees float in a sea of green in Nice, while in Almeria, the driest region of Spain, lawns cover the ground around ancient olive trees to attract tourists.

From the north of Europe to the south, and indeed in other parts of the world, the English garden model has become rooted in our collective unconscious as a symbol of happiness. In Wales and Ireland, magnificent lawns flourish apparently unaided, thanks to the regular rainfall. By contrast, in gardens in summer-dry regions a lawn can survive only at the cost of unending battles. Maintaining a beautiful green carpet in mediterranean-climate gardens requires copious watering in summer. The drier the climate, the higher the lawn's water consumption: in Montpellier or Marseilles a lawn needs almost 1,000 litres of water per square metre per year; in Andalucia or the Peloponnese, where the dryness is more intense, it needs more than 2,000 litres per square metre per year.

But it is not only water that a lawn requires. The grass species traditionally used for lawns are particularly greedy for nitrogen: so in order for them to form a dense carpet that is always green they need a regular application of fertilizer.

When you sow your first lawn you cannot imagine how demanding in terms of time and effort it will prove to be. The provision of water and fertilizer necessary for the lawn to survive, combined with the generous sunlight of the mediterranean climate, stimulates excessive growth. Watering, fertilizing, mowing: the mediterranean gardener is drawn into a cycle which comes close to the absurd despite his best intentions. Then on Sundays there's an urgent need to mow what he's done his utmost to grow during the week.

In the garden centres of southern Europe the array of products for the lawn is impressive: grass seed, fertilizers, weed-killers, treatments, irrigation equipment, not to mention dozens of lawn mowers from the simplest hand-pushed mower to the powerful ride-on machines. A gardener who has recently moved to a dry-climate region might well assume that lawns have always been an integral part of mediterranean gardens, and that these modern products represent welcome technological progress to lighten the ancestral task of maintaining a greensward. Nothing could be further from the truth. The lawn as we know it is a very recent invention.

For thousands of years magnificent gardens were created around the Mediterranean Sea without a lawn in sight. Lawns were unheard of in the gardens of Mesopotamia and Egypt, and non-existent in Roman and Islamic gardens – all places where the way of life is built around a respect for the relationship between man and nature. Looking at lawns from a historical perspective enables us to realize that the

1   2

Page 8
Tanacetum, Ipheion, Dorycnium and euphorbias colonize the gaps between paving stones on a green terrace. (Design by Pascal Cribier and Lionel Guibert for the Château Le Plaisir, Gard, France.)

Facing page
The garden of the Generalife, Granada.

1. In Wales and Ireland magnificent lawns flourish apparently unaided, thanks to the regular rainfall.

2. In Montpellier or Marseilles, watering a lawn requires almost 1,000 litres per square metre per year.

quest for a perfect lawn arises from a recent cultural context, which may indeed already be obsolete. With its high demands for water, an even carpet of lawn is unsuitable for mediterranean climates. It is a model which appeared relatively recently and nothing obliges us to follow it in the mediterranean gardens of the future.

Groundcover in the first gardens of the Western world

If there were no lawns, what covered the ground in the gardens of the past? Several centuries before the modern era, the first gardens in Persia were called *pairidaiza*, 'walled enclosures', from which is derived the Greek word *paradeisos*, and then our word 'paradise'. The paradise-garden, originally simply a hunting preserve protected from the outside world by walls, evolved into a refined place in which plantations of fruit trees and ornamental plants invited repose and sensual pleasure. A characteristic element is that the garden was not conceived of as simply a surface plane *on*

which one walked, but rather as a space made three-dimensional by the density of the planting *into* which one entered. The arrangement of the paths, which allowed one to move through the garden, corresponded to a symbolic organization of space and followed a geometric plan which was to inspire garden models for many centuries.

Following this Persian garden plan, the first Islamic gardens were divided into four planting areas by paths that converged in the centre at a pool. Whether plant or mineral, the choice of materials used to cover the ground demonstrates the particular care taken. Terraces, paths and steps express all the gardeners' skill. The diversity of the paving, the varied placing of terracotta tiles and the patterns created by cobbles, with tightly packed stones or pebbles placed vertically, transformed popular methods of covering the ground into works of art. On either side of these paths the beds contained species chosen for their flowers, their fruits, their foliage or their

scent: jasmine, damask roses, almond trees, citrons, pomegranates, figs, myrtle and oleander. Between the trees the ground was covered by a variety of low-growing or carpeting plants, prefiguring groundcover gardens: narcissus, violets, lavender, irises, acanthus, thyme, oregano, chamomile and clover. Clover, whose amazing qualities we are rediscovering today, was already appreciated as a flowering groundcover beneath fruit trees. Babur, the founder of the Moghul Dynasty, mentions it in his memoirs, in which he describes with pride the gardens he created. He lingers on the beauty of his garden in Kabul, the "Garden of Fidelity", where the pool was surrounded by pomegranates and orange trees set off by the carpet of clover which covered the soil.

Water was everywhere in the first gardens of the Mediterranean but sprinklers, of course, were unheard of. On the contrary, water was carefully channelled to feed pools and fountains, from which a network of rills allowed the traditional gravity-fed irrigation. The water was concentrated around the plants which needed it, for example citrus trees, by means of broad watering basins. The Mediterranean technique of gravity-fed irrigation allows deep watering at widely spaced intervals: it is not suited to the daily watering of a lawn. Water was always used frugally for it had to be raised from a river, a well or an underground cistern before it could be directed to the watering basins. Depending on the region, different methods of raising water were used. In Cordoba, the huge paddle-wheel which supplied water to the gardens of the Alcazar can still be seen beside the

Guadalquivir. In ancient Egypt, the *chadouf* technique, still employed today on the banks of the Nile, was used to irrigate the gardens of the New Empire: a long beam weighted with a clay counterpoise reduces the effort required to lift a bucket of water, which is then emptied into the irrigation channels. In Syria, along the River Orontes one can still see the magnificent norias used to raise water in order to irrigate the gardens that lined the river banks. According to legend, water for the Hanging Gardens of Babylon was raised from terrace to terrace using Archimedes screws, in other words constantly turning screws encased in cylindrical shafts, worked by slaves. Water was thus far too precious to be devoted to the surface irrigation of a lawn. In the great gardens which have marked the history of the Mediterranean the very idea of a lawn is meaningless. What is more, for long centuries the word 'lawn' quite simply didn't exist.

The first grass surfaces

One of the earliest references to the use of a grassy surface comes from the early Middle Ages. In about the year 800, Charlemagne decreed in his *Capitulare de villis* that monasteries must cultivate 94 plants, including medicinal or seasoning herbs, fruit trees, and plants used for textiles and dyes. Reflecting the strict organization of monastic life, the square or rectangular beds in which these plants were grown were regularly aligned to form a chequerboard plan. They were raised by planks or wattles to ensure good drainage and their dimensions were calculated so that half their width was equivalent to the length of a man's arm, in order

1. Overflowing with pomegranates, fig trees, olives and date palms, the gardens at the oasis of Palmyra in Syria allow us to imagine what the first paradise gardens of antiquity must have looked like.

2. The geometric layout of Persian gardens was a model for gardens for many centuries, such as here in the cloister of the San Juan de los Reyes monastery in Toledo.

1. A pool and fountain in the gardens of the Generalife, Granada. Water was present everywhere in the first Mediterranean gardens, but it was never used with a sprinkler to water lawns.

2. Ancient norias (waterwheels) line the banks of the River Orontes in Syria, some of which are still used to irrigate gardens on either side of the river.

3. The orange tree courtyard, or *Patio de los Naranjos*, in Cordoba. The Mediterranean gravity-fed irrigation technique allows deep watering at periodic intervals and is not suitable for the daily watering of a lawn.

The early form of the word lawn in English was "launde", meaning untilled land or wasteland. We find it used in this sense in the Middle English allegorical poem *Piers Plowman*, written towards the end of the 14th century. (It is worth noting that this meaning is preserved in the modern French word *lande*, denoting heathland.) By the 16th century the final d had been dropped and the meaning had changed, the word now signifying a woodland glade: in 1548 Elyot writes of "a place voyde of trees, as a laune in a parke or forrest". This meaning continued to apply for centuries. In Milton's *On the Morning of Christ's Nativity, Compos'd 1629* the phrase "The Shepherds on the Lawn […] Sate simply chatting in a rustick row" certainly doesn't refer to what we call a lawn today. William Morris also used the modern spelling for the old meaning when he wrote in 1876 "She came where the lawn of the woods lay wide in the flood of light". But by the end of the 19th century, the word lawn was already acquiring its modern meaning of "a flat and usually level area of mown and cultivated grass". In 1877, barely a year after William Morris wrote, The All England Croquet Club changed its name to The All England Croquet and Lawn Tennis Club.

In French, the meaning of the word *gazon* (now meaning "lawn") has also evolved over the centuries. It derives from the Old French word *wason* (first recorded in 1178), which in turn comes from the Frankish *waso*, signifying a sod of earth covered in grass. It was used as a legal term in transactions during the Gallo-Roman period: a sod of earth and a pair of gloves were offered when land changed hands.

By the end of the 14th century, by extension, the word *gazon* had come to mean not only the sod of earth covered with grass but the grass itself. It wasn't until the 18th century that *gazon* took on the meaning of "a surface covered in grass". Thus, when Louis XIV and André Le Nôtre designed in the Park of Versailles one of the first large lawns in the history of gardening, a vast green rectangle which emphasised the perspective of the Grand Canal, what they called it was a *tapis vert*, or "green carpet", since the word *gazon* had not yet acquired its current meaning.

In other Mediterranean languages we find the same evolution of meaning. In Spain lawns appeared much later than in France. Until the end of the 19th century the word *césped* meant a sod of earth covered in grass; it wasn't until 1899 that *césped* took on the meaning of "a surface covered in short, dense grass" with the first mention of *césped inglés* (an "English lawn"). When the first lawns were imported into Greece from France, the word for them was imported too, underlining the curious and exotic character of this strange green surface which had exploded into the landscape: the Greek word for lawn is γκαζόν, pronounced 'gazon' with the final n sounded. Lawns didn't become common in Greece, however, until the second half of the 20th century with the increased spread of water distribution networks in urban areas: the word γκαζόν first appeared in Modern Greek dictionaries in the 1960s. Similarly, in Portugal the word *gazão* derives directly from the French *gazon*.

In English the general word "grass" is widely used as an alternative to "lawn": we talk quite comfortably of sitting on, lying on or cutting the grass. The French word *pelouse* can also mean a surface covered in grass or a lawn, the two words *pelouse* and *gazon* being used almost interchangeably. We find this same double meaning of words equivalent to *grass* and *pelouse* in other languages too: for example in Turkish with the word *çimen*, in Portuguese with the word *relva*, in Italian with the word *prato*, in Arabic with the word مرج, *marj* and in Hebrew with the word דשא, *deshe*, which can signify both a lawn and a natural grassy expanse (*deshe* is used in the Bible to mean a simple expanse of green – Genesis 1, verses 11-12). But the French word *pelouse* has a broader meaning: to ecologists it signifies a stable formation comprising a wide cortège of herbaceous species: what in English is called a grassland.

In this book I shall use the words "lawn" or "conventional lawn" for the modern lawn composed of grass species such as English rye-grass, and the words "mixed lawn" or "wild lawn" to designate more diversified surfaces, such as mixed grassy areas including clover, daisies, plantains, self-heal and many other annual or perennial species.

1. The medieval orchard was thought of as a good place for lovers' trysts. In it were found raised turf benches, one of the first uses of grass surfaces in gardening history. (*Le Rustican* or *Livre des proffitz champestres et ruraulx par Pietro de' Crescenzi,* 15th century).

2. The series of tapestries known as The Lady and the Unicorn (La *Dame à la licorne*), today in the Musée de Cluny in Paris, show a medieval garden in which the ground is covered by a greensward or meadow studded with a multitude of flowers.

titude of flowers and bulbs. The *Dame à la licorne* tapestries depict a medieval garden and show a flowering greensward in which are mingled wild orchids, columbines, gillyflowers, jonquils, lilies, daisies, lily of the valley, pinks, periwinkles, violets, pot marigolds and primroses.

The use of grass to cover large areas first appeared in French gardens. In the gardens of the Chateau of Vaux-le-Vicomte the landscape architect André Le Nôtre used grass and clipped edging to create the complex design of his patterned parterres. In 1680, during the third expansion of the park of Versailles, Louis XIV had a long band of grass made on the axis of the Grand Canal in order to draw the eye towards the Apollo fountain, the principal point at which the park's perspectives converge. Of course, Louis XIV's grassy surface was very different from a modern lawn. It was called at

to make hand-weeding easier. These beds were separated by paths, which, according to the region, could be of beaten earth, stone or sometimes grass.

When attached to a manorial demesne, medieval orchards were used as places to walk in or for lovers' meetings. In them were to be found raised benches constructed of turf and covered in grass, forming green seats. These benches were seen in gardens where the climate was damp enough to keep the grass green throughout the year, and their limited surface area, of only a few square metres, meant that this grass could easily be cut to keep it low. The orchard itself was covered in grass or meadow, studded with a mul-

that time a 'green carpet', for the word 'lawn' in its current sense of 'a surface covered in grass' did not then exist; it was to appear a little later. At Versailles the green carpet was a simple meadow kept low by frequent scything. It consisted of a mixture of grasses accompanied by their natural floral companions: yarrows, clover, bird's foot trefoil, dandelions, dead-nettles, daisies, plantains, speedwells and self-heal. The frequent scything required in order to keep the grass low and even necessitated an extremely large workforce; hence in the time of Louis XIV an expanse of grass was a luxury to be found only in the gardens of chateaux.

In contrast to the formal style of French gardens, a new landscape aesthetic arose in England in the eighteenth century. Inspired by Romantic poetry and painting, it sought to recreate in gardens an idealised view of nature. Here, for the first time in garden history, grassy surfaces played a major part: they formed the link between the areas of the garden immediately adjacent to the house and the more distant perspective of the undulating landscape, punctuated with lakes and planted with copses of trees, whose purpose – although it was entirely man-made – was to imitate a natural landscape. The use of grass, made possible by the frequent rainfall and relatively mild temperatures of the English climate, was now applied to enormous areas. A technical artifice, the ha-ha, made it possible to maintain these large expanses of grass without the need for manual scything becoming excessive. A ha-ha is an invisible barrier separating a small area of grass around the house, whose limited dimensions make hand-scything feasible, from the huge stretches of grass fading into the distance where sheep and cattle are grazed to keep the grass short; it consists of a deep ditch, one of whose sides is vertical to prevent animals from crossing it. The levels of the grass around the house and of the surrounding pastures are adjusted so that the ha-ha is completely invisible to anyone walking in the gar-

The use of grass to cover the ground on a large scale first appeared in French gardens. In 1680, during the third expansion of the Park of Versailles, the landscape architect André Le Nôtre created for Louis XIV a "green carpet" to draw the eye along the axis of the Grand Canal. During this period, expanses of grass were found only in the gardens of chateaux because scything them by hand required a large workforce.

den, giving the illusion of perfect continuity between the scythed grass in the garden around the house and the long perspective of grazed meadows. Visitors invited to stroll in the garden would thus come upon this deep ditch suddenly, at which they'd exclaim "Ha!" in surprise, hence the word ha-ha. In France in the 17th century the name originally given to such ditches was *saut-de-loup*, or 'wolf's leap'.

When lawns became an obsession

The romantic landscape garden, whose ground is covered by a great expanse of green grass, became the dominant model for the vast estates of the British aristocracy in the 18th century. This model was copied in the United States by various aristocratic landowners inspired by the landscape art of Europe. George Washington, the first President of the United States, called upon the help of English gardeners to create a romantic garden at his Mount Vernon estate, where he had a ha-ha dug to separate the grassy area around the house from the distant pastures. In spite of its small area, however, the maintenance of the grass around his house posed great problems, until Washington solved them by installing kid goats to graze it. In fact until the 19th century, the need for manual scything remained the major limiting factor for maintaining grassy surfaces.

With the Industrial Revolution, the great story of the lawn left Europe and took off well and truly in North America. The first patent for a lawn mower was registered in the United States in 1868, following the invention of a mower in England by an engineer named Edwin Budding. Although his machine was a heavy manual mower with a spiral

The first lawn mower was invented in the 19th century by an English engineer, Edwin Budding. Although this was a heavy machine and awkward to handle, the invention of the lawn mower opened the way to a democratization of the lawn, first in England and then in the United States.

blade, unwieldy and hard to handle, the invention of the lawn mower opened the way to the democratization of the lawn. Having long been the preserve of the estates of the richest families, it now became a symbol of the social rise of middle-class families who were beginning to live outside towns. At the end of the 19th century an impressive steam-powered lawn mower was invented, and in 1919 a motor-driven mower. At the time when Ford was launching his Model T, Americans were enthusiastic about motorized tools and the motor-driven lawn mower was a spectacular success. The development of lawn mowers is a good measure of the way lawns became popular in the United States in only a few decades. At the end of the Second World War about 140,000 lawn movers per year were sold in the United States. Annual sales then rose dizzyingly to reach a million in 1950, four million in 1962, then up to seven million in 1974. Meanwhile, for North Americans the lawn had come to mean much more than a simple gardening activity, a means of relaxation or a leisure pursuit. It had become a symbol of integration, of respectability and of good neighbourliness, to the point where it turned into a national obsession. In entire neighbourhoods, lawns formed a continuous carpet from garden to garden. They became a source of rivalry between gardeners, involving hard work every weekend in the attempt to achieve a perfect lawn, if possible the finest in the neighbourhood. Regardless of the climate zone, from the East Coast to the West Coast of the USA garden lawns became almost obligatory. In some counties you can now be fined if you don't mow your lawn to the prescribed height.

A new standard of quality

The concept of a 'lawn' evolved over the course of the years. Until the Second World War, a lawn was a green expanse composed of a broad palette of plant species, mown fairly regularly. As well as grasses, it also included a great many weeds whose habit of growth as ground-hugging rosettes had evolved as an adaptation to grazing, enabling them equally to survive the blades of a lawn mower. However, after the end of the Second World War standards for lawns evolved rapidly. Chemical fertilizers and selective herbicides originally developed for intensive agriculture started to appear on the gardening market. Advertisements for lawns encouraged gardeners to seek to achieve a carpet as smooth

as velvet, composed of a restricted palette of grass species, carefully mown very short and maintaining a fine uniform colour throughout the year.

To help gardeners keep their lawns bright green in all seasons, a paint for lawns went on sale in the United States in the 1950s. It was welcomed as a miracle product: when the lawn naturally went dormant in winter, or when it was suffering from a temporary lack of water in summer, all that was necessary to make it once more a sumptuous emerald green was to spray-paint it. In 1965 the first synthetic grass appeared in America as a solution for covering large areas. It was promoted as a means of simplifying the gardener's life: no more mowing, no more watering, no more fertilizing – just the pleasure of a lawn without its inconveniences. Unfortunately, in the warm regions of the South-West of the United States synthetic lawn exposed to the sun becomes so burning hot that it can't be used during the day – unless, that is, you water it to cool it down.

From the 1980s onwards, more and more American gardeners who no longer had the time to take care of their front yards consigned the maintenance of their lawns to specialist firms known as "Mow & Blow"; once a week these companies send a team to look after a whole neighbourhood, moving from garden to garden to mow, blow away debris, apply fertilizer and treat the lawns. These lawns are then dotted with mandatory small flags, informing people that the grass has been treated with dangerous chemical products and that access to it is temporarily prohibited.

During this period, lawns in Europe advanced more modestly. At the end of the 19th century, as holiday homes and the first building developments took off, lawns became more widespread in temperate-climate gardens. However, they had difficulty advancing to the South, where the climate conditions were unsuitable for them. In their large properties on the Côte d'Azur wealthy English people created famous gardens, focusing their efforts in the 19th century on the acclimatization of exotic plants made possible by the mild winter temperatures. It was too hot and too dry for lawns to survive in summer, yet, despite this, some English people prided themselves on possessing a carpet of green in their Mediterranean gardens. In her book on the history of Serre de la Madone, a garden near Menton, Louisa Jones explains how they managed it. Every autumn they laid squares of turf, imported from England, to allow calm enjoyment of the lawn during the damp season. Then in summer they abandoned it completely, leaving it to dry out in the sun until autumn, when the ground was dug over and the lawn recreated with a new set of turves freshly imported from England.

It was only during the second half of the 20th century that lawns really became part of gardens in the Mediterranean. In the 1970s the technique of automatic irrigation spread everywhere, to the point where the installation of such a system was considered an obligatory stage in the creation of a dry-climate garden. Now, even before deciding what they are going to plant, people install a drip irrigation system and a sprinkler system just to be on the safe side, thus instantly

1. The idea of "the lawn" changed over time. It was not until after the Second World War, with the advent of chemical fertilizers and herbicides, that the lawn evolved into a uniform carpet composed entirely of grass species.

2. In mediterranean gardens artificial lawns can become so burning hot in summer that they have to be watered copiously to cool them down.

ruling out the countless Mediterranean species which cannot survive summer watering. Professional gardeners have turned into plumbers and throughout the whole of southern Europe, gardens and public spaces have been overrun by lawns. Some geographers speak of the 'Mcdonaldization' of the landscape, a turn of events with a certain justice to it: lawns ventured out from Europe to conquer the aristocratic gardens of the United States, then returned in force a couple of centuries later, borne on the vision of a standardized environment which is transmitted through American television serials.

But the history of the lawn isn't over yet. At the end of the 20th century, the pace of technical innovation accelerated. In 2000 the Scotts and Monsanto companies presented a transgenic lawn variety named Roundup Ready®, currently awaiting endorsement by the USDA, the American body which authorizes the marketing of products. It is a variety of lawn grass modified by the insertion of a gene conferring resistance to glyphosate, a broad-spectrum herbicide able to kill all plants indiscriminately. After four thousand years of gardening in the West, what is now being presented is the culmination of the quest for a perfect lawn: spray the entire garden with glyphosate, so that all that remains will be a single-species carpet free from weeds once and for all.

The emergence of an anti-lawn movement

If lawns reached their apogee in the United States in the 20th century, it was also in the United States that the first anti-lawn movements came into being. The American journalist Michael Pollan sees in the American obsession with lawns a fear of death and a sexual taboo. What is created is a landscape which is green at all seasons, where the natural cycle never reaches maturity – no flowers, no seeds – a fixed, static and smooth environment which has no sexuality and never grows old. Numerous voices have been raised to protest against an outdated social constraint which is less and less acceptable to the younger generation of gardeners. In the South-West states of the USA, water authorities are becoming worried by the excessive water consumption linked to the irrigation of lawns. In the urban zones of Southern California almost 60% of the total water consumption is used on lawns alone. In Las Vegas, a major programme to subsidize the removal of lawns was set up in 1999: gardeners receive 15 dollars for each square metre of lawn that they replace with water-wise groundcovers. According to the Southern Nevada Water Authority, in ten years almost 11 million square metres of lawn have been removed, bringing a saving of 26 million cubic metres of water per year. Ecological associations stress the environmental impact of all the fertilizers, herbicides, fungicides

1. The Mcdonaldization of the landscape: an artificial lawn in front of a fast-food restaurant in the South of France.

2. In urban areas in Southern California up to 60% of total water consumption is dedicated to watering lawns.

and insecticides required to achieve a perfect lawn. According to the EPA, the American Environmental Protection Agency, more than 30,000 tons of chemical products were spread over lawns in the United States in the single year of 1997, corresponding to a turnover of two billion dollars.

Some herbicides used to treat lawns, such as 2,4-D, are also the subject of a lively fight because of their impact on our health. What is 2,4-D? It is the molecule which constitutes one of the most widely sold herbicides in the world. It makes it possible to kill broad-leaved weeds, for instance clover and dandelions, without affecting the grass species of which the lawn is composed. In the United States the fight against this herbicide has a sensitive historical background: 2,4-D achieved unfortunate celebrity as one of the constituents of Agent Orange, a defoliant used during the Vietnam War with horrific consequences for the local people. The manufacturers assure us that 2,4-D, which was the least dangerous molecule in Agent Orange, presents no significant risk in gardens provided that certain precautions are taken (a protective mask, gloves and a waterproof overall). Neverthe-

less, the anti-herbicide campaigners remind us that 2,4-D is suspected of having many effects on gardeners' health, including for example damage to the reproductive system and anomalies in neurological development. The National Institute of Public Health of Quebec notes that there is still uncertainty as regards its potential to cause cancer in children, particularly if it is used in combination with other pesticide molecules, which is usually the case in gardens.

Behind this fight lies a substantial financial interest, for the sales volumes are huge. Dow, the American manufacturer of 2,4-D, is for example seeking two million dollars in damages and interest following the decision by the Province of Quebec to ban this herbicide. As a precaution, various other countries have also decided to forbid the use of 2,4-D, including Sweden, Norway and Denmark. Yet the battle over 2,4-D should not lead us to forget that numerous other herbicides, fungicides and insecticides used on lawn maintenance are as dangerous as 2,4-D, if not more so. To limit health risks, several states in America have passed legislation to make it mandatory to put up notices when a lawn

The impact on human health and the environment caused by pesticides used to obtain a perfect lawn were concealed for a long time. Today more and more questions are being asked.

has been chemically treated, forbidding all access to it for at least 24 hours. Some Canadian provinces have gone even further: for example, the use of any herbicide, insecticide or fungicide on private lawns is completely prohibited in the Province of Ontario.

In North America a huge movement has recently begun which has proposed an alternative to the industrial lawn ideal, namely the ecological meadow or *freedom lawn*. This is a grassy surface that still caters for the family use which is deeply rooted in the American way of life. However, its supporters refuse to use any chemical input, whether fertilizers, herbicides, fungicides or insecticides. The result is a meadow which is mown as infrequently as possible in order to allow flowering plants mingled with the traditional grass species to seed themselves generously. With the enthusiasm of new converts, the supporters of the freedom lawn are rediscovering the value of weeds such as clover, dandelions and daisies. Other solutions are envisaged in California, where the freedom lawn is too difficult to maintain because of dryness. In the Santa Barbara Botanic Garden a demonstration garden shows how to replace grass surfaces completely by groundcover beds consisting of native species with low water requirements. In Arizona and New Mexico a different style of gardening is becoming widespread, xeriscaping, or the art of gardening without water in a semi-desert climate.

Towards a new landscape model

In Europe, numerous initiatives have similarly proposed alternative solutions to the garden model based on lawns. Landscape designers are experimenting with new approaches to both private gardens and public spaces. In his nursery and garden in The Netherlands, Piet Oudolf mixes herbaceous plants and ornamental grasses to create beautiful scenes which evolve with the passage of the seasons, giving equal value to the succession of flowers in spring, autumn colours and frost on the golden haulms of the grasses in winter. In south-east England, Christopher Lloyd created a remarkable meadow at his garden, Great Dixter, composed of perennials, annuals and a profusion of bulbs, directly inspired by the flowering greenswards of the gardens depicted in medieval tapestries. Not far from Great Dixter, Beth Chatto transformed a stony car park into a gravel garden of great beauty, requiring minimal maintenance, which has inspired gardeners throughout the world. In France, Gilles Clément declared "I hate lawns" and turned to abandoned farmland or wasteland as a model of a dynamic garden, where the gardener observes and guides the natural trajectory of the evolving landscape. In several of his creations Erik Borja establishes a bridge between Japanese-inspired gardens and Mediterranean gardens, creating minimalist scenes with pared-down

1. Practitioners of the ecological lawn, or freedom lawn, avoid any chemical inputs, whether fertilizers, herbicides, fungicides or insecticides. The result is a cheerful scene in which "weeds" mingle with traditional grass species.

2. Inspired by the gardens depicted in medieval tapestries, Christopher Lloyd replaced lawns at Great Dixter, his famous garden in South-East England, with magnificent flowering meadows strewn with bulbs.

lines in which stone plays a major role. In Spain, Fernando Caruncho integrates cornfields into gardens, giving value to the yellow expanses of full summer and evoking the visual power of the landscapes of La Mancha. In Greece and in the South of France, a whole generation of young landscape designers are drawing on the wild flora of the Mediterranean Basin to create gardens requiring little water or maintenance, from which lawns have completely disappeared. Under the aegis of the Mediterranean Garden Society gardeners from all over the world share their research into climate-compatible gardening, put into practice at the Society's demonstration garden of Sparoza, near Athens. In this garden a circular natural meadow, resembling a threshing floor, is born anew each autumn after having dried out completely in summer. Other gardeners get rid of their lawns in order to devote a large part of the garden to the potager or vegetable garden, seen as a place of relaxation in which one can take a step back from the outside world; this creates a link with the very

first gardens of antiquity – Laertes, the father of Odysseus, cultivated his fruit-and-vegetable garden in the mountains of Ithaca as a place of retreat, and the garden of Epicurus in Athens, the site of a philosophy school named The Garden, was a vegetable garden.

The history of gardens through the ages gives us a sense of the development of man's relation to nature. Now that many gardeners are becoming aware of the ecological footprint of their activities, the model of a garden covered by a perfect lawn which is made possible only by a massive use of water, fertilizers and pesticides is reaching the end of its sway. Private individuals, landscape designers and the managers of public spaces are turning towards a kind of garden that better respects local soil and climate conditions. In all the mediterranean-climate regions of the world, gardeners are actively seeking alternatives to the lawn to create the gardens of the future.

All around the Mediterranean, gardeners seek alternatives to the lawn in order to create the gardens of the future.

GROUNDCOVER PLANTS IN THE WILD

When we speak of groundcover plants in gardens we tend to think of a limited range consisting in effect of perennial plants with a carpeting habit. Yet the term 'groundcover' can also be used in a wider sense, for the plants that cover the ground in natural or semi-natural environments belong to very diverse biological types. They include for example:

- annual plants, such as love-in-a-mist, poppies or borage, which can form magnificent carpets of flowers in spring, covering all the space available thanks to the density with which they grow, closely packed together;
- bulbs and related plants, such as narcissi, asphodels or cyclamen, which under certain conditions form great masses capable of covering the ground seasonally;
- herbaceous perennials, such as periwinkles or creeping potentilla, which colonize the ground by means of the lateral development of suckers, rhizomes or stolons;
- sub-shrubs such as common sage or lavender, whose spreading cushions cover the ground year-round thanks to their evergreen leaves;
- woody shrubs such as phillyrea or lentisk, sometimes become groundcovers as a result of extreme conditions which sculpt them into flattened masses, for example when they are exposed to strong salt-laden winds by the sea;
- climbing plants, such as ivy or honeysuckle, which romp over the ground when they find no supports on which to climb.

In this book I shall use the term 'groundcover' to denote all plants which can be used to cover the ground effectively in gardens, regardless of their shape, their height and their biological type. It is indeed the diversity of ground-covering plants in nature that broadens the range of alternatives to lawns in mediterranean gardens.

How do groundcover plants live in the wild?

All around the Mediterranean we see a great variety of plants which can serve as groundcovers in gardens: carpeting plants like *Artemisia pedemontana* in the mountains of Spain, cushion-forming plants like *Rhodanthemum hosmariense* in Morocco, or ball-shaped plants like *Thymbra capitata* in Crete. A cushion- or ball-shaped habit of growth is a frequent adaptation to an arid environment: the sphere is the geometric form that exposes the smallest surface area for a given volume, thus limiting the plant's water losses while optimizing its photosynthesis. The diversity of groundcover plants is also seen in their different heights: *Arenaria balearica* is a miniature carpet just a few millimetres high, while *Sarcopoterium spinosum* is a massive plant which, in favourable conditions, can reach a metre in height and several metres in spread. Observing groundcover plants in nature provides the gardener with a wealth of information. It enables us to understand how to cultivate them so that they require minimal maintenance.

Facing page
Sarcopoterium spinosum colonizes abandoned terraces on the island of Amorgos in the Cyclades.

1. *Crocus goulimyi* colonizes stony soil beneath olive trees in autumn on the Mani peninsula in the Southern Peloponnese.

2. On Cape Creus, in Spanish Catalonia, the force of the salt spray sculpts the shrubby vegetation of phillyrea into a fine groundcover carpet. Groundcover plants that inhabit natural environments belong to a wide variety of biological types.

1. A relict oak forest on the slopes of Mount Zas on the island of Naxos in the Cyclades. The competition between plant species, reinforced by environmental stresses and recurrent disturbances, creates a dynamic that leads to the constant evolution of landscapes.

2. The Larzac plateau in the South of France. To escape competition, *Thymus praecox* spreads over rocks where taller plants cannot gain a foothold.

3. The Sierra de Cazorla in Southern Spain. *Juniperus sabina* is not at all vulnerable to competition because its dense vegetation shades the ground completely.

Plants are in constant competition for space, light and nutrients. In nature, this competition creates a dynamic that leads to the progressive modification of landscapes: depending on the soil and climate, the vegetation of a given place always seeks to evolve and attain its potential mature stage. In the mediterranean climate, when conditions are optimal, this mature stage generally comprises forest. In this landscape dynamic, groundcover plants are at risk of being rapidly overtaken by taller plants, which would take their place; in order to survive, they need to adopt strategies that allow them to fight off competition. Knowledge of these strategies is useful when we are planning a low-maintenance groundcover garden. In gardens the competition between plants is just as intense – the whole problem of dealing with weeds in a flowerbed is an example of it.

The density of their vegetation is one of the factors that enable groundcover plants to resist competition. If a plant's foliage remains thoroughly dense throughout the year, a height of 30-40 centimetres will be enough to limit to a great extent the germination of competing species. For example, in the mountains of Southern Spain the vigorous vegetation of *Juniperus sabina* forms large spreading masses which eliminate all competition: the leaves completely cut out the light from the soil under them, and seeds are unable to germinate beneath the plant. Another strategy consists of producing chemical substances that inhibit germination. This strategy forms part of the phenomenon of allelopathy, in other words a chemical reaction between plants (from the

Greek *allelon*, reciprocal, and *pathos*, suffering). This allows some plants to maintain a fine ground-covering carpet, in spite of the fact that the low density of their vegetation could have been rapidly invaded by more aggressive species.

Plants with allelopathic properties are particularly numerous in regions with a mediterranean climate. They include species as widely different as *Callistemon* in Australia and *Salvia leucophylla* in the chaparral of Southern California, as well as garrigue plants like rue, *Cistus*, *Phlomis* and thyme. These plants disperse their phytotoxic compounds in various ways. In *Salvia leucophylla* they are volatile and are deposited on the ground like a dew; in rue they are leached from the leaves by rain; in *Cistus* and *Phlomis* they

are liberated during the decomposition of the dead leaves which form a litter round the base of the plant; finally, in thyme they are directly exuded into the soil by the plant's roots. In the garigue, plants with allelopathic properties often have aromatic leaves. Apart from thyme, they include for instance rosemary, sage, oregano, lavender and savory. This is one of the many reasons to incorporate aromatic plants into the composition of large groundcover displays – because they require less weeding. Some species possess such effective allelopathic properties that they have large-scale uses in agriculture. Mouse-ear hawkweed (*Pilosella officinarum*) or annual grasses like wall barley (*Hordeum murinum*) and drooping brome (*Bromus tectorum*) have the potential to be 'herbicidal plants', which could be planted as grass cover in orchards and between vines to limit the use of synthetic pesticides.

Other groundcover plants are less well equipped to fight off competitors, having neither allelopathic properties nor sufficiently dense vegetation to limit competition. Hence they develop strategies that allow them to survive where taller plants have difficulty gaining a foothold. Such strategies can be divided into two groups:

• the development of resistance to environmental stresses, so that they can grow in hostile environments where competition is limited;
• adaptation to the frequent disturbances which prevent other plants from developing.

1

Environmental stresses and repeated disturbances contribute to the formation of an 'open landscape' whose evolving dynamic is temporarily blocked. For as long as this block continues, ground-covering plants with low potential competitiveness can establish and propagate themselves. All around the Mediterranean, from the Syrian steppes to the Larzac plateau, from the mountains of Morocco to the rocky coasts of the Greek islands, Clara and I have studied the multiple facets of these open landscapes for some time. They have been for us one of the best sources of inspiration as we reflect on the techniques of drought-adapted gardening. They have also inspired us as we consider alternatives to lawns in mediterranean gardens.

1. Mouse-ear hawkweed, *Pilosella officinarum*, is a groundcover plant renowned for its allelopathic properties: it diffuses chemical substances which inhibit the germination of competing species.

2. *Asphodelus microcarpus* is able to withstand outbreaks of fire. Its tuberous roots conserve water and nutrients when the vegetation above ground has been destroyed by the flames.

3. When fires recur, the asphodel ends up dominating the landscape, as here on the Gardiole mountain in the South of France.

1. Some groundcover plants use strategies to adapt to environmental stresses and survive in hostile environments thus eliminating the problem of competition. *Globularia alypum* thrives in the poor and rocky soils of the *calanques* (creeks) of Marseilles.

2. *Helichrysum orientale* ensconces itself in fissures in sea cliffs on Mediterranean islands.

3. *Santolina magonica* thrives on the arid coast of the Levant peninsula in Mallorca.

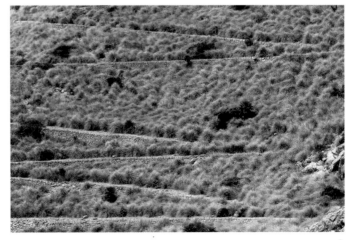

Here are some of the factors that contribute to making an open environment that favours groundcover plants: poor and stony soil, dryness, cold, wind, salt in coastal areas, as well as over-grazing, the frequency of forest fires, disturbed soil or agricultural activities such as recurrent ploughing. It is generally a combination of factors that keeps a landscape open. For example, in dry-climate regions *Ampelodesmos mauritanicus* covers vast expanses of grazing land subject to regular fires. This grass isn't bothered by the pressure of grazing because its leaf margins are equipped with fine downward-pointing teeth that make the plant unpalatable to sheep and goats. Its deep root system enables it to withstand drought perfectly. Thanks to its powerful suckering

1. The Revellata peninsula, near Calvi in Corsica. Environmental stresses and repeated disturbances help maintain an "open landscape" in which evolutionary progress is temporarily blocked. This type of open landscape offers inspiration to gardeners looking to create a groundcover garden that requires little maintenance.

2. Resistant to grazing, drought and fire, *Ampelodesmos mauritanicus* is able to colonize areas where few other species can survive. On the Formentor peninsula in Mallorca it covers vast expanses that are otherwise punctuated only by the dark shapes of a few dwarf palms.

2

rootstock, the plant is also able to sprout again rapidly after a fire. The combination of over-grazing, drought and fire thus enables *Ampelodesmos mauritanicus* to thrive in environments where few other plants can survive, so much so that it may form a single-species groundcover stretching as far as the eye can see, as on the Formentor peninsula in Mallorca.

From the wild to the garden

In gardens, it is often impossible to reproduce the combination of factors which create ideal conditions for different groundcover species in the wild. It's hard to imagine setting fire to the garden once a year in order to help the bed of *Ampelodesmos* to prosper. However, it is entirely possible to plan the garden according to the types of groundcover envisaged, in order to come close to the natural conditions in which the plants grow without any need for maintenance.

Poor and stony soil, although often seen by gardeners as a disadvantage, proves to be a true bonus in gardens where you want to grow a wide range of groundcover plants native to the stony hillsides of the Mediterranean with little main-

In some parts of the garden, allow the natural dynamics of the landscape free expression: do not try to create a fixed picture but rather allow the groundcover to evolve from year to year. Here *Stipa barbata*, with its supple and silvery inflorescences, self-seeds freely in a large bed of perennials.

tenance. Weeds grow less easily than they would in a rich soil, and the groundcover plants can spread comfortably without the risk of being swamped by competitors. The gravel garden is a good option when the soil in the garden is not naturally stony: the thickness of this layer of mineral mulch suppresses the germination of weeds almost entirely, thus eliminating to a great extent the need for weeding in a groundcover bed

When combined with a long period of summer drought, stony soil can become the basis of a flowering steppe, one of the most original techniques for creating a surface which can be walked on, is ornamental throughout the year and requires minimal maintenance. The balance between plant and stone, so characteristic of the landscapes around the Mediterranean, can also inspire countless garden examples – in steps and low walls or in the cracks between the paving stones on a terrace

The grazing of livestock is one of the most common ways in which the environment is disturbed in the southern regions of the Mediterranean Basin. In the garden, grazing can easily be replaced by occasional scything or clipping. Natural dry grasslands include a whole range of plants adapted to grazing by means of their rosette form or ground-hugging habit. In small areas, some of these plants can be used as carpets of green which withstand foot traffic and look very ornamental. Goats, wind and salt spray sculpt dense masses of mediterranean evergreen shrubs to create amazing groundcover landscapes. The gardener can mimic these external factors by clipping large beds of shrubs to keep them flat and compact in habit.

Before the use of selective herbicides became widespread, tilling – the main means by which the environment became open in agricultural landscapes – favoured a great many flowering plants that co-existed with crops. In the garden, a

simple autumn digging over of the soil, using even the most basic tools, allows us to sow a flowering meadow which will look magnificent in spring with the minimum of maintenance. Finally, in some areas of the garden why not give free rein to the dynamic evolution of the landscape? Instead of trying to create a fixed picture, leave the groundcover to evolve from year to year in a scheme that will take its lead from the soil, climate and palette of pioneer plants which are able to establish themselves in your particular garden.

By taking inspiration from nature, it's possible to adapt your approach to managing garden surfaces and opt for a 'groundcover garden' that is adapted to local conditions and easy to maintain. The different lawn alternatives I'm going to put forward in the following pages result from our observations of groundcover plants in their native environment. I propose a range of solutions that fit different requirements in terms of their use, amount of foot traffic, aesthetics and maintenance time.

In some parts of the garden, allow the natural dynamics of the landscape free expression: do not try to create a fixed picture but rather allow the groundcover to evolve from year to year. Here *Stipa barbata*, with its supple and silvery inflorescences, self-seeds freely in a large bed of perennials.

LESS WATER AND LOW MAINTENANCE: THE GROUNDCOVER GARDEN

How can one cut down on lawn maintenance? The first answer is simply to reduce the size of the lawn. Consider how much lawn is absolutely necessary in your garden and eliminate it from places where its presence can't really be justified. You may want to have a large lawn for aesthetic reasons. But why should a 21st-century gardener living in a dry climate be obliged to follow a landscape aesthetic developed in England in the 18th century? When it is not an aesthetic choice, the need for a surface which can be walked on is often used to justify a large area of lawn. People want to walk, run and play in their gardens, so there needs to be lawn everywhere – but the areas required for regular foot traffic are usually greatly overestimated.

To determine the real need for a surface which can be walked on in a family garden, it is useful to define the degree of foot traffic by zone. The lowest category relates to areas that are almost never walked on, such as steep slopes, the margins of the garden and the parts of it that are not easily accessible. An intermediate category covers parts of the garden that are frequently walked on, such as the children's play area, the transition between the terrace and the garden, and the area surrounding the swimming pool. Finally come the parts that receive a great deal of foot traffic: paths used every day giving access to the entrance of the house, to the garage, to the woodpile or to the kitchen garden. There is no reason to use grass everywhere; depending on the degree of foot traffic, a different arrangement may be suitable for each zone. Lawn has a place only in areas where the foot traffic is intermediate. It is ill-suited to areas with intense foot traffic and pointless in places that are rarely walked on.

This analysis of the degree of foot traffic can also be applied to public spaces. One often sees lawn used to cover spaces that cannot be walked on because they are either inaccessible or dangerous. For example, the only person who ever walks on the grass on the roundabouts at the entrance to French villages is the municipal employee who is obliged to go over them with a lawn mower in the midst of all the noise and exhaust fumes of passing cars. And to make the most of the soft grass between the tram rails by lying in the sun would be tantamount to suicide. The management of public spaces sometimes borders on the absurd: lawns that look as if they were made to be walked on but are forbidden territory, as we are rapidly made aware of by countless little signs, sometimes translated into other languages for the benefit of tourists: *Do not walk on the grass*, *gazon interdit*, *césped prohibido*. Reducing the number of pointless lawns remains the easiest way to economize on water and limit maintenance in gardens and public spaces around the Mediterranean.

Facing page
Since it requires neither watering nor pesticides, the groundcover garden requires less maintenance. Among the plants that make up this scene are *Achillea coarctata, Achillea nobilis, Achillea crithmifolia, Thymus ciliatus, Centaurea bella* and *Geranium sanguineum*.

1. There is no reason to use lawn everywhere: an analysis of the degree of foot traffic allows us to work out different approaches for the various zones of the garden.

2. The need for a surface that can be walked on, which is frequently used to justify large areas of uniform lawn, is often greatly overestimated in gardens. Here a simple path has been made by mowing to create a passage through taller vegetation.

3. In a large town in the South of France, this four-lane highway is divided by a central reservation, inaccessible and yet covered in grass. When the mistral blows, the sprinkler system floods not only the lawn but also the adjacent road surface.

4. The crowning glory for a lawn in a public space is when people are forbidden to walk on it.

1. Tramlines are often set in magnificent carpets of lawn in Mediterranean countries. Intended to create an image of "nature" in the city centre, these lawns consume an inordinate amount of water, fertilizer and herbicides for very limited returns in terms of social use.

2. Reducing the surface area of pointless lawns remains the easiest way of economizing on water and reducing maintenance in public spaces in mediterranean regions.

3. Depending on the areas to be covered and the needs of each zone, there are many practical solutions for replacing a lawn.

4. A wild lawn that requires less maintenance can be used to cover a large area that gets a moderate amount of foot traffic.

banal uniformity in gardens and public spaces in mediterranean regions. To set off on the fascinating journey towards lawn alternatives marks first and foremost a rejection of this standardization of the landscape. Lawn alternatives allow multiple groundcover solutions to suit personal taste and you don't have to adopt one solution for your garden but can choose a variety to suit the needs of each garden zone. In this book I am going to propose ten ideas for lawn alternatives to suit different parts of a garden depending on their use and degree of foot traffic.

1. For diehard lawn lovers, I propose warm-season grass species that require less water and maintenance than conventional lawn plants.

2. To liberate you from the restrictions of a grass lawn, I describe mat-forming plants suitable for growing green carpets that can be walked on.

In search of lawn alternatives

The next stage in reducing the maintenance demands of a lawn is the most interesting but also the most complex: setting out to find lawn alternatives. When creating a new garden, a lawn may seem the easy way out. A rarely admitted reason for a lawn is that it offers an easy way of dealing with the garden when we don't know what to plant. We cover the ground with a lawn so that we don't have to start reflecting on the whole concept of the garden. By contrast, replacing a lawn enables us to regain the entire surface of the garden; the downside is that this involves a lot of research and thought: if we take the lawn away, what should we put in its place?

The answer is to consider not just one alternative to the lawn but many. During the last 50 years lawns have led to a

3. To reduce the maintenance of these green carpets, I show how to create a mixed carpet where the diversity of foliage limits the problem of weeding.

4. For those who are ready to abandon the perfect lawn and turn to a more natural grass cover, I explain how to cultivate weeds as the most extreme version of the mixed lawn. This biodiverse option consists of a multitude of annual, perennial and bulbous plants and can be managed in two ways in mediterranean climates: occasional watering to keep it more or less green in summer; or zero watering and acceptance of total summer dormancy, even to the point where it is just beaten earth in the driest regions.

5. To avoid the problem of a dried-out grass surface in summer, I propose a flowering steppe on a bed of gravel. This is a space that can be walked on and requires minimal maintenance. There will be some visual impact during the summer resting period but not the extreme of beaten earth.

6. Expand the idea of a flowering steppe to create an entire gravel garden consisting of plants with a variety of forms – carpets, cushions and balls – highlighted by emerging perennials and bulbs. The plants are spaced out in order to allow one to walk all over the garden and to set off the contrast between gravel and plant.

7. Add plants to hard landscaped areas, such as terraces, paths, steps and parking spaces, to create areas suitable for foot traffic. Take inspiration from traditional Mediterranean ground-covering techniques such as paving, decorative pebble work, and other hard surfaces that are permeable thanks to the planted cracks that allow for better water management.

8. In areas where there is no foot traffic, create large beds of perennials and shrubs whose dense foliage prevents light getting through to the ground, thus limiting competition.

9. Leave part of the garden free and semi-wild and add self-seeding pioneer plants to rapidly colonize empty space.

Maintenance consists of guiding the evolution of this area and intervening to accept or get rid of woody species that emerge and tend to close up the environment.

10. Create a mediterranean flowering meadow with changing seasonal interest as it passes from an explosion of spring flowers to a dry meadow in summer. There are many techniques for planting and managing an annual or semi-perennial meadow.

Towards a groundcover garden

All these options for replacing lawns have one thing in common: they give rise to a new way of managing space. Instead of treating the surface of the garden simply as a flat expanse to be covered by a uniform lawn, the use of a variety of groundcover plants allows us to compose layers of vegetation of different heights. These layers, accentuated by the pronounced play of light and shadow, which is typical of mediterranean regions, draw the eye and increase the sense of depth in the garden. The Romantic landscape

Lawn alternatives lead to different ways of managing space. Instead of the surface of the garden being viewed on a single plane and covered with a uniform carpet of lawn, by using a variety of groundcover plants you can create layers of vegetation at different heights.

from which the lawn-based garden model arose is organized around a static scene which imitates an idealized nature. By contrast, the groundcover garden is inspired by the changing mosaic of Mediterranean landscapes. It lends itself to the creation of a succession of planes, spaces and volumes that evolve over time and lead from one to another, weaving in a multitude of perspectives that arise from shifting viewing points. The paths that link the different parts of the garden complement these visual perspectives by providing a multi-sensory experience, in which scent plays a major part in summer, recalling the original tradition of the Mediterranean garden.

The mosaic of landscapes which provides the inspiration for groundcover gardens consists of a broad palette of colours in which stone alternates with plants: white limestone, dark schist or terra rossa, the subtle dark greens of myrtle and lentisk, the spectrum of greys and silvers in downy-leaved plants, the brilliant yellow of harvested cereal crops, with the dark trunks of almond trees or the dense mass of holm oaks as counterpoint. Whereas the perfect lawn is required to remain absolutely the same colour throughout the year, lawn alternatives on the contrary break with the dominance of green in the garden to reflect better the changing diversity of colours in the Mediterranean landscape. A groundcover garden recognises the value of seasonal changes in the appearance of a landscape. It embraces drought or cold, with their respective periods of dormancy, as driving forces behind the changing face of the garden. It invites us to stray from imposed garden models, and try a kaleidoscope of shapes and colours which are less usual in a traditional garden: the yellow carpet of *Zoysia* in winter,

The broad palette of colours available in a groundcover garden make it possible to break up the dominance of green in gardens.

the silvery laciness of *Cerastium* spreading over a bed of black pozzolana, the opulent mass of *Sarcopoterium* which in summer reveals its thorny brown skeleton, the dense golden fleece which covers *Phlomis chrysophylla* during the dry period, or the transitory carpets of bulbs which dramatically break the austerity of the dry meadow with the arrival of the first autumn rains.

Many carpeting groundcover plants, whether tolerant of foot traffic or not, make striking alternatives to the lawn. But the range of groundcover plants is not restricted to those with a carpeting habit. Depending on the degree to which they are walked on, different parts of the garden can be home to a great variety of groundcover plants which can be used alone or in association to create an almost infinite number of possible combinations. And for these plants there are also complementary hardscape options – terraces, paths, gravel. In traditional gardens, hardscaping and planting solutions are often isolated from one other and sited in distinct parts of the garden but the groundcover garden integrates them.

Of the different ideas offered here, none is a miracle solution that will solve the problem of a lawn in a dry climate. Each solution has its advantages and its disadvantages and it is important is to weigh up the pros and the cons when choosing a lawn alternative for a specific part of the garden. You need to check that the solution is on the one hand compatible with the climate and soil conditions, and on the other hand suitable for the particular needs defined for this area in terms of foot traffic, maintenance level, irrigation, aesthetics and period of use during the year. The main error is to replace a large area of lawn with an alternative that is just as unsuitable. A few dozen square metres of *Zoysia*

tenuifolia make an ideal play area for children. A carpet of *Frankenia laevis* measuring a few square metres may provide a green carpet perfect for stretching out on in the sun beside a swimming pool. However, it would be a major mistake to plant *Frankenia* or *Zoysia* on a large scale on an inaccessible roundabout. Each solution is suitable for filling a particular need, but one solution does not fit all. They are however complementary and may be combined within a garden. In the following chapter, my purpose in presenting these different solutions in detail is not to offer ready-made prescriptions that can simply be copied in your garden. Every garden is different – it is up to you to find the option best for your particular situation.

The seasonal colour changes in a groundcover garden evoke the shifting mosaics of Mediterranean landscapes:

1. Olives and cultivated fields are interspersed with patches of garrigue in this winter landscape on the island of Naxos in the Cyclades.

2. A landscape in La Mancha, south of Madrid, in the burning June light.

3. The amazing colours of a landscape parched by drought at Cap Corse, Corsica, September 2007.

4. All gardens are different and it is up to each gardener to invent his or her own lawn alternative.

4

GROUNDCOVER GARDENS
FOR DRY CLIMATES

LAWNS WITH WARM-SEASON GROUNDCOVERS

ADVANTAGES: Lower maintenance and water requirements than a conventional lawn. Species adapted to high summer temperatures. Low height means less frequent mowing (no mowing is required for *Zoysia* if it is walked on regularly).

DRAWBACKS: complete yellowing of leaves during the period of winter dormancy. Planting, which can be by cuttings directly put in the ground, by pot-grown plants or by laying pre-grown squares of turf, involves significant labour and expense. Newly planted lawns require assiduous care during their first year.

RECOMMENDED SURFACE AREA: depends on the species chosen. Small areas (a few dozen square metres) for *Zoysia tenuifolia* when pot-raised plants are planted; a medium-sized area (50 to 100 square metres) for *Stenotaphrum secundatum*; a large area (several hundred square metres, or much more for some professional uses) for hybrid *Cynodon*.

Lawns are often vaunted for their functional qualities. They limit run-off, filter water, cool the air, retain dust and contribute to trapping carbon. Their even surface makes them suitable for many sporting activities. However, they also possess numerous drawbacks, especially in regions with a dry climate. Hence the question arises for mediterranean gardeners: is it possible to preserve the functional qualities of a lawn while at the same time limiting its drawbacks? One of the first things to be examined is the diversity of grass species in order to identify those which could be used for lawns that consume less water, less fertilizer and fewer pesticides. To explore this idea, we have for several years been testing many different warm-season grass species, including *Zoysia tenuifolia*, *Stenotaphrum secundatum* and *Cynodon* 'Santa Ana'. These grasses enjoy the high temperatures of mediterranean summers. Although they still require summer irrigation, their resistance to drought is markedly better than conventional lawn grasses. Nevertheless, although they possess many good qualities, warm-season grass species are not miracle plants: they have some serious drawbacks which one needs to bear in mind before making one's choice. An examination of these grasses may thus serve as a model for the process to be followed when we are considering many other lawn alternatives.

Microthermic and macrothermic grasses

Agronomists make a distinction between two large groups of lawn grass species: cool-season (or *microthermic* grasses) and warm-season (or *macrothermic* grasses). These grass species behave quite differently in the garden since they don't both demand the same growing conditions. Cool-season grasses include all the species of which conventional lawns are composed, for example English rye grass, Kentucky bluegrass, *Agrostis* species and various fescues. Warm-season grasses include species such as *Zoysia tenuifolia*, *Pennisetum clandestinum*, *Stenotaphrum secundatum*, *Paspalum vaginatum* and various species of *Cynodon* and their hybrids.

Cool-season grasses are called microthermic because they are adapted to relatively low temperatures: they withstand winter cold very well and their optimal growing temperature is between 15 and 23 °C. By contrast, when the summer temperatures are too high they cease to grow and gradually become dormant. Their leaves turn yellow and they stop all photosynthesis; their dormant buds are able to sprout again in autumn if the period of dormancy has not been too prolonged. These cool-season grasses are particularly sensitive to high temperatures at root level: soil temperatures of 30 to 35 °C cause the roots to die with the result that they will not then sprout again in autumn. So, no matter how much a conventional lawn is watered, it's possible that the high temperatures of a mediterranean heat wave may cause irrevocable die-back followed by death.

Page 38
There are many ways of using groundcovers as alternatives to a lawn and the choice depends on the personal taste of each gardener. Among the plants that make up this scene are *Salvia lavandulifolia* subsp. *blancoana*, *Tanacetum densum*, *Lavandula* × *intermedia* and *Lavandula dentata*.

Facing page
Zoysia tenuifolia forms a bumpy carpet whose colour changes over the seasons.

Page 41
Zoysia tenuifolia makes a lawn that withstands foot traffic very well but it is slow-growing so best for covering small areas. It can be mixed with other species, as here with *Achillea coarctata*.

1. A lawn of
*Stenotaphrum
secundatum* at
Kirstenbosch Botanical
Garden in South
Africa. Although
its appearance is
relatively coarse,
Stenotaphrum requires
less maintenance
than a conventional
lawn. However, it can
be used only in mild
climates as it is not
hardy.

2. Like all warm-season
or "macrothermic"
grasses, *Zoysia
tenuifolia* becomes
dormant in winter.
Its leaves turn totally
yellow during the cold
season. It survives, just
ticking over, by means
of its rhizomes which
serve as storage organs.

3. The first young
green shoots of
*Stenotaphrum
secundatum* appear
after the period of
winter dormancy.
Stenotaphrum does
not start sprouting
again until mid-spring,
when the soil has
warmed up.

1

Warm-season grasses are called macrothermic because, on the contrary, they like the heat of mediterranean summers. Their optimal growing temperature is between 25 and 32 °C and they can tolerate even higher temperatures perfectly well. Their period of dormancy is the inverse of that of cool-season grasses: they are dormant in winter. When the mean soil temperature falls below 10 to 12 °C, they stop the process of photosynthesis. Their leaves turn completely yellow and they remain in a suspended state, simply ticking over, thanks to their powerful rhizomes which act as storage organs. Once they have entered into dormancy they are able to withstand temperatures below zero, of the order of –5 to –12 °C according to the species. In spring they do not start putting out new shoots until the mean soil temperature reaches above 10 to 12 °C. The new shoots which then sprout

from the rhizomes and stolons rapidly refurnish an entirely green carpet.

The advantages of macrothermic grasses

Plants obtain water from the soil by means of absorbent hairs situated at the tips of their roots. Water is then carried up to the leaves in the sap. It is lost from the leaves through the stomata in the form of water vapour during the gaseous exchange that is connected with the process of photosynthesis. Water also evaporates directly from the soil and the leaf surfaces. The cumulative loss of water by these routes is called 'evapotranspiration'. It makes it possible for us to calculate the water needs of a plant in a given climate. In the South of France, for example, the evapotranspiration in summer from a lawn composed of microthermic grasses is about 6-8 mm per day, which means the lawn loses on average 6 to 8 litres of water per square metre every day in summer. The rate of this water loss varies a lot depending on local conditions of heat, wind and orientation. In the countries of the Southern Mediterranean, when a dry wind blows for several days the evapotranspiration from a conventional lawn can exceed 10 litres of water per square metre per day.

Macrothermic grasses are less greedy of water than microthermic grasses. Originating from warm regions, they have developed various strategies to resist drought which temperate-climate grasses lack. The first of these strategies is the leaf structure: the stomata are concentrated on the inner

face of the leaves. In a period of drought the leaf margins roll up to form a tight gutter protecting the stomata, thus reducing water loss. The second strategy has to do with a modification of the photosynthesis cycle: macrothermic grasses close their stomata during the day and open them at night when temperatures are lower, in order to limit transpiration. Warm-season grasses can thus offer the same green expanse as a conventional lawn while losing less water through evapotranspiration. According to the grass species used, the reduction in water loss may be from 30 to 50%.

The drought resistance of lawn grasses depends not only on their ability to limit water loss but also on the depth of their root system. Macrothermic grasses are equipped with strong rhizomes which enable them to probe the deep layers of the soil. Hybrid *Cynodon*, for example, has a root system that penetrates to a depth of more than two metres. These rhizomes are capable of drawing on the small amounts of moisture available in the lowest layers of the soil, even when the surface is suffering from intense drought. They also act as storage organs, enabling *Cynodon* to survive in extreme conditions. In Mediterranean regions, hybrid *Cynodon* is the only macrothermic grass which can be used for a lawn that is intermittently irrigated in summer. It can even tolerate not being irrigated at all once it is well established. By partially yellowing, it is able to withstand long periods of drought while awaiting the first autumn rains.

Macrothermic grasses propagate themselves easily through the lateral spreading of their rhizomes and stolons. This means of vegetal propagation is so effective that in nature propagation by seed becomes secondary in some species, or even non-existent. *Zoysia tenuifolia*, for example, produces few seeds, and these have a very low germination rate into the bargain. The slow increase of its rhizomes is enough to ensure the plant's long-term survival without any need for self-seeding. Similarly, the *Stenotaphrum secundatum* grown in the South of France is a sterile form; this species multiplies so well through its vigorous surface stolons that many of its varieties produce little, if any, seed. Finally, one of the best macrothermic grasses used for lawns in dry climates, *Cynodon* 'Santa Ana', is a sterile hybrid which produces no seed. This absence of seeds can be an advantage. The plant cannot self-seed elsewhere in the garden, where it could be considered an undesirable weed. Nor can it migrate outside the garden and sow itself in natural sites where it could become invasive, with long-term negative effects.

Moreover, the multiplication by rhizomes and stolons of macrothermic grasses has other advantages for the gardener. Instead of growing vertically, macrothermic grasses grow laterally and require significantly less mowing than conventional lawns. From this point of view, *Zoysia tenuifolia* is the best species: depending on the desired effect, one may very well decide not to mow it at all. In this case it will take on the appearance of a humpy carpet, most striking, where flat areas alternate with mini-hillocks, in a sort of tectonic confrontation between the different layers of rhizomes as they

1. Macrothermic grasses spread by their rhizomes and stolons: the detail here shows the rhizomes of *Zoysia tenuifolia*.

2. A path of *Zoysia tenuifolia that receives* heavy foot traffic. The rhizomes of *Zoysia tenuifolia* form an extremely dense network, giving this species an exceptional ability to withstand pedestrians but it cannot self-seed as it produces almost no seeds.

1

2

ride over one another. These rhizomes give macrothermic grasses an exceptional resistance to foot traffic. Here once again *Zoysia tenuifolia* wins the prize: for small areas where nothing else will grow, beneath a swing for example, *Zoysia tenuifolia* is capable of forming a very thick lawn, no matter how much it is walked on. Finally, in some species, the rhizomes and stolons allow a plant to become established very rapidly. When the conditions of heat and humidity are favourable, the speed with which *Stenotaphrum secundatum* or *Cynodon* 'Santa Ana' grow is remarkable – it's as if one can actually see the plant spreading from one day to the next.

The drawbacks of macrothermic grasses

Unfortunately, macrothermic grasses are not without disadvantages. The best macrothermic species can be established solely by vegetative means, not by sowing. So establishing a macrothermic grass lawn is labour intensive, expensive and needs scrupulous maintenance during its first year. There are three possible planting methods, each with its own drawbacks:

- *In situ* planting of cuttings. On a small scale, the cuttings are planted manually. You see this method used in Morocco or Spain to create the dense lawns of *Stenotaphrum secundatum* seen frequently there. Long cuttings are laid horizontally in damp furrows about 30 or 40 cm apart. When the furrows are filled in with soil, only the tip of the cutting should appear above ground in order to limit water loss during the rooting period. Cuttings are planted at a time of year when the soil is warm, and daily watering is necessary for a few weeks to ensure a good take-up rate. In the United States, Spain and Italy industrial techniques make it possible to plant cuttings *in situ* using specialized machines that can distribute and bury the rhizomes over extensive areas. In Italy, thanks to the availability of this technique for *in situ* planting

1. *Cynodon* 'Santa Ana' is a hybrid Bermuda grass whose spikelets are sterile. It cannot be grown from seed like a conventional lawn.

2. Hybrid *Cynodon* on a golf course near Brindisi, in Southern Italy in January when the winter dormancy of *Cynodon* causes a complete yellowing of the landscape. For this kind of large-scale installation, hybrid *Cynodon* is planted in place by cuttings, using a special machine that distributes and buries the rhizomes.

of cuttings and because of its low requirements for water and chemical inputs, hybrid *Cynodon* is widely used to cover large areas. The most iconic *Cynodon* lawn is without doubt that of the Olympic stadium in Rome. Hybrid *Cynodon* lawns also cover the football pitches of Genoa, Lecca and Reggio di Calabria, as well as the golf courses of Brindisi in Apulia, and Savona in Liguria. As far as we know, no company in the South of France offers this mechanized method of planting cuttings, thus drastically limiting the area that can be planted.

• Planting young plants grown in pots. A planting density of 4 to 9 pots per square metre, depending on the species used, will achieve total coverage in a year (see page 127). Thorough weeding is necessary before the young plants are put in, and regular irrigation while they are becoming established. The area that can be planted is limited mainly by the maintenance required during the first year; larger areas of lawn may be achieved by successive planting over several years. More and more nurseries in the South of France offer young macrothermic grass plants for sale. For someone who wants to reduce the expense of installing a lawn, it is perfectly possible to produce one's own stock of young plants, starting from a first small patch of lawn that serves as the mother plant.

• Laying pre-cultivated squares of turf. In Portugal, Spain and Italy major lawn firms produce different species of macrothermic grasses in the form of pre-cultivated squares or turves, ready for laying. In France, the climatic conditions make this kind of enterprise less economically viable than in warmer regions, where the period of winter dormancy is reduced. It is nevertheless possible to find imported turves of *Zoysia tenuifolia*. Laying squares of *Zoysia* provides a very attractive solution as it makes it possible to have an instant result. However, the high cost of the turves generally limits the area to be planted. Great care must be taken with laying the turves and watering them during the establishment phase, since squares of *Zoysia* give disappointing results when the ideal conditions are not met. The best time to plant *Zoysia* turves is between May and September, when the soil is warm. Abundant watering is needed to ensure a good take-up rate. During the following years maintenance must also be strict, for without it the newly established lawn may rapidly fail.

There are other disadvantages to macrothermic grasses. The yellowing of the lawn in winter, during its natural period of dormancy, is often perceived as a major problem by gardeners new to the world of macrothermic grasses. Although this is subjective and some gardeners may consider it of secondary importance, winter yellowing is something you need to be aware of before planting this type of lawn. In the Montpellier region of France, yellowing generally begins in December or January, but it may start earlier if there is a cold snap in November. In our experience, it is towards the end of the period of yellowing that gardeners start to tire

1. In Morocco and Spain, *Stenotaphrum secundatum* lawns are traditionally planted by cuttings placed directly in the ground. Long cuttings are inserted into damp furrows, where they will root in a few weeks. Only the tips of the cuttings should be above ground when the furrows are filled in.

2. A new planting of *Stenotaphrum secundatum* in a garden in Oujda, Morocco. Once they have rooted, the cuttings put out long stolons which spread in every direction. Regular watering is necessary during the whole planting process.

3. Once established, macrothermic grasses can give an expanse of green which consumes less water than a conventional lawn. Shown here is a lawn of *Stenotaphrum secundatum* in the garden of the Alcazar in Seville.

1　　　　　　　　　　2　　　　　　　　　　3

1   2   3

of it. In our own garden, the macrothermic grasses don't begin to show signs of life until the first half of April, when the rest of the garden is already staggering under the weight of the flowering *Cistus* and *Phlomis* species. For grass species which are relatively hardy, like *Zoysia tenuifolia*, it is the length of the dormant period that limits their use outside mediterranean-climate regions. In areas where winters are long and harsh, there's a risk that *Zoysia* would effectively remain dormant, with yellow leaves, for more than half the year. For other macrothermic species and varieties, such as *Stenotaphrum secundatum* and *Cynodon* 'Santa Ana', the problem doesn't arise because their sensitivity to cold makes it impossible for them to survive in places with a harsh winter.

Among the different macrothermic grass species, a few utilize two methods of multiplying: on the one hand powerful vegetative spreading by rhizomes and stolons, and on the other easy propagation by seed. This apparent advantage (they can be sown directly in place, like a conventional lawn) can sometimes be a real problem in that these species can become invasive. *Pennisetum clandestinum* (Kikuyu grass) can become a weed that is hard to control in gardens with a mild winter climate (this species is very sensitive to cold) and where the soil remains relatively moist in summer (it is fairly greedy for water). Another macrothermic grass which can become invasive, particularly in coastal gardens, is *Paspalum vaginatum*. In some cases, thanks to their ability to self-seed, these species can escape gardens and seed themselves in natural or semi-natural areas. For example, when *Paspalum vaginatum* finds favourable environments (estuaries and coastal salt marshes), it has a potential for invasiveness that makes it very difficult to control. It is important to assess the risks very carefully before planting species that may easily escape from gardens (see the chapter on invasive plants, page 159). Our advice is that these species should be avoided in gardens situated near natural areas in order to prevent them from becoming invasive and having a negative impact on the environment. As alternatives,

Pennisetum clandestinum (Kikuyu grass) can be replaced by *Stenotaphrum secundatum* (false Kikuyu grass) and *Paspalum vaginatum* by hybrid *Cynodon*, neither of which can escape from gardens since they don't self-seed.

Reconciling advantages and drawbacks
To reconcile the advantages and drawbacks of macrothermic grasses, one of the best solutions is to mix several different species instead of planting just one. In a mediterranean garden, even the idea of replacing an 'English' lawn with a large expanse of *Zoysia* or *Cynodon* is questionable. To get away from the image of a perfectly regular lawn, a first step could be to plant a mixture of macrothermic grasses, for instance *Cynodon* and *Stenotaphrum* which go together very well. The second step could be to introduce other perennial plants whose very different appearance breaks up the uniformity of the patch and whose complementary foliage goes a long way towards limiting the disadvantages of macrothermic grasses.

The major drawback of a traditional planting of pot-grown *Zoysia tenuifolia* is its slow growth during the first year. By mixing *Zoysia tenuifolia* with a fast-growing groundcover plant, like *Achillea coarctata* or *Frankenia laevis*, one gets several successive stages of cover, with the balance between the different species changing progressively. In the early months the ground is colonized by the fast-growing plant which is gradually replaced by the extremely dense vegetation of the *Zoysia*. In a few years' time a wonderfully ornamental picture is achieved, with the flowers of the perennial plants emerging through the ground-hugging carpet of *Zoysia*. In our garden we overcame the problem of the slow establishment of *Zoysia tenuifolia* by planting it with *Achillea coarctata* and *Verbena rigida*, the three species forming a striking flowering lawn in spring which is one of the most successful scenes in our garden. In time, the powerful *Zoysia* strangled its competitors, so that the achillea and the verbena were relegated to the periphery where the carpet of *Zoysia* is less dense.

1. A lawn of macrothermic grasses can be made using young pot-raised plants.

2. A new planting of *Zoysia tenuifolia*. During the first year, careful weeding between the young plants is necessary.

3. To reduce the cost of planting the lawn, you can prepare a stock of pot-grown plants in advance. Although relatively slow, propagation is easy for the amateur gardener.

1

2

3

Cynodon 'Santa Ana' is another species that lends itself to mixing with herbaceous perennials. One such plant is *Trifolium fragiferum*, a carpeting clover whose ability to resist drought is comparable to that of *Cynodon*. The two plants have an inverse cycle: *Trifolium* becomes dormant when *Cynodon* is in full leaf in summer and forms a dense green carpet just when *Cynodon* turns yellow in winter. These two plants are also complementary in terms of their nutrient needs. Like all grasses, *Cynodon* needs nitrogen and *Trifolium* fixes nitrogen from the air and restores it to the soil by means of the bacterial nodules on its roots (see page 119).

Trifolium fragiferum thus encourages the growth of *Cynodon*, while *Cynodon* in turn moderates the *Trifolium*, whose sometimes excessive growth in spring means that it needs frequent mowing if planted on its own. In the garden, the combination of *Cynodon* and *Trifolium fragiferum* may serve as the basis for other mixtures, including for example *Achillea crithmifolia* and *Phyla canescens*. All these fast-growing species withstand heavy foot traffic. They can be combined to create a wild-looking groundcover that requires little maintenance, for example in children's play areas or permeable car ports (see also page 58).

1. As an alternative to planting cuttings or plug plants, ready-grown turf squares of *Zoysia tenuifolia* can be laid to give an instant result.

2. If you are not looking for a perfectly even lawn, a mixture of macrothermic grasses can be planted. *Cynodon* and *Stenotaphrum, for example, do very well together.*

3. By planting *Zoysia tenuifolia* with a fast-growing groundcover plant such as *Achillea coarctata*, you can achieve several successive stages of groundcover. The achillea gives a rapid preliminary greening of the patch allowing time for the dense vegetation of *Zoysia* to slowly colonize the entire area.

4. *Zoysia tenuifolia, Achillea coarctata* and *Verbena rigida* 'Lilacina'. The combination of a macrothermic grass and perennial flowering plants offers striking ornamental scenes. In time, *Zoysia becomes* dominant and the other species are relegated to the peripheries.

4

GREEN CARPETS: PLANTS YOU CAN WALK ON

ADVANTAGES: no mowing is necessary. Reduced watering compared to a conventional lawn. Groundcover that is adapted to being walked on (degree of foot traffic according to species). Very attractive appearance, easy to integrate into a mediterranean garden.

DRAWBACKS: planting pot-grown plants may involve a lot of labour and high costs. For some species, hand-weeding is a significant limitation. New plantings require attentive care during their first year.

RECOMMENDED SURFACE AREA: a few dozen square metres.

In addition to grasses, numerous other plants may be used to cover the ground in mediterranean gardens. The lowest growing of these hug the ground to form real green carpets, and some of them withstand foot traffic perfectly well. Creeping thymes, *Frankenia laevis* or scented achillea, for example, form flat carpets that are inviting to walk or lie on. These groundcover plants can replace small areas of lawn very satisfactorily. By covering the soil continuously with their regular vegetation, they reduce the problems of dust in summer and mud in winter. They provide an open space that extends the reception area of the terrace and can serve as a green carpet for children to play on.

One of the points of interest of carpeting groundcover plants is that they offer a completely different appearance

from the conventional lawn. The green of the lawn, identical in every garden, seeks to evoke the perfect colour of an English meadow, regardless of its climate zone. By contrast, carpeting groundcover plants offer the opportunity to create a different identity for each garden. Thanks to the variety of their colours and leaf textures, they make it possible for us to diversify our landscaping approaches to groundcover. They integrate well into the concept of a mediterranean garden by acting as a foreground to beds of dry-climate perennials and shrubs and providing visual continuity between different parts of the garden. The dark green of *Thymus hirsutus* evokes the sombre colour of evergreen shrubs such as myrtle and lentisk, while the downy carpet of mouse-ear hawkweed or scented achillea marries perfectly with *Nepeta* species, artemisias or *Stachys* species. Carpeting groundcovers create a changing landscape, in harmony with the passage of the rest of the garden through the seasons. The grey foliage of *Thymus ciliatus* takes on an amazing violet hue in winter, when the new shoots of box are reddish and the lentisks become bronze. With the arrival of the first cold weather, the dark green carpet of *Frankenia laevis* becomes marbled with shades of red, orange and violet which lighten its dark foliage, just as the pomegranates and *Cotinus* are decked in their autumn colours.

Carpeting groundcover plants differ from lawns because in addition to their handsome evergreen foliage, they often have very ornamental flowers. The flowers of *Thymus*

Facing page
The velvety foliage of *Thymus ciliatus* makes a thick, soft carpet.

1. The carpeting vegetation of *Thymus serpyllum* 'Elfin' is good for replacing lawn in small areas.

2. A carpet of *Matricaria tchihatchewii*. Carpets of vegetation are easily integrated into the mediterranean garden and when used in the foreground with beds of dry-climate perennials and shrubs behind, they create a visual continuity between the different parts of the garden.

The flowering of
carpeting groundcover
plants is often very
ornamental:

1. *Thymus ciliatus*
is covered in downy
flowers in May.

2. Of all carpeting
groundcovers, *Phyla
canescens* flowers the
longest: its countless
small pinkish-white
flowers are produced
in succession almost
ceaselessly from June to
September.

3. *Potentilla
neumanniana* flowers
right at the beginning
of spring.

3

praecox are so tightly packed that they almost submerge the entire plant, which is transformed into a magnificent carpet of bright pink. At the end of winter, spring cinquefoil blooms with pretty luminous yellow flowers that mix with the tender green of the new shoots. *Matricaria tchihatchewii* is covered with white daisy flowers in spring, making the patch of groundcover resemble a wild meadow. The pale pink flowers of the strawberry clover, *Trifolium fragiferum*, open in June, followed by curious paper-like fruits whose pale colour contrasts with the dark green leaves through summer. Of all groundcover plants, *Phyla canescens* blooms longest: its countless small pinkish-white flowers, decorative

and scented, go on appearing almost endlessly throughout the whole summer.

To make the most of the ornamental qualities of the different carpeting groundcover plants, vary the species used in different parts of the garden. As they all have different needs, first take the time to carefully weigh up their advantages and disadvantages and choose the right plant for the right place. Tolerance of foot traffic varies depending on the species so bear in mind the degree to which an area will be walked on when choosing groundcover plants for it. For instance, the area surrounding a swimming pool is well

Phyla canescens is a groundcover plant that can withstand intensive foot traffic. Here the carpet of *Phyla* colonizes a path that is used daily. Irregular planting of *Limonium pruinosum* softens the edges of the path, adding a wild note to the scene.

suited to the soft carpet of a creeping thyme such as *Thymus hirsutus*, while an area subject to heavy foot traffic responds well to carpets of *Phyla* or *Achillea odorata*. The ornamental value of groundcover carpets can be used in this way to enhance the different parts of the garden with a range of complementary surfaces.

Most of the plants which can be used as green carpets are markedly more resistant to drought than the conventional lawn. Many of them are native to the lands around the Mediterranean Basin, such as *Frankenia laevis* which grows in Corsica or *Thymus ciliatus* which comes from Morocco. Like all plants adapted to the mediterranean climate, they are able to tolerate long periods of drought but it may be necessary to give them an occasional watering in summer. One of the strategies used by carpeting plants to enable them to withstand drought is the partial loss of their foliage during summer dormancy. On the Larzac plateau, *Thymus praecox* forms lovely expanses of pink in the spring, then loses its leaves during the hottest time of summer; the foliage grows again with the first rains of autumn and by winter the plant is once more a superb carpet, dense and even. If we allow the plant to follow its natural cycle in the garden, it is a lot less attractive in summer: its thin wiry brown stems among more or less dried out leaves do not in the least resemble the thick green carpet that we'd anticipated. Most gardeners are thus led to water carpeting plants, even if in their natural habitat they withstand drought well, in order to do away with the resting period during which the plant is less ornamental in the garden. So when considering drought resistance from the gardener's point of view there are two factors: on the one hand their absolute drought resistance, which corresponds to the plants' ability to survive in their natural environment, and on the other hand their drought resistance as a garden plant which depends on several factors, among them the gardener's expectations in terms of summer foliage.

Carpeting plants can easily let undesirable weeds appear through their low-growing foliage. Planting too large an area with this type of groundcover is an error frequently made by novice gardeners. The amount of time needed for hand weeding may be more than the gardener is willing to devote to it. However, the degree of competition by weeds varies between different species, so the amount of weeding required is a factor which needs to be taken into consideration when we are choosing plants, according to the objectives and the intended area over which they will be planted. A solution that provides an alternative to hand weeding is to plant on a bed of gravel (see page 129). This method partially

1. *Frankenia laevis* in its natural habitat, at Cap Corse, Corsica, at the end of August. To withstand drought, *Frankenia* loses almost all its leaves in summer thereby also losing its ornamental value.

2. In gardens in the South of France, *Frankenia laevis* needs watering occasionally in order to maintain dense vegetation during the summer.

1

2

reproduces the natural conditions in which carpeting plants grow on their own, without any maintenance. In the wild, these plants are happy in a stony environment which is not subject to competition from weeds (see page 31). Gravel also has the advantage of limiting evaporation from the surface of the soil, creating perfect drainage and encouraging the surface rooting of some carpeting plants like thymes and *Frankenia*, which grow even faster during their first year.

To prevent the pressure of weeding or watering becoming too great, carpeting plants are best used in small areas. On sites measuring a few dozen square metres – near a terrace, beside a swimming pool or in children's play areas – they can form magnificent and visually striking effects. But these plants are just a taste of the fascinating world of lawn alternatives and various other solutions now take up the baton for covering larger areas of ground. To sum up the advice on green carpets, instead of going for a uniform carpet, choose a variety of plants to get a groundcover which requires markedly less maintenance than a single-species carpet (see the following chapter). To limit the weed problem, plants such as strawberry clover or mouse-ear hawkweed can act as the basis for a very different kind of management which is nearer a wild lawn consisting only of 'weeds' (see page 63). Finally, planting on gravel offers the opportunity for stun-

ning landscaping possibilities, among which the 'flowering steppe' is without doubt the most advanced means of covering large areas with minimal maintenance (see page 71).

Over twenty years of experimenting, we have tested countless carpeting plants, not all of which gave satisfactory results. We have selected the following species as most suitable for dry-climate gardens.

PLANTS FOR GREEN CARPETS

Achillea crithmifolia
Achillea millefolium
Achillea odorata
Achillea tomentosa
Chamaemelum nobile
Dichondra repens
Dymondia margaretae
Frankenia laevis
Herniaria glabra
Matricaria tchihatchewii

Phyla canescens
Pilosella officinarum
Thymus ciliatus
Thymus herba-barona
Thymus leucotrichus subsp.
  neicefii
Thymus hirsutus
Thymus serpyllum 'Elfin'
Trifolium fragiferum

---

1. A new planting of a carpeting thyme. Planting on gravel reduces competition from weeds, provides perfect drainage and limits direct evaporation from the soil.

2. Demonstration squares of carpeting plants at the Los Angeles County Arboretum, California. In the foreground, the even carpet of *Thymus hirsutus*.

FLOWERING CARPETS:
A MIXTURE OF GROUNDCOVER PLANTS

ADVANTAGES: less maintenance and less frequent watering than for uniform green carpets. Withstands foot traffic (degree of resistance to foot traffic depends on the mixture). Very striking appearance, great variety of possible mixtures.

DRAWBACKS: planting pot-grown specimens involves significant labour and expense. New plantings require attentive care during the first year.

RECOMMENDED SURFACE AREA: from a few dozen square metres to several hundred square metres, depending on the maintenance needs of the chosen mixture.

A mixture of groundcover plants requires less maintenance than a single-species carpet and is therefore a practical option for covering large areas. These mixed plantings have a very different appearance offering a tapestry of varied foliage in all shades of green and grey. The first positive effect is psychological: weeds become less irksome. If a few weeds manage to infiltrate the groundcover carpet, they don't seem so shocking because they are camouflaged among the diversity of foliage. Weeding thus becomes less of a chore since it doesn't have to be so painstaking. If competition from weeds becomes too pronounced at certain times of year, it is easy to supplement hand-weeding with a simple mowing process which reduces the height of the weeds without it being necessary to remove them altogether.

A second positive effect of mixed plantings has to do with irrigation. If we allow the plants to enter into partial dormancy, groundcover remains more ornamental when it consists of mixed species rather than one species. Since different species don't all share the same resting period, they can stand in for one another and create a picture that evolves over the course of the seasons. Irrigation generally remains necessary, but it can be given at more widely spaced intervals: a varied groundcover consumes significantly less water than a single-species carpet. Mixed planting also allows us to use more drought-tolerant plants, such as *Centaurea bella* or *Tanacetum densum,* which would be ill-suited to single-species carpets but integrate perfectly into a diversified composition.

Mixed groundcovers allow us to play with the micro-contours among different plants whose vegetation may be of varying thickness. If, for example, we mix several different thymes, some of them will be perfectly flat and ground-hugging while others, like *Thymus ciliatus*, have thicker vegetation. Instead of having a flat carpet, it becomes animated by movement which draws the eye and reinforces a sense of depth in the planted area.

The examples that follow are not intended as models for all gardens. On the contrary, I invite each gardener to invent his or her own mixture to suit the surrounding landscape, the size of the plot and awareness of how the plants will look in summer. Don't be afraid to experiment with an unexpected mixture. By using several different species to cover the ground, you reduce the risk of error as there is a greater chance that there will be at least one species which

Facing page
A mixed groundcover, consisting of *Thymus hirsutus, Thymus ciliatus* and *Phyla canescens.* (Bourjas Garden, design by Jean-Laurent Felizia.)

A "weed" is considered a nuisance when it emerges in the middle of a uniform carpet, while it often passes unnoticed in a mixed carpet:

1. Dandelions in the middle of a carpet of *Frankenia laevis.*

2. Dandelions in a mixed planting of *Frankenia laevis* and *Phyla canescens.*

and the slightly staggered flowering times prolong the period when the carpet is in bloom: *Thymus ciliatus* from the end of April, *Thymus leucotrichus* subsp. *neicefii* from mid-May, *Thymus hirsutus* and *Thymus praecox* in June.

An aromatic groundcover composed of plants rich in essential oils: *Thymus serpyllum* 'Lemon Curd' (lemon-scented), *Thymus herba-barona* (cumin-scented) and *Thymus praecox* subsp. *polytrichus* (bergamot-scented). This mixture can be completed by *Achillea odorata*, smelling of camphor, and *Chamaemelum nobile*, which gives off a powerful fruity scent dominated by green apple. Walking on this patch crushes the plants and releases the scent of the leaves. This kind of aromatic groundcover can later be punctuated by taller plants with strong scent potential, such as *Calamintha nepeta* or rue, to create an original scent garden.

A groundcover with thick vegetation, very decorative and effective at preventing weeds from growing through it: *Centaurea bella*, *Tanacetum densum*, *Achillea odorata* and *Achillea crithmifolia*. These plants form a thick carpet, 5 to 10 cm high, and their very dense vegetation effectively prevents competition from weeds, in part through the chemical compounds they diffuse in the soil which inhibit the germination of competing species (allelopathy). Achilleas have a good tolerance of foot traffic, while *Centaurea bella* and *Tanacetum* only moderately so. In this kind of mixture, the density of the planting does not have to preserve a regular balance between the different species: depending on the lay-

1. The many possible mixtures of carpeting plants allow us to approach the landscaping of a mediterranean garden in different ways. Here carpets of *Thymus ciliatus*, *Tanacetum densum* and *Potentilla neumanniana* invade the paths between the squares of a small vegetable garden. (Garden of Jeanne and Jean Burger.)

2. The delicate vegetation of *Frankenia laevis* slips through thick cushions of *Tanacetum densum*. The diversity of foliage makes a multitude of striking combinations possible.

3. The grey-green and silver tones of the foliage of *Centaurea bella* and *Tanacetum densum* complement one another perfectly. These two species, both of them drought-resistant, have dense vegetation that effectively prevents grass from growing through them.

is perfectly happy in the particular conditions and will form the basis of the groundcover carpet requiring little maintenance. It is always possible to improve the mixture later on by introducing complementary new species after a few years to complete the planting. In this way, mixed groundcovers allow us to approach garden making not in terms of a fixed picture whose initial appearance must remain unchanged, but rather as a place of experimentation, open to evolving in the future. Among the plant mixtures we have tried out, here are a few which we have found especially successful:

A carpet of mixed thymes: *Thymus hirsutus* (green foliage), *Thymus ciliatus* (downy grey-green foliage), *Thymus leucotrichus* subsp. *neicefii* (grey foliage), *Thymus praecox* (dark green foliage). The foliage colours complement one another

out, it should be possible to allow achilleas to dominate in the places walked on most frequently.

A cameo in grey: *Achillea crithmifolia, Achillea odorata, Pilosella officinarum, Thymus ciliatus*. This carpet of grey or grey-green foliage can be set off by a counterpoint of dark green, for example by a few cushions of *Teucrium × lucidrys* or *Thymus camphoratus* emerging from it. One could also envisage the negative of this picture, in other words a groundcover carpet forming a cameo of shades of green (for example *Thymus praecox, Frankenia laevis* and *Potentilla neumanniana*), punctuated by cushions of grey-leaved plants, *Teucrium marum, Rhodanthemum hosmariense* or *Artemisia* 'Canescens'.

A silver carpet: *Artemisia pedemontana* and *Achillea tomentosa*. These plants form a striking carpet, ideal for making a strong contrast with surrounding areas of green-leaved plants. However, their cultivation is more demanding than that of most other carpeting plants since, like many silver-leaved species, they require perfect drainage. If the soil is heavy, the first thing to be done is to add a fairly large amount of sand or gravel in order to achieve a light, very well-drained soil to a depth of at least 15 to 20 cm. These plants do best when they are planted in a bed of gravel which continues the work of the surface drainage (see page 129). To create the effect of a sculpted relief, the silver carpet may be punctuated by a few cushions of *Tanacetum densum* or *Achillea umbellata*, whose leaves become almost white in summer. In a mild climate, waves of *Dichondra argentea* or *Cotula lineariloba* can be added.

A garrigue effect for poor and stony soils: a mixture of *Carex halleriana, Potentilla neumanniana* and *Brachypodium retusum*. Many garrigue plants can be incorporated in small patches into this kind of mixture: *Iris lutescens, Euphorbia cyparissias, Teucrium chamaedrys, Thymus vulgaris, Sedum sediforme* or *Salvia verbenaca*. Bulbous plants naturalize easily among groundcover plants: *Muscari, Narcissus dubius* and wild orchids.

A mixture of *Phyla canescens* and *Achillea crithmifolia*: the growth cycles of these two species are complementary, which allows us to have a good coverage of the soil throughout the year. The *Phyla* is deciduous in winter, just at the time when the achillea is in full growth. By contrast, the *Phyla* grows vigorously in summer when the achillea enters into partial dormancy to cope with drought. This mixture of two rapidly growing species can be used to cover fairly large areas because, once established, it requires little maintenance: an occasional mowing can replace weeding, while watering can be adjusted to suit the limited irrigation needs of *Phyla* (watering once or twice a month in summer in the

1. The balance between species can vary in different parts of the same patch. By using a mixture of *Tanacetum densum* and *Achillea crithmifolia*, it is possible to create paths through the planting where the achillea will be dominant, since it withstands foot traffic better.

A mixture of silver-leaved groundcovers can create a strong visual contrast if they are planted among plants with dark-coloured leaves:

2. The leaves of *Achillea tomentosa* change over the seasons: grey-green in winter, they are covered in silver hairs as soon as the heat arrives.

3. *Achillea umbellata* forms a compact cushion whose silver foliage turns almost white in summer.

4. With its lacy silver foliage, *Tanacetum densum* is one of the best groundcovers for mediterranean gardens.

Montpellier region of France). This plant association can also serve as the basis for numerous secondary mixtures, including for example mouse-ear hawkweed (*Pilosella officinarum),* various thymes (*Thymus ciliatus, Thymus hirsutus* and several other achillea species (*Achillea coarctata, Achillea odorata*).

When one is looking for a solution to cover large areas that are regularly walked on, with a minimum of maintenance, another interesting mixture consists of *Cynodon* 'Santa Ana' and *Trifolium fragiferum.* To this mixture can be added *Phyla* and *Achillea crithmifolia* for extensive colonization of large areas. As regards the visual aspect, the groundcover can be completed by over-sowing with wild species, such as *Plantago coronopus, Lotus corniculatus* or *Sanguisorba minor,* which brings us to the subject of the wild lawn (see page 63).

A mixture for shade, consisting of three carpeting plants that tolerate deep shade: *Dichondra repens,* with tender green foliage, *Glechoma hederacea,* whose fine spikes of violet-blue flowers open in spring, and *Viola hederacea,* whose abundant small bicoloured flowers, mauve and white, open in successive waves, in spring and again in autumn. This carpet can be punctuated with some taller perennials that like shade, such as *Geranium macrorrhizum* or *Salvia spathacea.*

Another mixture for shade: *Ophiopogon japonicus* and *Soleirolia soleirolii. Ophiopogon* grows slowly and takes several years to become established. *Soleirolia* is faster-growing and

provides a first cover for the ground. Both these species like relatively damp shade.

All these basic mixtures of plants can develop into countless variations. One could emphasize foliage colour, with the dominant note being grey (*Achillea crithmifolia, Thymus ciliatus*) light green, (*Chamaemelum nobile, Matricaria tchihatchewii*) or dark green (*Thymus herba-barona, Thymus hirsutus*). The diversity of textures makes it possible to cre-

ate different effects: a mossy carpet for a Japanese-inspired garden using *Thymus serpyllum* 'Elfin' or *Soleirolia soleirolii*, soft carpets using *Achillea tomentosa* or *Cotula lineariloba*, a flat, ground-hugging carpet using *Herniaria glabra*, or luxuriant vegetation using *Carex halleriana*. One could also play on a succession of flowers, mixing spring-flowering plants such as thymes, potentilla or chamomile with summer-flowering species like *Phyla*. To complete this flowering mixture, the groundcover plants can be combined with a broad range of bulbs, capable of pushing through the low-growing groundcover to produce their brightly coloured flowers. By making a careful selection of plants by flowering season, one can create very decorative combinations of bulbs and carpeting plants. For example, *Ipheion uniflorum* 'Rolf Fiedler'

could be planted in a carpet of *Potentilla neumanniana*: the bright blue flowers of the *Ipheion* open at exactly the same time as the luminous yellow flowers of the potentilla. Autumn-flowering bulbs such as *Sternbergia lutea*, *Cyclamen persicum*, *Colchicum lusitanum*, *Crocus goulimyi* or *Crocus sativus* are particularly useful for creating patches of colour out of season.

One might also envisage a garden in which different areas are given different mixtures of plants in such a way that the groundcover layer plays a part in the overall diversity of the landscape. Even within a single area one could vary the density of the components from one place to another. In one section, the dominant plants could be complemented by

Carpeting groundcover plants can be combined with a large range of bulbous species. In early April, the bright blue flowers of *Ipheion uniflorum* 'Rolf Fiedler' emerge from the yellow carpet of *Potentilla neumanniana*.

secondary species providing a simple visual counterpoint, while in another section these secondary plants could in turn predominate. In this way, the different species enable us to weave a fabric in constant movement, whose irregular weft alternates light and dark, grey and dark green foliage. In a large area, one could also create a visual progression, starting with a single-species foreground and gradually evolving into a diverse mixture of plants of greater height, which serves as a transition to beds of tall plants.

Groundcover plantings that start off highly diversified generally evolve into a simpler mix because some species will be happier with the particular conditions of the garden and over time come to predominate. The more one var-ies the number of species, the more one can reduce irrigation, adjusting the watering schedule to the needs of the most drought-resistant plants. These will then be the species that will gradually dominate in summer when some of the other species become partially dormant, without any significant loss in terms of aesthetics. So the mixed ground-cover solution offers two distinct advantages over single-species carpets: weeding can be replaced by an occasional mowing; and irrigation can be reduced to the level needed by the species most resistant to drought. Using a mixture of carpeting plants makes it possible to cover a larger area without increasing water consumption or time spent on maintenance.

Thymus hirsutus and *Phyla canescens*. Plantings that are initially very diverse tend to evolve into a simpler mixture because, depending on the particular conditions in each garden, in time some species become dominant.

When you are creating large areas of groundcover, the two limiting factors remain the cost of the plants and the maintenance required in the first year. Even for mixtures that need minimal maintenance once they are established, new plantings require regular hand weeding, which can take up quite a lot of time. The wisest approach, if you want to cover a large area with groundcover plants, is to carry out the planting in successive stages. Every year you can expand an existing patch of groundcover by adding a small area of new planting which will, by virtue of its size, require only a modest amount of maintenance. An added advantage is that instead of deciding at the start which plants will make up your mixture for the entire planned area, you can adapt your choice of plants for a newly added section by selecting those that have already given the best results. The whole business of creating an area of groundcover can now be seen in a new light: earlier plantings can provide mother plants from which future plantings can be propagated. Most groundcover plants suitable for large mixed carpets are easy to propagate, since either they root wherever their horizontal stems are in contact with the soil or they have a suckering habit which makes them easy to divide. In the A-Z plant directory (pages 167-227) I include information on the propagation of each species. By propagating carpeting plants yourself, you not only reduce the cost of the planting but also get the satisfaction of creating a lawn alternative virtually single-handed.

PLANTS FOR A MIXED GROUNDCOVER

Achillea coarctata
Achillea crithmifolia
Achillea millefolium
Achillea odorata
Achillea tomentosa
Achillea umbellata
Artemisia pedemontana
Carex halleriana
Centaurea bella
Chamaemelum nobile
Cotula lineariloba
Dichondra argentea
Dichondra repens
Frankenia laevis
Glechoma hederacea
Herniaria glabra
Lotus corniculatus
Matricaria tchihatchewii
Ophiopogon japonicus

Phyla canescens
Pilosella officinarum
Potentilla neumanniana
Soleirolia soleirolii
Tanacetum densum
Thymus ciliatus
Thymus herba-barona
Thymus leucotrichus subsp. *neicefii*
Thymus praecox
Thymus praecos subsp. *polytrichus*
Thymus hirsutus
Thymus serpyllum 'Elfin'
Thymus serpyllum 'Lemon Curd'
Trifolium fragiferum
Viola hederacea

The grey rosettes of *Achillea crithmifolia* are set off by the reddish hue of the carpet of *Frankenia laevis.* A mixed groundcover has two decisive advantages over a single-species carpet: less weeding and less water are required.

MIXED GRASSLAND "LAWNS":
THE ART OF CULTIVATING WEEDS

ADVANTAGES: u ed in the same way as a conventional lawn but requires less maintenance. Reduced irrigation and less frequent mowing Does not require either fertilizers or pesticides. Ornamental spring flowering. Provides habitat for beneficial insects and pollinators.

DRAWBACKS: growing some perennial species from seed can sometimes give disappointing results because of the slowness of germination. Pot-grown plants can be used instead, which involves more work and a higher cost.

RECOMMENDED SURFACE AREA: unlimited apart from the constraints of mowing and occasional watering, depending on the appearance desired.

In regions with a dry climate, the perfect lawn is always on the verge of reverting to a mixed grassland – it is only the gardener's ceaseless work that prevents it from returning to this stage which is much richer in species and infinitely easier to maintain. Replacing a lawn composed entirely of grass species with a mixed lawn containing a multitude of wild flowers is one of the simplest solutions for a groundcover that requires little maintenance. It is easy to implement, having more to do with the gardener than the garden. What is needed is a change in your expectations, modifying the standard of lawn that you seek to achieve. By putting behind you the goal of a perfect lawn, you will discover the unexpected pleasure of a more natural 'lawn'. The progression from the one to the other translates into various

complementary practical changes: reduce the frequency of watering, eliminate fertilizers, abandon herbicides and mow less often.

To transform a conventional lawn into a mixed lawn, start by watering it less often. The frequency with which it is irrigated and the amount of water given each time affect the composition of the lawn. In very hot weather, each irrigation by sprinkler causes a serious loss of water through evaporation, even if one takes care to water the lawn at night: because of the capillary action bringing water upwards through the soil, a lot of evaporation occurs during the following day. The more frequently one waters a lawn, the more evaporation increases – from this point of view, in mediterranean gardens watering a lawn daily is the very worst thing one can do. By contrast, if a natural lawn is watered deeply at widely spaced intervals, water use is optimized because less is lost through evaporation. This modified watering regime leads to a change in the range of plants that make up the lawn, particularly if the use of fertilizers stops at the same time. The conventional lawn grasses, which in the mediterranean climate require very frequent watering and abundant feeding, rapidly lose their vigour. They give way to other species which are less greedy for fertilizers and more resistant to drought, in fact precisely the plants one welcomes in order to achieve a mixed lawn that is easier to maintain.

To encourage the growth of a mixed lawn, mow it less often

Facing page
A mixed lawn is much easier to maintain than one consisting of only grass species.

1. In abandoning the goal of a perfect lawn, gardeners find that more natural lawns bring unexpected pleasures.

2. A playing field in a village in the South of France. By mowing less frequently, reducing the use of fertilizers and eliminating herbicides and pesticides, it is possible to transform a single-species lawn into a mixed lawn which serves the same social uses but requires markedly less maintenance. Deep watering at periodic intervals is necessary if the lawn is to remain green in summer.

and allow the grass to grow taller. You can also mow it in varying ways, for example by close mowing pathways and clearings that get pedestrian traffic and leaving the rest of the grass to grow taller. These mown and non-mown areas may change over the course of the seasons, allowing different parts of the garden to be mown alternately. A manual lawn mower with a spiral blade and without a grass-collecting box is suitable for this work. Grass cuttings left on the spot constitute a supply of organic material which will be absorbed by the soil to enhance the growth of a mixed lawn. If you have stopped applying chemical herbicides, this adjustment of the height of the mowing favours species that may flower and self-seed more or less all over the lawn – the famous 'weeds' against which a whole army of gardeners has been struggling for the last fifty years.

Some of these plants which are considered weeds are in fact extremely valuable allies to the gardener that should not just be tolerated in the lawn but actively encouraged. Clovers, for example, have the remarkable ability to fertilize the soil thanks to the nitrogen-fixing nodules arranged like strings of beads on their roots. The flowers of the bird's foot trefoil produce abundant nectar that attracts pollinators, particularly welcome if fruit trees are grown in the vicinity. Other weeds contribute to making chemical treatments against various insect pests superfluous. Daisies and dandelions, for instance, are important sources of pollen which, early in the year when other flowers are few and far between,

serve as food for a multitude of beneficial insects, such as lacewings, hoverflies and ladybirds, whose larvae will subsequently devour whole colonies of aphids. Finally, some lawn weeds have very ornamental flowers. Bulbous plants able to colonize lawns, for example anemones, ornithogalums and grape hyacinths, can transform the monotony of a lawn into a succession of lovely flowery scenes over the course of the seasons.

By adjusting the frequency of watering, by mowing less often and by eliminating fertilizers and herbicides, one creates an environment in which the grasses that make up conventional lawns are unable to maintain a dense carpet. Among them a whole procession of complementary plants develops – annuals, perennials and bulbs – which progressively transform the single-species lawn into a mixed lawn

1. Many lawn "weeds" are valuable allies of the gardener. Clovers fertilize the soil and the bird's-foot trefoil, rich in nectar, encourages the presence of pollinators.

2. The composition of the lawn plays a direct role in the overall management of the garden. Dandelions, for example, are an important source of pollen and food for a host of beneficial insects such as lacewings, hoverflies and ladybirds.

3. A lacewing (*Chrysoperla* sp.) eats an aphid under the attentive gaze of the next aphid that patiently waits its turn. Like many beneficial insects, the lacewing is very sensitive to the pesticides used to treat lawns consisting of grass species.

that is very interesting from aesthetic and ecological points of view. However, if the lawn has been heavily treated with herbicides for years, the natural seedbank in the soil will sometimes be so scanty that the lawn will have difficulty becoming more diverse. In this case the lawn in transition may look little better than a sad and rather bare carpet. The plants which most easily colonize a lawn are those whose seeds are carried long distances by the wind, like daisies and dandelions. But other species whose seeds are not dispersed over great distances may not appear in the lawn unless they are present in neighbouring gardens. In this case one can give nature a helping hand by introducing complementary species to hasten the transformation of a single-species lawn into a mixed grassland lawn.

Various methods can be used to introduce new species into an existing lawn: sowing seed, planting plug plants or, for some species, planting bulbs. For species that germinate very easily, the simplest method is to sow seed directly on to the existing lawn, called over-sowing. The gardener shifts roles: instead of battling against weeds, he or she on the contrary now begins to examine the ornamental species that naturally colonize wild grasslands in the neighbourhood in order to collect a few handfuls of seed. If, for example, dandelions generally appear in the lawn by themselves, one might want to add some of their cousins, such as hawksbeard (*Crepis sancta*) or smooth golden fleece (*Urospermum dalechampii*), which are of interest not only for their flowers but also for their edible young rosettes that make delicious wild salads in early spring. Harvesting ripe seeds, followed by sowing in small patches in the more open areas of the lawn, will introduce the desired species. If the soil is very compact, a light scarification and the addition of a small amount of sand just before sowing can be useful. The following year, after a complete growth cycle, the new species will be able to self-seed throughout the lawn. For the best chance of success, seed should be sown in early autumn, when the soil is still warm and the first rains ensure the regular water necessary for germination.

To introduce bulbous species into a mixed lawn, the simplest way is to buy bulbs from a supplier who specializes in mediterranean bulbs and to plant them during their dormant period. For most drought-adapted bulbs this dormant period is at the beginning of summer. Planting bulbs in the middle of existing grass is easy. Use a bulb planter to

1. *Anemone hortensis* and *Bellis perennis* in the Monti Madoni, Sicily. By choosing bulbous plants capable of naturalizing in a mixed lawn, gardeners can create effects that call to mind the magnificent wild grasslands of Mediterranean mountains.

2. At Great Dixter in England large expanses of narcissi colonize the meadow in winter, when mowing is not necessary. Later in the season, the withered leaves of the narcissi disappear just when the wild lawn requires its first mowing.

1

2

3

open holes into which you can slip the bulbs. They should be planted at a depth equal to approximately twice their height and covered with fine soil mixed with sand. Bulbous

1. Although its flowers appear delicate, *Ornithogalum umbellatum* is a robust species that naturalizes easily in wild lawns.

2. In March, the blue-mauve flowers of *Muscari armeniacum* decorate the wild lawn.

3. *Narcissus tazetta* grows wild in the South of France. Very adaptable, it is equally happy in dry ground or damper soils.

4. The strawberry clover (*Trifolium fragiferum*) is one of many ornamental perennials that can be included in a wild lawn.

There are several techniques for creating a mixed lawn: sowing a wild flower seed mix, planting plug plants in carefully prepared soil, or planting plug plants in the middle of an existing lawn, which will then produce seed and spread.

FORAGING ON YOUR LAWN: WEEDS AND WILD SALADS

With a pinch of salt and a generous drizzle of olive oil, wild salads make a delicious dish at the end of winter. Many food-lovers, reviving an ancient tradition, scramble over hills, grasslands and garrigue to collect the young shoots of various delicately flavoured plants. Some of these species can easily naturalize in a mixed lawn, and the keen gardener can easily encourage them and turn the lawn into an ornamental larder. Here are some of the edible species that can be eaten raw or cooked: daisy (*Bellis perennis*), dandelion (*Taraxacum officinale*), salad burnet (*Sanguisorba minor*), buck's-horn plantain (*Plantago coronopus*), hawksbeard (*Crepis sancta*) and smooth golden fleece (*Urospermum dalechampii*). Other taller wild salad plants, borage, poppies, common brighteyes and many more, can be grown in parts of the garden which are not mown, for example in a small patch of flowering meadow next to the lawn (see page 107). French-speaking enthusiasts can consult the guide published by Les Ecologistes de l'Euzière, *Les Salades sauvages. L'Ensalada champanèla* (see bibliography). Greek gourmets sing the praises of the white mustard (*Sinapis alba*) and the Mediterranean hartwort (*Tordylium apulum*), and I'm sure that in many other parts of the mediterranean world, gardeners will know other edible wild plants that can easily be grown in a mixed lawn.

plants naturalize well in grass if they are allowed to complete their growth cycle. Leave them to set seed and accumulate reserves in their bulbs without cutting off the leaves until they have turned completely yellow.

For perennial species that multiply by means of suckers or stolons, such as achilleas, bugles, clovers and potentillas, over-sowing is sometimes disappointing since the results are open to many variables. Germination rates are poor, if not zero, if the ideal conditions of warmth and humidity are not present at the time of sowing. As an alternative to growing from seed, we have tried the method recommended by Christopher Lloyd for introducing perennial plants into mixed lawns, namely by planting young pot-raised specimens here and there in the lawn. Planting can be at a fairly low density, about 3 or 4 plants to every 10 square metres, for their purpose is simply to serve as mother plants in an existing lawn. Subsequently they will progressively spread by themselves into different parts of the lawn, in part by

4

means of their colons and in part through self-seeding when the temperature and moisture conditions that each species needs are optimal. To plant young perennials into an existing lawn all that is required is to remove the grass and dig over the soil in an area about 25 cm square. Planting in autumn allows the plants to benefit from the rains that will ensure the watering they need in order to become established. In our experience, this simple and inexpensive method appears to be the most effective for introducing perennial plants, which are slow to arrive naturally and add to the diversity of the lawn. If you take cuttings or root buds from mixed lawns in your neighbourhood, you can raise young plants yourself in a corner of the garden that might temporarily be named "the weed nursery".

If you want to create a mixed lawn from scratch on bare ground, it is possible to do so in small areas starting with pot-raised specimens of the perennials which will form the basis of the lawn, for example, clover, bird's foot trefoil, potentilla, self-heal or mouse-ear hawkweed. Planting can be at a density of 4 to 6 plants per square metre, just as for a green carpet of thymes or *Frankenia*. The maintenance of the mixed lawn planting is by contrast a lot less than it is for a green carpet. There is no need to battle against weeds since the plants you have put in are themselves weeds: every species happy to grow here is welcome in a mixed grassland lawn. An occasional mowing simply helps avoid the growth of taller plants that might compete for light too powerfully or have unattractive foliage like thistles. This first planting

In the renowned botanic garden of the Villa Thuret in Antibes, in the South of France, the huge central lawn is home to a multitude of "weeds" including dandelions, plantains, anemones and narcissi that make a wonderfully ornamental sight in spring. This lawn is not irrigated and dries out completely in summer: here the seasonal change in the appearance of the lawn is accepted as part of the landscape's Mediterranean identity.

of perennials will then serve as the basis for over-sowing with annuals and for the subsequent addition of bulbous plants that will contribute to the diversity of the mixed lawn. It is also possible to follow the planting of the pot-grown perennials with a light over-sowing of rye grass, at a much lower density than would be used for a conventional lawn. The rye grass will temporarily fill the spaces between the young perennials as they start to colonize the lawn; its vegetation will quickly become dormant when the heat and drought of the first summer arrive.

Converting a conventional lawn into a mixed lawn reduces the labour of mowing and eliminates the application of fer-tilizers and herbicides. In regions where summer drought is not very significant, a mixed lawn does not need any water-ing. And where summer drought is severe the gardener has two options: either to accept that the mixed lawn will progressively dry out during the summer until it becomes completely yellow in August, or to give it a deep watering at widely spaced intervals in order to prevent it from becoming fully dormant in summer. The frequence of such watering will depend on the length and intensity of the dry period. For example, in the Montpellier region of France a deep watering once a fortnight from June to August is enough to keep a mixed lawn reasonably green, except in unusual heat waves when it needs to be watered more often.

Natural grasslands on the Larzac plateau in the South of France. The structure of this landscape, in which open grasslands alternate with dark-leaved shrubs, continues to have a strong visual impact even when the grasslands turn golden in summer.

Kew, the centuries-old trees were in fact much more beautiful when set against a golden lawn. English gardeners don't seem to worry too much when their gardens turn yellow: on the contrary, they are enthusiastic about the fine weather, as if granted a tiny bit of mediterranean climate.

In dry-climate gardens it is possible to set off the yellow colour of the dry lawn by using dark-leaved shrubs such as myrtle, phillyrea or lentisk as feature plants. The contrast between the pale lawn and the dark evergreens emphasizes the play of light and shade that is so characteristic of mediterranean gardens in summer. In parts which are not irrigated, the mixed grassland lawn can play different roles over the seasons offering ornamental and ecological interest in autumn, winter and spring, then in the hot season becoming a simple open space that serves as a golden counterpoint to the surrounding plantings.

To limit water consumption, the mixed grassland lawn can be divided into different sections, with irrigation given only to the areas most used in summer, for instance a poolside area or shady terrace. Other areas can be left to follow their natural cycle and become dormant. They will still be more resistant to drought than a conventional lawn, capable of turning completely yellow in summer and then greening up again with the arrival of the first autumn rains. In mediterranean regions, a lawn that turns yellow seems to drive a lot of gardeners crazy. But in southern England lawns can also turn yellow in summer. Clara and I have been in England during particularly dry summers and seen vast lawns in prestigious gardens such as Hampton Court and Kew become a fine straw colour. In the magnificent arboretum at

---

SPECIES THAT CAN BE USED IN A MIXED LAWN TO COMPLEMENT GRASSES

Perennial species
Achillea millefolium
Ajuga reptans
Bellis perennis
Glechoma hederacea
Lotus corniculatus
Pilosella officinarum
Plantago coronopus
Plantago lanceolata
Plantago major
Potentilla neumanniana
Potentilla reptans
Prunella vulgaris
Sanguisorba minor
Taraxacum officinale
Trifolium fragiferum
Trifolium pratense
Trifolium repens

Annual species
Crepis sancta
Medicago lupulina
Urospermum dalechampii
Veronica filiformis

Bulbous species
Allium neapolitanum
Anemone coronaria
Anemone hortensis
Crocus tommasinianus
Leopoldia comosa
Muscari armeniacum
Muscari neglectum
Narcissus hybrids
Narcissus tazetta
Ornithogalum umbellatum

Ajuga reptans is a very ornamental species but it needs occasional watering in summer. To limit its water consumption, a mixed lawn can be divided into several sectors, with irrigation being given only to the zones most used in summer.

ADVANTAGES: a surface that can be walked on which requires minimal maintenance. Does not need any watering in summer. Appearance always visually interesting, even during summer dormancy. Low density planting limits the cost of purchasing plants.

DRAWBACKS: labour and cost of initial investment related to laying the gravel.

RECOMMENDED SURFACE AREA: unlimited, apart from the labour involved in laying the gravel and planting.

In regions where extreme drought makes natural lawns unsuitable, a flowering steppe is one of the easiest alternatives to maintain. The concept of the flowering steppe is inspired by the high plateaux in the mountains of the Mediterranean, where large expanses frequented by sheep are home to a specialized vegetation that resists grazing, drought, wind, cold and being walked on. Near where we live we are lucky enough to have the Larzac plateau which has a very rich flora and provides a remarkable landscape model. Every year, Clara and I go and camp on this plateau for a few days to study its botanical diversity. On one of these botanizing expeditions we were struck by how the steppe landscapes seemed to offer interesting options in our quest for dry-garden groundcovers that require little maintenance and remain ornamental throughout the year.

The steppe zones of the Larzac plateau occur where conditions are particularly harsh and the stony, shallow soil does not allow rich grasslands with orchids to develop. Instead, the vegetation takes the form of sparse tufts that leave stony ground exposed and trodden by sheep. There is a mixture of carpeting plants, bulbs and grasses. In order to replicate the visual impact of this balance between stone and plants, we have attempted to turn one of the experimental areas in our garden into a flowering steppe by planting an assortment of groundcover plants at a low density on a thick layer of gravel. The result, in our opinion, has been spectacular: the little steppe in our garden, covering about 200 m², remains attractive throughout the year despite receiving no water during the long months of summer drought. We are now interested in examining close-up the floral diversity of steppe zones around the Mediterranean, in particular in Morocco, Turkey and Syria, the ancestral steppes of the Fertile Crescent. Studying these areas has led us to add to our original planting autumn-flowering bulbs such as *Crocus goulimyi*, fine-leaved grasses such as *Stipa barbata*, and extremely tough plants native to the desert steppes of the Middle East such as *Limonium pruinosum*.

One of the characteristics of a steppe is the strong seasonality of its visual appearance. As soon as autumn arrives, early bulb species break the austerity of summer with a multitude of small patches of brightly coloured flowers. In

Facing page
A flowering steppe is an ornamental space that can be walked on and is adapted to the dry summers of the Mediterranean.

1. A steppic landscape on the Larzac *plateau:* the stony soil is dotted with widely spaced patches of vegetation, including thyme, germander, bird's-foot trefoil, cinquefoil and *Stipa.*

2. *Crocus* flowering in November in the stony steppes of Mount Taygetos in the Southern Peloponnese.

1

2

1. A steppic landscape in the high plateaux of the Middle Atlas, near Midelt in Morocco. The pressure of over-grazing has left the soil here almost bare: the stony landscape is interrupted only by a few species not eaten by sheep, such as asphodels and euphorbias.

2. Natural steppic landscapes can easily be adapted for the garden, creating areas that can be walked on composed of carpeting plants and bulbs on a bed of gravel. The steppe needs minimal maintenance and does not require any watering in summer.

3. One of the characteristics of a steppe is the strong seasonality of its appearance. At the end of summer, early-flowering bulbs such as *Colchicum lusitanum* or *Sternbergia lutea* break the dryness of summer and transform the austere landscape into an explosion of ephemeral colour.

3

winter, plants that are summer-dormant slowly come to life again in the wet season. Although flowers are absent, the steppe is very beautiful at this time of year when the contrasts in texture and colour of foliage of the various species comes to the fore. In spring, the steppe is transformed into a landscape overflowing with colour. The harsh conditions seem to increase the intensity of the flowering in order to attract pollinating insects within a short timeframe. Then, when the summer heat sets in, the steppe plants gradually become dormant.

The creation of a flowering steppe is carried out in several stages. The first step is to break up the soil thoroughly and incorporate sand to improve the drainage that is so vital. All the species which can be used for a flowering steppe require excellent drainage because in their natural habitat they grow in very stony conditions. The second step is to lay a bed of gravel about 6 to 8 cm thick, before planting. This gravel serves several purposes: it conserves moisture in the soil during the dry period by reducing direct evaporation from the soil; it improves surface drainage during heavy autumn rains; it prevents the germination of the majority of weeds; it acts as a uniform surface that can be walked on, independent of the plant cover whose density may vary from season to season; and it creates a visual harmony between stone and plants which gives the flowering steppe a landscaping impact that is interesting throughout the year. The third step consists of planting, preferably in early autumn, a range of carpeting plants, cushion-shaped plants and bulbs whose vegetation will spread above the gravel. The planting density is low compared to that of an ordinary carpet of groundcover since, once established, the plants don't have to cover the ground entirely. We can thus see a flowering steppe as the reverse image of stepping stones: instead of having a carpet of plants with stones between them, we create a stone carpet with clumps of carpeting plants here and there.

In our experience, making a flowering steppe is one of the best ways of covering the ground in a mediterranean garden if you want a surface that can be walked and needs no irrigation. One of the advantages of a flowering steppe is that during a prolonged summer drought it does not become an

A flowering steppe can be thought of as the negative image of stepping stones: instead of having the soil covered by carpeting plants and punctuated by a path of stones, we create a stony groundcover – gravel – punctuated by patches of carpeting plants.

The four seasons of a flowering steppe in our experimental garden:

1. Spring. Irregular paths over lower-growing plants are traced among the billowing flowers.

2. Summer. The achilleas, so generous in springtime, are now dormant during the hot season. Their faded inflorescences have been clipped off to reveal the gravel, sparsely punctuated by cushions of *Centaurea bella* and *Tanacetum densum*, which retain their leaves in spite of the drought.

3. Autumn. The foliage of the carpeting plants is gradually refurbished with the arrival of the first autumn rains. The autumn leaves of nearby trees are strewn over the steppe, adding a touch of colour.

4. Winter. The snow has melted on the gravel but still covers the carpeting plants. Here and there the leaves of narcissi are emerging, whose lovely flowers will soon brighten the steppe at the end of winter.

expanse of beaten earth which can be the case with a mixed lawn that receives no water. Unlike the plants that make up a mixed lawn, the plants in a steppe do not have to provide permanent groundcover since the gravel serves throughout the whole year as an underlying base on which to walk, regardless of the state of the vegetation. The most drought-resistant carpeting plants, which in summer form islands on the gravel surface, create a striking landscape that remains attractive even in periods of the most extreme drought.

The flowering steppe can include both carpeting plants and those that form somewhat flattened cushions, whose height varies according to the amount of foot traffic. Some cushion plants may actually take on varied forms in the wild: they may grow as flat ground-huggers in places frequented by goats, or as cushions in areas protected from grazing.

These plants are able to shoot from the rootstock, putting out suckers that make new leaves if the upper parts of the plant have been crushed by too much foot traffic. In winter, the varying heights of the carpeting plants excel in aesthetic terms; interspersed among gravel expanses, they create a succession of undulating light whose rhythm changes over the course of the day as the slanting rays of the winter sun grow lower in the sky.

The height of some species is limited not by the amount of foot traffic but by the availability of water over the course of the seasons. *Achillea crithmifolia*, for example, almost never flowers in the driest gardens but instead its leaves form a suckering carpet which remains flat and close to the ground. However, in gardens where the soil remains moist, its stems may reach 20 cm or so and it flowers abundantly in May-

June. In spring, when flowering is most profuse, the flowering steppe can take on the appearance of waves as routes regularly used to cross it form lower-growing paths in the midst of the undulating vegetation. After flowering, all the taller plants can be cut back hard to re-establish the initial structure of a much flatter carpet. Depending on the size of the area, spent flowers can be removed by mowing or simply cut off by hand with secateurs or small scissors. The resulting clippings should preferably be removed, in order to preserve the mineral nature of the steppe by limiting the addition of organic matter: in the wild, the species that are used for this kind of groundcover grow in eroded soils where organic matter does not accumulate. In our garden, for certain species like the various achilleas that colonize our flowering steppe, we prefer to pull out the stems with spent flowers. This is a swift and easy way of dealing with them

and it allows us to remove the woody bases of the stems which the lawn mower would miss – making it much more comfortable to walk barefoot on the steppe in summer after flowering. We have also noticed that pulling up their spent flowering stems seems to increase tenfold the colonizing power of the achilleas, which sucker even more vigorously to reconquer all the available space.

The flowering steppe offers a very different approach to groundcover than the mixed lawn and they represent ecosystems with distinct evolutionary pathways. If a mixed lawn is abandoned, it very quickly turns into a transient wasteland, which is the first stage of its evolution towards forest. If, on the other hand, one abandons a steppe, it will remain relatively unchanged, without any notable evolution, for a long time. For a number of reasons, among

The flowering steppe can be home to both carpeting and cushion-shaped plants, whose height varies depending on the amount of foot traffic.

1. In the wild, steppes are maintained by poor and stony soil, tough climate conditions and grazing. Here we see the summer appearance of steppes, pared down by the heat and drought, in the semi-desert landscapes north of Damascus, Syria.

2. In the garden we can artificially mimic the tough soil conditions with a bed of gravel, which eliminates competition from weeds.

3. If a steppe is abandoned, it will remain relatively unchanged for a long time, without any marked evolution: the steppe more or less maintains itself.

them the tough soil and climate conditions, the steppe is an ecosystem which has reached a plateau in its evolutionary trajectory. This translates into a significant advantage for the gardener: maintenance requirements are low since the steppe more or less looks after itself. In the wild, the steppe maintains itself thanks to poor and stony soil, harsh climate conditions and grazing animals. In the garden, we reproduce the tough soil conditions by creating a bed of gravel, which just about eliminates competition from weeds. All that remains is for the gardener to replace the grazing sheep by mowing the steppe once or twice a year, in order to cut off the spent flowers of the taller species and mow down any weeds which might have managed to emerge through the gravel.

It could be an advantage to create a flowering steppe in small sections over time. This would make it possible to spread the main work – laying the gravel – and select from the first set of plants those that give the most interesting visual effects. In this way, later plantings could be influenced by earlier ones, making it possible to modify the plant palette or density. Making a flowering steppe section by section also allows you to collect seeds or suckers from the earlier sections to plant out in autumn in the new sections thus limiting the outlay to the cost of the gravel.

SPECIES THAT CAN BE USED IN A FLOWERING STEPPE

Achillea coarctata	*Matricaria tchihatchewii*
Achillea crithmifolia	*Muscari armeniacum*
Achillea odorata	*Muscari neglectum*
Achillea tomentosa	*Narcissus tazetta*
Achillea umbellata	*Potentilla neumanniana*
Allium moly	*Prunella hyssopifolia*
Allium tuberosum	*Salvia multicaulis*
Artemisia 'Canescens'	*Salvia verbenaca*
Artemisia pedemontana	*Scabiosa argentea*
Brachypodium retusum	*Sternbergia lutea*
Centaurea bella	*Stipa barbata*
Chamaemelum nobile	*Stipa juncea*
Colchicum lusitanum	*Stipa pennata*
Crocus goulimyi	*Tanacetum densum*
Crocus sativus	*Teucrium aureum*
Dymondia margaretae	*Teucrium chamaedrys*
Erigeron karvinskianus	*Teucrium luteum*
Erodium trifolium	*Teucrium montanum*
Geranium sanguineum	*Thymus ciliatus*
Geranium × cantabrigiense	*Thymus herba-barona*
Goniolimon speciosum	*Thymus leucotrichus* subsp.
Iris lutescens	*neicefii*
Leopoldia comosa	*Thymus praecox*
Limonium pruinosum	*Thymus praecox* subsp.
Lotus corniculatus	*polytrichus*

A flowering steppe can act as a foreground for a taller layer composed of groundcover shrubs such as rosemary, cistus or *Phlomis*. The variety of lawn alternatives creates a mosaic of landscapes within the garden that set off each other.

ADVANTAGES: Limited maintenance. No watering needed after the first year. Low-density planting means less money spent on buying plants. The wide range of plants allows for a great variety of styles.

DRAWBACKS: labour and cost of laying the gravel. Weeding of new planting if the gravel is not laid until the end of the first year (see the various options, page 127 and following pages).

RECOMMENDED SURFACE AREA: unlimited apart from the cost of the initial investment (gravel and drainage work) and maintenance during the first year.

A gravel garden is the natural progression from a flowering steppe for parts of the garden that are rarely walked on. These two groundcover techniques share the same landscaping approach: spaced-out planting in soil covered with a thick layer of gravel. Both have the advantage of not requiring any water in summer. They differ mainly in the range of plants used, which changes according to the degree of foot traffic. The flowering steppe is conceived of as a space that can be walked on using mostly carpeting plants capable of withstanding relatively frequent foot traffic. The gravel garden, by contrast, uses a much wider range of plant forms. As well as carpeting plants, it can be home to plants which form cushions or balls, as well as perennials and sub-shrubs whose taller silhouettes emerge from the lower-growing plants.

In our experimental garden, the practice of growing plants in gravel rapidly became the most effective solution to the planting of large areas, because of the limited amount of maintenance needed. Year after year, the recurrent work of weeding by hand is one of the most demanding maintenance tasks in a mediterranean garden. Spring and autumn, when the climate is mild and damp, are seasons that favour the germination of weeds. In the space of a few weeks, plants can be overrun by exuberant vegetation that provides serious competition to smaller plants. So we must hand weed, which in large gardens and public spaces can be a well-nigh insurmountable task. The demands imposed by weeding can lead to a uniformity in the range of groundcover plants

used in gardens: small-sized plants, relatively sensitive to competition by weeds, are often rejected as being too difficult to maintain. The gravel garden, in which the surface of the soil is covered by a thick mineral mulch, is very effective at reducing the amount of weeding needed. It can thus be home to a more extensive range of groundcover plants, often little known and yet highly ornamental.

The gravel mulch makes it possible to increase the distance between plants, without the need to achieve the continuous plant cover of a traditional groundcover bed. Part of the gravel surface remains visible between the plants, thus establishing a balance between stone and plants which is even more attractive than that of a flowering steppe, thanks to the diversity of heights and plant forms. A great many groundcover species have a natural cushion- or ball-shaped growth habit, which is better set off when they are not crowded together. The open spaces between the plants offer visually restful areas that emphasize the ornamental qualities of each plant. These open areas can also be colonized by numerous bulbous plants that fleetingly transform the landscape when they flower, such as *Allium cristophii*, with its spectacular flower heads reminiscent of fireworks. The gravel garden is thus the lawn alternative best suited to cultivating the amazing diversity of groundcover plants and bulbs that are adapted to drought and grow wild in the poor and rocky soil of the hills and mountains of the Mediterranean.

Facing page
A thick layer of gravel covers the ground between plants in a gravel garden.

Allium cristophii and *Stachys byzantina* emerge from a carpet of *Tanacetum densum*. As an inorganic mulch, which effectively limits competition from weeds, the gravel garden can include a great variety of plants with different forms: carpeting plants and those with cushion or ball shapes, as well as the elegant silhouettes of many bulbous plants.

garden better into the surrounding landscape, but there are countless aesthetic possibilities depending on the style of garden that you want to create. The colours of the gravel are complemented by the diversity of colours and textures that characterize the foliage of mediterranean groundcover plants. Their leaf colour comes in all shades, ranging from the sombre dark green of, for example, *Cneorum tricoccon*, to the ashen white of *Cerastium candidissimum*, passing though the magnificent grey tones of the artemisias, ballotas and helichrysums.

Gravel gardens can also be made in temperate regions. In England, Beth Chatto was one of the first to put this kind of gardening into practice. She introduced many species originating from the Mediterranean into her famous gravel garden, which serves as a demonstration area at the entrance to her nursery. These species have been able to acclimatize to South-East England thanks to the poor stony soil, the garden having been made on what was once a pebbly car park. The famous rock garden at The Royal Botanic Gardens, Kew is another good example of a gravel garden. It consists of a series of raised beds with paths running between them and drainage is assured by the great blocks of stone that imitate a natural rocky landscape. In spite of the temperate climate in this suburb of London, the perfect drainage enables Kew to maintain a collection of plants which in the wild live in a very dry climate, such as *Hypericum empetrifolium*, the Cretan St John's wort, or *Rosmarinus × mendizabalii*, the amazing rosemary with downy grey leaves that is native to the cliffs of southern Andalucia.

Unlike the garden model focused on a lawn, where green is the dominant colour at all seasons, the gravel garden allows us to highlight an extended palette of colours. First of all there is the background colour of the gravel. The vast range of commercially available gravels, from dark schist, white quartz, red pozzolana to black basalt, makes it possible to play with a great variety of colours and contrasts. In our own garden, we have preferred to stick to a palette of soft-coloured calcareous gravels in order to integrate the

1. The gravel garden is the lawn alternative best suited to the extraordinary variety of groundcover plants that grow wild in the rocky soils on the hillsides and mountains of the Mediterranean.

2. The gravel garden does not require any watering in summer which makes it suitable for covering large areas of a mediterranean garden with minimal maintenance.

Flower performance also excels in gravel gardens. The gravel mulch not only improves surface drainage but also helps retain water deep in the soil using capillary action to prevent evaporation from the surface. So flowering is often markedly more abundant because the plants are under less stress. Some groundcover plants flower with extraordinary vigour, for example *Teucrium cossonii*, whose mauve flowers cover the fine silvery foliage in spring, *Bupleurum spinosum*, whose acid-green flowers seem impervious to the summer heat, or *Globularia alypum*, whose bright blue flowers open in the

middle of winter, when the rest of the garden is still sleeping. Grey- or downy-leaved plants are particularly happy on gravel. In the wild, these plants live for the most part in well-drained stony soil, where water quickly vanishes even after the heaviest rains. The greyness of the foliage is due to the dense network of hairs that covers the epidermis of the leaves. These hairs protect the plant from extreme heat and light, and effectively limit water loss through transpiration. However, the coating of hairs that covers the leaves and the bases of the stems tends to become sodden if the surface of the soil remains damp and stagnant. When grown in poorly drained soil, grey-leaved plants are prone to various kinds of wilt caused by cryptogamic diseases that develop when the foliage remains wet for too long. A gravel garden on the other hand, thanks to the perfect surface drainage it provides, is the ideal place to show grey-leaved plants to their best advantage. In our garden we have made the most of this asset to create a huge bed composed entirely of plants with grey, blueish or silver foliage. Its visual impact at all seasons, irrespective of whether the plants are in flower, makes it one of the most attractive parts of our garden.

A gravel garden is a good option for extensive coverage of parts of the garden that don't receive much foot traffic. To allow some access, leave pathways where the plants are less dense, so it's possible to walk through the plants just as one does when one hiking across a young garrigue. These pathways can have stepping stones placed among the gravel to guide the way. You could also leave broad

Cushions of light-coloured foliage grow in steely grey pozzolano on the volcanic slopes of Mount Etna. Drawing inspiration from the natural landscapes found around the Mediterranean, we can create very different styles in the garden that make the most of the various colours of gravel.

1. Thanks to the perfect surface drainage that it gives, the gravel garden is the ideal place to show off the great variety of grey-leaved plants that dislike winter wet.

2. Carpeting plants flow between taller plants, marking out a passage across the gravel. The combination of a flowering steppe with a gravel garden is one of the most successful solutions for covering the ground in a mediterranean garden.

3. The gravel garden is suitable for areas which do not receive much foot traffic. Paths allow one to walk through the plants.

expanses of gravel with just a few plants as focal points to guide the eye and create unexpected perspectives. Another idea would be to replace the stepping stones with a pathway of carpeting plants that intersect the gravel. Or you could introduce patches of flowering steppe to create a visual continuity between the parts of the garden that can or cannot be walked on: the balance between plants and gravel, the richness of the plant palette and the reduced maintenance make this one of the best groundcover solutions for gardens that are not irrigated.

Here is a list of species that are particularly happy in a gravel garden. It is far from exhaustive: there are hundreds, if not thousands, of native mediterranean species that live in the wild in conditions similar to those they find in a gravel garden. You can add the species listed in the chapter on flowering steppes too, for all of them are equally suitable for a gravel garden.

PLANTS FOR A GRAVEL GARDEN

Allium cristophii
Allium neapolitanum
Antirrhinum hispanicum
Asphodelus microcarpus
Cerastium candidissimum
Ceratostigma plumbaginoides
Cistus creticus 'Calcosalto'
Cistus × florentinus 'Tramontane'
Cistus × pauranthus 'Natacha'
Convolvulus cneorum
Coronilla minima
Cyclamen hederifolium
Delosperma cooperi
Drosanthemum hispidum
Euphorbia characias subsp. *wulfenii*
Euphorbia 'Copton Ash'
Euphorbia myrsinites
Euphorbia rigida
Euphorbia spinosa
Globularia alypum
Helichrysum orientale
Hertia cheirifolia
Hypericum empetrifolium
Hypericum olympicum 'Citrinum'
Iris unguicularis
Lavandula dentata
Lavandula × chaytorae
Lavandula × ginginsii 'Goodwin Creek Grey'
Lavandula × losae
Origanum dictamnus
Origanum laevigatum
Origanum majorana var. *tenuifolium*
Origanum microphyllum

Origanum scabrum subsp. *pulchrum*
Origanum vulgare
Pallenis maritima
Phlomis lychnitis
Rhodanthemum catananche
Rhodanthemum hosmariense
Rosmarinus × noeanus
Rosmarinus × mendizabalii
Salvia 'Bee's Bliss'
Salvia chamaedryoides
Salvia clevelandii
Salvia fruticosa
Salvia interrupta
Salvia lavandulifolia
Salvia pomifera
Santolina magonica
Santolina insularis
Santolina × lindavica
Santolina viridis 'Primrose Gem'
Scabiosa cretica
Scabiosa hymettia
Scabiosa minoana
Senecio viravira
Sideritis cypria
Stachys byzantina
Stachys cretica
Teucrium cossonii
Teucrium divaricatum
Teucrium lusitanicum
Teucrium marum
Teucrium montanum
Thymbra capitata
Thymus camphoratus
Thymus mastichina
Thymus vulgaris
Verbena rigida
Veronica polifolia

The gravel garden remains attractive even outside the flowering season, thanks to the visual balance between stone and plants.

TERRACES, PATHS AND STEPS:
THE GREENING OF STONE SURFACES

ADVANTAGES: minimal or no maintenance. Withstand intense foot traffic. A great variety of styles possible. Most of the suitable plants require no watering after their first year.

DRAWBACKS: requires major work.

RECOMMENDED SURFACE AREA: generally small, because of the labour and cost involved.

During our botanical expeditions around the Mediterranean, Clara and I noticed again and again stone surfaces partially invaded by the natural vegetation. We were struck by ancient mule paths taken over by flowers in the Cyclades, tiers of ancient theatres home now to *Cyclamen* lost in the Taurus mountains, and the extraordinary network of paths, walls and steps, interspersed with tiny olive groves or flows of wild plants, that cover the slopes of the Sierra de Tramuntana in the Balearcs. These stone surfaces are evidence of a long history of human occupation of the landscape and they prompted us to think about lawn alternatives in new ways.

Planted terraces

We noticed that carefully constructed, ancient threshing floors weather the dilapidations of time remarkably well. They often survive when the hamlets around them have been reduced to ruins. There are two main methods of laying the stone in threshing floors: heavy slabs laid flat on the ground, or small stones or pebbles placed vertically to form cobbles. These traditional stoneworking techniques use no

mortar and thus allow plants to grow spontaneously in the cracks, outlining the stones. The roots of these plants spread below the stone surface, making use of the moisture trapped beneath the stones which protect the soil from evaporation. When the threshing floor begins to disintegrate, pioneer plants move in between the broken paving slabs or gaps between the cobbles and these often form cushion or ball shapes, creating a bulkier mass that complements the tracery of green in the cracks. These ancient threshing floors sometimes present magnificent miniature landscapes, real models for green terraces in dry gardens.

In the gardens of Andalucia, such as the Alhambra in Granada or the patios of Cordoba, many paths, steps and terraces are cobbled. But here the traditional technique takes on another dimension. As well as its functional role, the stonework becomes a place for artistic expression as cobbles have been worked into complicated patterns, sometimes emphasized by the use of different coloured pebbles. In the South of France, there is a revived interest in traditional stone-working techniques and an excellent practical guide, *Calades. Les sols de pierre* (see the bibliography), gives all the information needed to create your own cobblestone design at home. However, making a cobbled area takes time and is often not a priority when one begins to create a garden. In this case make it a longer-term project and allow for it in the initial lay-out. In our own garden, we waited for more than fifteen years before embarking on the fascinating adventure of using cobbles to replace a small gravel garden in which we had temporarily planted a collection of oreganos. To limit the work involved, a small patch of cobbles can be integrated into more extensive paved or gravelled areas. Some contemporary landscape designers like Erik Borja or Jean-Jacques Derboux combine different kinds of stonework or mineral groundcovers in the same designs that are often Japanese inspired. The paving, gravel and cobbles, whose varied textures are in themselves ornamental, need nothing more than a light counterpoint of plants to set them off.

Laying broad paving stones on a bed of sand remains the quickest way of dealing with large areas of greened terraces. The width of the cracks between the slabs determine the type of planting. In narrow cracks, use carpeting plants that

Facing page
A green terrace paved with cyclopic slabs. The wide gaps between the paving have been colonized by pioneer plants which constitute the first stage in an evolving landscape whose appearance changes from year to year according to random self-seeding. In the foreground: *Glaucium flavum*, *Euphorbia myrsinites*, *Euphorbia cyparissias*, *Scabiosa cretica* and *Centranthus ruber*. (Design by Pascal Cribier and Lionel Guibert for the Château Le Plaisir, Gard, France.)

A mule path overgrown with plants on the island of Amorgos in the Cyclades. The stone surfaces that one finds in garrigues all around the Mediterranean, vestiges of the human occupation of the landscape, prompt new ideas for lawn alternatives. These kinds of surfaces can be used to cover the ground in parts of the garden where there is a lot of foot traffic.

1. This ancient threshing floor, high up near a pass in the mountains of Greece, uses traditional dry-stone-walling techniques.

2. An ancient threshing floor in Corsica on the Revellata peninsula which overlooks the Bay of Calvi. The broken paving has been colonized by cushions of *Teucrium marum*, with silvery foliage, and *Cistus monspeliensis*, whose dark balls have been sculpted by the salt spray. Ruined threshing floors can serve as a model for green terraces in dry gardens.

3. Taking inspiration from natural scenes around the Mediterranean, one can introduce a remarkable variety of plants into the stone surfaces of the garden. Here *Thymus ciliatus, Santolina viridis* 'Primrose Gem' and *Erigeron karvinskianus* climb a flight of steps. (Sidler garden, design by ADELFO, Jean-Baptiste Pasquet.)

root wherever they are in contact with the soil and progressively colonize all the cracks, such as *Thymus serpyllum* 'Elfin', *Herniaria glabra* or *Zoysia tenuifolia*. Or if you are using pot-grown plants, slice them vertically to produce rooted fragments which can then be inserted between the paving stones. If there are occasional wider gaps (10 cm or more) you can break up the spread of carpeting plants by planting small pot-grown plants such as *Thymus ciliatus* or *Thymus hirsutus*, and other plants that form balls or cushions such as *Convolvulus cneorum* or *Teucrium marum*.

Paths, walls and steps

To complement the terraces, you can also use paths, dry-stone walls and steps as supports for this kind of planting. A great many species can be slipped in between steps and in the cracks between the stones in walls, as for example ivy-leaved toadflax (*Cymbalaria muralis*), *Euphorbia myrsinites* or *Erigeron karvinskianus*. Flowering steps, which are spectacular in spring, can also be used to create visual continuity between green terraces on different levels.

Stepping stones, paths and steps also lend themselves to being planted with strongly scented aromatic plants that overflow on to the places where people walk. Every time someone passes, brushing against the foliage, a cascade of scents is released. Try plants with a fresh and minty scent such as *Calamintha nepeta*, a spicy scent such as *Helichrysum italicum*, a powerful sharp scent such as *Salvia clevelandii*, an almost unpleasant scent such as *Ruta graveolens*, or a delicate and powdery scent such as *Origanum majorana* var. *tenuifolium*. This type of planting appeals to many of the senses and this is one of the greatest attractions of the Mediterranean landscape in summer. The scents, intensified by the heat and the drying effects of the sun, add to the interest of the foliage when few plants are in flower.

The dry-stone retaining walls of terraces can also provide a home for plants. Those that self-seed into the cracks and crevices include valerian, wallflowers, snapdragons, throatwort (*Trachelium*) or houseleeks (*Sempervivum*). Since it is often difficult to plant directly into a wall, the best thing is

1. Elegant raised cobbles set off by the green gaps between them. The *Soleirolia soleirolii* used here requires shade and relative damp if it is to do well. (Erik Borja's garden in Beaumont-Monteux, France.)

2. *Achillea crithmifolia* marks the outlines of heavy paving stones laid on a bed of sand. (Design by Pascal Cribier and Lionel Guibert for the Château Le Plaisir, Gard, France.)

3. Making the most of the moisture trapped beneath the stones, carpets of *Thymus hirsutus* and *Thymus ciliatus* thrive in the gaps between the paving on a terrace. (Sidler garden, design by ADELFO, Jean-Baptiste Pasquet.)

4. Kept low by foot traffic, *Thymus serpyllum* 'Elfin' makes a fragmented carpet that overflows irregularly on to the stones.

5. The mossy vegetation of *Soleirolia soleirolii* softens the rectilinear shape of granite paving stones.

to put in a few plants just above the wall, so that they can seed themselves or spread naturally by suckers and in a few years' time will appear here and there among the stones of the wall. The colonization of the wall is made complete by planting a few species with a cascading habit on top of the wall, such as *Clematis flammula*, which flowers in summer, or *Clematis cirrhosa*, which flowers magnificently in winter. Taking inspiration from natural scenes is an excellent way to add plants to terraces, paths, steps and walls. This harmonizing of stone and plants is one of the most origi-

nal ways of replacing lawns in gardens where there is heavy foot traffic.

Parking spaces

To take this a step further, let's have a look at alternatives to the lawn that could be used for parking spaces and drives. To make a permeable parking space in a garden, one solution is to remove the soil to a depth of about 30 cm and replace it with a mixture of earth and stone. This type of mixture offers a favourable environment to a range of specialized

The successive levels of large limestone slabs are enhanced by edgings of vegetation including *Thymus hirsutus*, *Thymus serpyllum* 'Elfin', *Artemisia pedemontana*, *Sedum album* and *Phyla canescens*. (Roubinet garden, design by ADELFO, Jean-Baptiste Pasquet.)

plants whose vegetation insinuates itself between the surface stones during the course of being crushed by car wheels. It consists of one-third topsoil and two-thirds crushed stone with a grade of about 40 to 80 mm. By resting on top of one another the stones form a rigid structure that acts as reinforcement to the weight-bearing surface. The stones prevent the compaction of the interstitial spaces, which are full of earth and in which the plants' roots can grow comfortably. The mixture of earth and stone thus forms a structure that is both weight-bearing and nourishing.

Plants suitable for this type of surface include the strawberry clover, *Trifolium fragiferum*, the buck's-horn plantain, *Plantago coronopus*, and the spring cinquefoil, *Potentilla neumannia*. These species can be sown directly *in situ* and will mingle with the natural vegetation, which differs from region to region, to complete the colonization of the earth-stone mixture over time. For small areas it is sometimes simpler to incorporate plants in pots at a low density to act as seed-bearers and result in a natural colonization of the patch after a few years. The pots should be positioned slightly below the level of the weight-bearing surface so that they won't be crushed by the wheels of cars. A mixture of hybrid Bermuda grass, *Cynodon* 'Santa Ana', lippia, *Phyla canescens* and strawberry clover can also be used on this type of surface to form pretty flowering lawns able to withstand the movement and parking of cars.

Here are some examples of plants that can be used on terraces, paths and dry-stone steps.

1

2

1. By allowing aromatic plants to flow freely, a flight of steps can be transformed into a cascade of scents. In the mediterranean garden, aromatic leaves give off their scent in summer, enriching our multi-sensory experience of the garden at a time when not much is flowering. (Sidler garden, design by ADELFO, Jean-Baptiste Pasquet.)

2. A permeable parking space. The earth-stone mixture that forms the weight-bearing structure can be home to a specialized range of groundcover plants. *Potentilla neumanniana* in full flower in spring, has seasonal vegetation: it becomes dormant in summer, losing its leaves when it is very hot, then greening up again with the first rains of autumn.

1. Spontaneous plants colonize this stone-laid surface, occasionally used for parking a car. The dominant vegetation consists of a mixture of strawberry clover and plantains. Various annuals and bulbs make a miniature garden between the stones in spring.

2. In a mediterranean garden all the terraces, paths, steps and walls can be planted. This combination of stone and plants makes one of the most striking alternatives to lawn for covering areas with a lot of foot traffic. (Aslangul garden, design by Jean-Jacques Derboux.)

PLANTS FOR TERRACES, PATHS AND DRY-STONE STEPS

Narrow cracks between paving or cobbles on terraces
Achillea tomentosa
Arenaria balearica
Herniaria glabra
Soleirolia soleirolii
Thymus serpyllum 'Elfin'
Zoysia tenuifolia

Wide cracks (10 cm and more) between paving on terraces
Achillea coarctata
Achillea crithmifolia
Asphodelus microcarpus
Carex halleriana
Cistus creticus 'Calcosalto'
Cistus salviifolius 'Bonifacio'
Coronilla minima
Dorycnium hirsutum
Dymondia margaretae
Euphorbia cyparissias
Glaucium flavum
Globularia alypum
Goniolimon speciosum
Helichrysum orientale
Hypericum olympicum 'Citrinum'
Ipheion uniflorum 'Rolf Fiedler'
Iris unguicularis
Lavandula × chaytorae
Limonium pruinosum
Origanum laevigatum
Pallenis maritima
Phlomis lychnitis

Phyla canescens
Salvia lavandulifolia
Santolina magonica
Santolina viridis
Scabiosa argentea
Scabiosa hymettia
Sedum: many species
Stachys byzantina
Teucrium flavum
Teucrium lusitanicum
Teucrium marum
Thymus ciliatus
Thymus hirsutus
Trifolium fragiferum
Veronica polifolia

Flowering steps: planting between the treads and the risers
Achillea umbellata
Antirrhinum barrelierii
Antirrhinum hispanicum
Antirrhinum majus
Artemisia pedemontana
Campanula portenschlagiana
Centaurea bella
Cerastium candidissimum
Ceratostigma plumbaginoides
Convolvulus sabatius
Cotula lineariloba
Cyclamen hederifolium
Cymbalaria muralis
Erigeron karvinskianus
Erodium trifolium
Euphorbia myrsinites
Geranium sanguineum
Hypericum aegypticum

Nepeta racemosa
Origanum dictamnus
Origanum microphyllum
Potentilla neumanniana
Sedum: many species
Sempervivum sp.
Tanacetum densum
Teucrium aureum
Teucrium cossonii

Plants cascading down low walls
Clematis cirrhosa
Clematis flammula
Delosperma cooperi
Dichondra argentea
Drosanthemum hispidum
Hertia cheirifolia
Jasminum nudiflorum
Lantana montevidensis
Osteospermum fruticosum
Phyla canescens
Putoria calabrica
Rosmarinus officinalis (prostrate varieties)

A cascade of scents: aromatic steps
Calamintha nepeta
Chamaemelum nobile
Geranium macrorrhizum
Helichrysum italicum subsp. *serotinum*
Nepeta × faasenii
Rosmarinus officinalis 'Montagnette'
Ruta graveolens

Salvia 'Bee's Bliss'
Salvia clevelandii
Salvia dominica
Salvia pomifera
Salvia sclarea
Salvia spathacea
Santolina insularis
Thymus mastichina
Thymus serpyllum 'Lemon Curd'

Parking areas: earth-stone mixture
Achillea crithmifolia
Brachypodium retusum
Cynodon 'Santa Ana'
Phyla canescens
Plantago coronopus
Potentilla neumanniana
Sanguisorba minor
Trifolium fragiferum

Plants that self-seed in walls
Antirrhinum barrelierii
Antirrhinum majus
Campanula portenschlagiana
Centranthus ruber
Cymbalaria muralis
Erigeron karvinskianus
Erysimum × cheiri
Sempervivum tectorum
Trachelium caeruleum

PERENNIAL AND SHRUB GROUNDCOVERS FOR LARGE AREAS

ADVANTAGES: groundcover for large spaces with limited maintenance. No watering after the first year.

DRAWBACKS: cannot be walked on. Weeding maintenance required during the first two or three years (unless the soil is covered with a mulch).

RECOMMENDED SURFACE AREA: unlimited apart from the labour involved in planting and maintenance during the first years.

One of the stages in the evolution of the mediterranean vegetation is a dense cover in which evergreen plants form a thick and almost impenetrable mass. This kind of vegetation is found in all the mediterranean-climate regions of the world: it is called *garrigue* or *maquis* around the Mediter-

Facing page
A large bed composed of evergreen plants, which can cover the ground in areas of the garden that are not much used.

1. Landscape in Southern Greece: dense garrigue, regularly grazed by goats. All around the Mediterranean we find this type of vegetation, consisting of very dense evergreen plants that close the environment and cover the ground.

2. Taking our inspiration from garrigue landscapes, we can create large groundcover beds to occupy the space in parts of the garden that are not very accessible: here it is not so much the individual plants that act as groundcover but rather the continuous mass of shrubs that completely covers the ground. In the foreground *Cistus laurifolius* and *Cistus × argenteus* 'Blushing Peggy Sammons'.

2

ranean, *chaparral* in California, *matorral* in Chile, *fynbos* in South Africa and *kwongan* in Australia. In the garden, we can replicate it in large plantings of perennials and evergreen shrubs. These plantings require little maintenance and are perfectly drought-resistant; they can be used to replace lawns in more remote parts of the garden. They complement the walkable areas with a taller groundcover, whose dense vegetation can act as a background that enriches the structure of a mediterranean garden.

While the gravel garden and the flowering steppe are inspired by open environments that preserve a visual balance between stone and plants, the evergreen bed creates a closed environment in which the vegetation covers the

1. In a dry garden the springtime flowering, often spectacular, lasts for a relatively short time. When planning a large groundcover bed, it is better to focus on the visual quality of the evergreen foliage, which remains attractive throughout the year.

2. The wider the range of species a bed contains, the more we can highlight contrasts in the colour, height and texture of their foliage.

soil entirely. By preventing the light from penetrating to the ground, the dense foliage eliminates competition from undesirable plants and blocks the germination of weeds. As a result, beds of evergreens can be used to cover large areas of the garden, with a very limited amount of maintenance since they eliminate the problem of weeding. In order for the groundcover to be effective, the plants must be sufficiently thick: they need to have dense foliage and a minimum height of 20 to 30 cm to prevent all light from reaching the soil. The plant palette we can use does not consist only of plants with a spreading habit. It can also include taller plants, such as *Phillyrea angustifolia* or *Teucrium fruticans*, which, when planted in groups, can make a continuous mass with a height of 1 m or 1.50 m. It is not these plants

individually that serve as groundcovers, but rather the dense masses they form when planted in groups whose successive waves can be ranged at different heights.

Some species, like prostrate rosemary or cistus, have a spreading habit and such effective ground-covering potential that it is tempting to use them for single-species plantings on a large scale, for instance in public parks. But it is always better to plant a large variety of different species. Mono-specific plantings are vulnerable to outbreaks of pests and diseases that find ideal breeding conditions in a planting containing only one species (see page 145). Diversified planting on the contrary favours equilibrium: diseases or pests are much less frequent and are resolved naturally,

Diversified planting is an insurance policy for the long-term life of the planting. It lasts longer, reduces maintenance, and minimizes the cost of replacing plants. In the foreground *Bupleurum fruticosum* is in full flower in early summer.

The idea of large beds of evergreen plants lends itself to many different landscaping approaches:

1. The supple foliage of euphorbia, cistus, scabious, artemisia and *Phlomis* mingle in a free and exuberant scene. In the foreground are the bright flowers of *Cistus × tardiflorens*.

2. Clipped into dense balls, lentisks form a dark counterpoint in front of the silvery mass of olive trees. A small wild lawn, green in winter and golden in summer, accentuates the successive layers that make up the scene. (Demoustier garden, Saleccia Park, near L'Ile-Rousse, in Corsica.)

3. The elegant silhouettes of *Nolina, Brahea* and *Dasylirion* emerge from the grey or silver masses of lower-growing groundcover plants.

often before the gardener has even had time to spot them. By using a variety of species, the planting will continue to evolve over time ensuring a longer life for the plants and reducing maintenance requirements and the expense of replacing plants.

The evergreen foliage typical of so many mediterranean species enables the plants to prolong their growth during the wet seasons of autumn, winter and spring. This allows them to become dormant during the difficult summer period, when they merely tick over, adopting various strategies to resist drought. These strategies are expressed in the extraordinary variety of their foliage. Some plants with dark green foliage, such as myrtle, lentisk and *Rhamnus alaternus,* have leaves covered with a shiny cuticle that reduces transpiration in times of great heat. Other plants, such as *Salvia pomif-*

era and *Phlomis chrysophylla,* have leaf surfaces covered in a thick coating of grey, silver or golden hairs, which reflect the rays of the sun and reduce water loss during photosynthesis.

The wider the range of species, the more you can show off contrasts in colour, height and foliage texture to best advantage. These contrasts allow us to create attractive effects throughout the year, not just during the flowering season, which is often limited to spring. When planning a large groundcover bed, it is worth focusing on the different kinds of foliage rather than on flowers alone. The flowering of each species generally lasts for just a few weeks and, although they may be spectacular for a brief period, succeed one another all too quickly. Foliage, on the contrary, constitutes the permanent framework and provides year-round

The dark masses of myrtles, lentisks and laurustinus are regularly clipped to make this billowing landscape evoke garrigues grazed by goats. (Eleni Martinos' garden.)

visual interest in a large groundcover bed. In the plant descriptions (pages 167-227), I emphasize the visual quality of the leaves over the course of the seasons. The prize goes to species whose foliage remains handsome throughout the year, even during the summer resting period, regardless of heat and drought.

A network of narrow paths among the plants, barely visible, is useful to maintain access to the centre of the bed, for example for pruning. These narrow paths are also a joy to children, for whom the large beds are an adventure playground and a dream for making secret houses. This type of bed can also act as the transition between lower-growing parts of the garden, such as a flowering steppe or a gravel garden, and taller features like a free-growing hedge that marks the garden's boundary. In our garden, we have created many different zones that intersect with one another, gravel gardens or flowering steppes separated by dense plantings of evergreen plants. The network of paths that link these areas means that one can walk freely all over the garden. The plants used in the different areas go together perfectly and form a harmonious visual whole. Evergreen plants give a permanent structure throughout the year, and the gravelled parts of the garden are home to complementary species whose groundcover potential is less but whose summer flowering is irreplaceable, thanks to plants such as *Perovskia* 'Blue Spire', *Origanum scabrum* subsp. *pulchrum* or *Epilobium canum* 'Western Hills'.

Large groundcover beds can be interspersed with areas of gravel garden: the evergreen plants provide the permanent structure throughout the year, and the gravel garden is home to complementary plants, whose groundcover potential is less but whose summer flowering is unbeatable, like that of *Perovskia* 'Blue Spire'.

Irrigation of groundcover plants in large beds, as for all dry-climate plants, should be given only during the first year to ensure that the plants become established. The best method is always hand watering into large watering basins created around the base of the plant. If planting has been carried out in good conditions in autumn, in a soil that has been thoroughly decompacted to a good depth, it will be necessary to water only about once a month during the first summer. In our garden we water as little as possible, maybe a total of three or four times during the first summer and thereafter not at all. In a modest-size garden, it is easy to water by hand but when large beds are created, for example on the scale of a public park or along suburban roads, it is tempting to do away with this task by installing an automatic drip irrigation system. Quite apart from the question of the appropriateness of installing a drip system that will be used for only a limited number of waterings, there is a real danger that it will do more harm than good making the plants frailer instead of preparing them to cope with drought. This important subject will be discussed in detail in the chapter entitled "Economizing on Water" (page 133).

SPECIES FOR LARGE BEDS OF EVERGREEN PLANTS

Acanthus mollis
Ampelodesmos mauritanicus
Artemisia alba
Artemisia arborescens 'Carcassonne'
Artemisia thuscula
Ballota acetabulosa
Ballota hirsuta
Ballota pseudodictamnus
Choisya 'Aztec Pearl'
Cistus × *florentinus* 'Tramontane'
Cistus × *ledon*
Cistus × *pauranthus* 'Natacha'
Cistus × *pulverulentus*
Cistus × *purpureus*
Cistus × *skanbergii*
Cistus × *tardiflorens*
Cistus × *verguinii* 'Paul Pècherat'
Epilobium canum 'Western Hills'
Erica manipuliflora
Euphorbia ceratocarpa
Euphorbia dendroides
Geranium macrorrhizum
Geranium 'Rambling Robin'
Hedera helix
Hypericum balearicum
Iris × *germanica*
Jasminum nudiflorum
Juniperus horizontalis 'Blue Chips'
Lavandula dentata 'Adrar M'Korn'

Lavandula × *intermedia*
Leucophyllum langmaniae
Limoniastrum monopetalum 'Carnaval'
Lonicera splendida
Myrtus communis subsp. *tarentina*
Olea europaea subsp. *cuspidata*
Olea europaea var. *sylvestris*
Phillyrea angustifolia
Phlomis chrysophylla
Phlomis 'Edward Bowles'
Phlomis purpurea
Phlomis purpurea 'Alba'
Phlomis purpurea subsp. *almeriensis*
Phlomis × *cytherea*
Pistacia lentiscus
Rosmarinus officinalis, prostrate forms
Rosmarinus officinalis 'Spice Islands', as well as all ball-shaped rosemary
Salvia fruticosa and its hybrids
Salvia microphylla and its hybrids
Santolina chamaecyparissus
Santolina magonica
Santolina × *lindavica*
Sarcopoterium spinosum
Stipa tenuissima
Teucrium fruticans
Teucrium × *lucidrys*
Viburnum tinus
Vinca major

Small narrow paths, barely visible amid the mass of vegetation, can be useful to maintain access to the middle of a large groundcover bed, for example for pruning.

PIONEER PLANTS FOR SLOPES AND WILD GARDENS

ADVANTAGES: independent colonization of land that is degraded or hard to access. Inexpensive planting for large areas in wild gardens. Habitat for fauna and beneficial insects.

DRAWBACKS: colonization by pioneer plants can take several years. When the environment starts to become closed, maintenance may be required to remove unwanted plants.

RECOMMENDED SURFACE AREA: unlimited.

Pioneer plants are species that spread quickly through self-seeding, even when the soil conditions are unfavourable. In the wild, they often establish themselves on severely degraded land. Valerian, for example, spontaneously colonizes rocky slopes left bare by road construction. Fennel and mulleins are capable of invading clay soils that have been compacted by heavy machinery. Sticky fleabane self-seeds easily in disturbed environments where infertile subsoil has been brought to the surface. *Dorycnium* species and lucernes have the ability to fertilize the land they colonize thanks to the nitrogen-fixing nodules along the length of their roots. Pioneer plants can thus in some cases provide easy solutions to groundcover problems. In mediterranean climates they offer alternatives to the lawn on inaccessible slopes and in areas where the soil is particularly poor. They are also suitable for planting large areas of wild garden, where the distinction between weeds and garden plants becomes secondary, inexpensively and without the need for irrigation.

The pioneer plants that self-seed most rapidly are relatively short-lived. They generally constitute a simple first stage in the dynamic evolution of the vegetation on degraded soils. Their presence will contribute to a gradual modification of the environment, through improving the soil structure, adding organic material and regenerating bacterial life in the upper layers of the soil. The establishment of the first patches of vegetation, which trap dust and seeds carried by the wind, create favourable conditions for the subsequent development of a more varied floral composition. Pioneer plants are the first to arrive in an evolving landscape whose changing appearance from year to year represents the successive stages in the evolution of the environment. In the garden context, this means that planting a range of pioneer plants corresponds to the first phase of colonization, which will be followed by other stages when the gardener decides to remove or leave certain plants depending on the long-term effect desired.

To start off colonization by pioneer plants, the simplest method is to make a small-scale initial planting consisting of islands of seed-bearing plants. Depending on the size of the area to be planted, these islands can be spaced about 10 to 15 m apart, giving an approximate density of one island for every 100 to 200 m². The creation of these islands reduces the work involved, since it allows us to concentrate in the first year on soil preparation and follow-up for very small areas. The size of each island can vary depending on the number of species chosen. Islands of about 4 to 5 m² are

1

2

large enough to contain about ten pioneer species. To have a more varied plant palette, one can create several islands with complementary vegetation.

Depending on the colonizing strategies of the different pioneer species, they will take a longer or shorter time to spread. The plants need time to flower, to produce the first generation of seeds and to self-seed. In the second stage, the plants grown from these first seeds flower, producing and

disseminating their own seed in turn. In this way, the vegetation spreads incrementally as the patch of land becomes colonized. Many pioneer species flower in their first year and seed themselves a few months later. If we plant them in autumn, they flower in spring, disseminate their seed in summer and germinate in autumn, in other words just a year after being planted. By choosing very prolific species, such as valerian, clary sage, *Dorycnium hirsutum*, *Euphorbia characias* or *Coronilla valentina* subsp. *glauca*, we can

Pioneer species that self-seed rapidly such as euphorbia, clary sage and *Dorycnium hirsutum,* make it possible to plant wild areas of the garden or inaccessible slopes at a low cost:

1. *Euphorbia characias* subsp. *wulfenii.*

2. New inflorescence of *Salvia sclarea.*

3. *Dorycnium hirsutum* and *Achillea coarctata*: a seeding species and a rhizomatous species mingle in a wild area of the garden.

4. *Stipa tenuissima* self-seeds very easily on dry ground. Its supple vegetation forms an undulating mass, from which the stiff inflorescences of *Eremurus* × *isabellinus* 'Pinokkio' emerge. (Sidler garden, design by ADELFO, Jean-Baptiste Pasquet.)

achieve quick colonization of a large piece of land. To these rapidly proliferating pioneer plants can be added some woody species that grow more slowly, such as *Bupleurum* or *Phillyrea*. These secondary species create diversity and after a few years will form a lasting thread in the fabric of the evolving landscape.

Some pioneer plants not only self-seed but also spread laterally by means of vigorous stolons (*Potentilla reptans*) or rhizomes (*Euphorbia cyparissias*). These species can help to reduce erosion on slopes that have been newly created with imported soil. Several achilleas, such as *Achillea nobilis*, *Achillea crithmifolia* and *Achillea coarctata* are very invasive on loose soil but particularly effective for stabilizing slopes, thanks to their spectacular lateral growth. By planting a diversity of species, one can create interesting scenes that combine effective stablization of the soil with ornamental spring flowers.

Other methods can be used to plant slopes where access is difficult. The first of these consists of making flat shelves at various points on the slope, underpinned by interwoven horizontal branches attached to stakes that are driven into the soil. These make it possible to prepare the soil for our islands of pioneer plants. Sited along the contours of the slope, these elongated islands need to be just wide enough to allow traditional planting with a watering basin. To economize on width, the basins can be oval-shaped with their centres above the base of the plant. The shelves not only provide planting places for pioneer plants which will then seed themselves over the slope, but also help reduce erosion and trap sediments washed downhill.

Achillea nobilis is an extremely vigorous plant with invasive rhizomes. Planted together with other pioneer species, it helps to reduce erosion on slopes where soil has been added.

When the slope is too steep for supports of this kind, then simply plant a line of seed-bearing plants along the top. Seeds will be dispersed down the slope by gravity or by run-off from rain. For large-scale areas such as along motorways or railways, pioneer plants can be sown by a technique called hydroseeding, carried out by specialist companies. This involves using a cannon to fire a mixture of water and seeds at long range. To prevent the seeds becoming rapidly lost due to erosion, the mixture often includes a cellulose-based fixative and an anti-erosion matrix made of vegetable fibres.

Pioneer plants can also be useful to occupy space in wilder parts, for example at the bottom of a large garden. For this purpose, I recommend mixed islands containing both seed-bearing plants and those that spread by rhizomes and stolons. The different species will mix freely as they gradually colonize the space available. In our garden, we have achieved quite by chance an interesting association of *Achillea nobilis*, which has taken over a huge area by means of its very powerful rhizomes, with a mixture of *Centranthus*, *Dorycnium* and *Teucrium flavum*, which self-seed liberally into the carpet of achillea. This kind of plant association creates a landscape that evolves from year to year, progressively enriched by taller species. Pioneer plants can thus form the beginning of a wild garden, which will also act as a wildlife refuge for many beneficial creatures – butterflies, birds and hedgehogs.

Some species are of interest for their specfic ecological functions. Sticky fleabane, one of the first species to seed itself in disturbed ground, encourages the presence of *Eupelmus urozonus*, a parasitical insect that helps limit the population of olive flies. Several pioneer species, such as shrubby hare's ear, fennel or *Dorycnium*, have flowers rich in nectar that attract a host of beneficial insects. Trees in the planting zone will provide habitats for birds that disseminate the seeds of plants with fleshy fruits. We could thus plant one of our islands with pioneeer species such as *Pistacia lentiscus*, *Phillyrea angustifolia*, *Viburnum tinus*, *Lonicera etrusca* and *Rhamnus alaternus*, whose berries attract sparrows. Birds are welcome not only for their graceful flight and lovely song but also because, when they are not feeding on berries, they

1. In our garden *Coronilla valentina* subsp. *glauca* self-seeds in small gaps in our large groundcover beds.

2. The rhizomatous *Euphorbia cyparissias* has invaded a whole area of our garden.

hard to live with, like brambles and sarsaparilla, but also other pioneer plants that have escaped from neighbouring gardens, such as *Buddleja* or pampas grass. Managing a wild area in the garden thus becomes a lot more interesting than it might at first appear. Technical questions (how and when should one prune or clip?) are followed by ethical questions (which plants does one consider welcome, and which undesirable invaders?). Using pioneer plants in an evolving landscape can make us question our own perception of nature.

consume vast numbers of insects and thus contribute to the ecological equilibrium of the garden.

In this type of evolving landscape, you will rapidly be faced with the question of maintenance. To what extent do you accept this part of the garden becoming really wild? When the plants start to fill out, judicious use of a lawn mower or strimmer can make paths that allow access to the middle. Woody plants can be pruned to form a permanent structure, which will develop over time into a large groundcover stand of evergreen plant (see the preceding chapter). You may find it necessary to remove species you consider undesirable. But your idealized vision of a natural garden that flourishes without any intervention can indeed fade when the planting evolves in a direction quite different from the one you intended. What started as a harmonious mixture of fennel, valerian and *Coronilla*, may a few years later become overwhelmed by an enormous mass of impenetrable brambles.

Depending on the environment that surrounds the garden, other unplanned plants may also make their appearance, brought by the wind or by birds. For example, birds can spread seed of *Pyracantha* from neighbouring gardens very efficiently. The wind too carries seeds from a large number of pioneer plants, which germinate easily in disturbed soil and seek a wild part of the garden where they can establish themselves. So in a remote part of the garden that you wish to leave more or less untouched, you must be prepared to welcome not only the plants that gardeners usually find

PIONEER SPECIES FOR SLOPES AND DRY GARDENS

Seed-bearing plants for slopes and wild gardens
Asphodelus fistulosus
Bupleurum fruticosum
Centranthus ruber
Cistus albidus
Cistus creticus
Cistus monspeliensis
Clematis flammula
Coronilla valentina subsp. *glauca*
Dittrichia viscosa
Dorycnium hirsutum
Dorycnium pentaphyllum
Erigeron karvinskianus
Eschscholzia californica
Euphorbia characias
Euphorbia myrsinites
Euphorbia rigida
Foeniculum vulgare
Gaura lindheimeri
Glaucium flavum
Goniolimon speciosum
Lavandula dentata
Limonium pruinosum
Lonicera etrusca
Malva sylvestris
Medicago arborea
Medicago sativa

Melilotus officinalis
Phillyrea angustifolia
Rhamnus alaternus
Salvia sclarea
Santolina × *lindavica*
Spartium junceum
Stipa tenuissima
Teucrium flavum
Verbascum sinuatum
Viburnum tinus

Plants that spread vigorously by rhizomes or stolons, enabling them to combat erosion on loose slopes made from imported soil
Achillea coarctata
Achillea crithmifolia
Achillea nobilis
Artemisia ludoviciana 'Silver Queen'
Brachypodium phoenicoides
Euphorbia cyparissias
Lepidium draba
Malvastrum lateritium
Potentilla reptans
Securigera varia

Clematis flammula is able to spread over long distances: its seeds, equipped with silky plumes, are dispersed by the wind. When you leave a zone of the garden to evolve by itself, new species will appear whose seeds have been brought by the wind or birds.

FLOWERING MEADOWS IN DRY CLIMATES

ADVANTAGES: very ornamental spring flowering. Low maintenance; no watering required. Important ecological role: provides a refuge for insects and birds. Low cost allows large areas to be covered.

DRAWBACKS: summer appearance not very attractive in mediterranean regions, unless the plan is to make a virtue of the yellow colour of the dried meadow.

RECOMMENDED SURFACE AREA: unlimited.

Flowering meadows do not need any irrigation. They consume neither fertilizers nor pesticides and require very little maintenance. Once they have been sown, no further intervention is needed until the time comes to scythe them after they have finished flowering. In the South of France many municipalities have turned towards this method of cover-

ing the ground as they adopt different approaches to public spaces. Near the town centre, a horticultural approach is maintained, while in more outlying zones groundcover solutions are used. In these zones, flowering meadows pro-

Facing page
Flowering meadows enable us to cover large areas while reducing maintenance.

1. A seven-spotted ladybird feeds on nectar on a newly opening flower of the wild carrot. An area of flowering meadow constitutes an important refuge for beneficial insects.

2. Flowering meadows can provide a transition between suburban zones and agricultural areas or natural spaces.

In the mediterranean climate, a flowering meadow is characterized by the strong seasonality of its appearance. Here you can see the changing appearance of meadows in olive groves:

1. In April the white daisies of *Matricaria*, the yellow daisies of *Glebionis* and poppies form swathes of colour between the trunks of the trees. The wider variety of species the meadow includes, the more successive flowerings will continue over a long period in spring.

2. In September the golden straw has been ploughed into the soil. The new meadow is ready to grow again from seed.

3. In December, making the most of the winter humidity, the newly growing meadow resembles a great expanse of wild lawn.

vide an excellent lawn alternative for covering large areas. They can be used, for example, for roadsides or for creating large ornamental areas in urban parks, where they are much appreciated by the public for their natural appearance. They can also be used on a smaller scale in private gardens, for example to make ecological strips that act as refuges for beneficial insects near a vegetable garden or small orchard.

The summer appearance of flowering meadows differs widely according to climatic zone. In temperate or oceanic climates, the relatively mild and damp conditions in summer make it possible for flowering to continue uninterrupted, from spring to autumn. In his book *Meadows*, which has become a reference work for countless gardeners in northern Europe, Christopher Lloyd lists the whole range of perennials, annuals and biennials that resulted in a virtually year-round flowering scene at Great Dixter, his vast experimental garden in the south of England. By contrast, in a mediterranean climate, the flowering of a meadow is distinctly seasonal and, because of the dry summers, very much shorter than in a temperate climate. Almost all the flowers are concentrated in spring and, although often of an extraordinary intensity, relatively fleeting. By the end of June almost all flowering is over, and with the arrival of the hot weather the exuberant spring scenes are transformed into an expanse of dry vegetation. To reduce the risk of fire, the meadow should be scythed quickly. Throughout the summer its appearance is that of a simple field of yellowed grass mown to the ground.

One of the challenges of landscape managers is to integrate the yellow expanse of the scythed meadow into a green space that needs to be ornamental in summer at the height of the tourist season. For this reason, managing a flowering meadow in dry climates is more complicated than it is in a temperate climate. There are two key lessons to learn: first, you must get to know the species that give the longest possible succession of flowerings from the end of winter to early summer and second, you must learn to apply landscaping techniques that enhance the yellow colour of the dry summer meadow.

Annual meadows and semi-perennial meadows

In the mediterranean climate, there are two broad types of flowering meadow: annual and semi-perennial. The cultivation cycle of the annual meadow passes through four distinct phases, which correspond to the passage of the seasons. It begins in autumn with the preparation of the ground followed by the sowing of a mixture of annual plants that flower freely. In winter, the green expanse of the germinating meadow resembles a large wild lawn. In spring, brilliant and multicoloured flowers appear one after the other, often

MEADOW, WASTE GROUND OR FALLOW?

"Flowering meadow" seems to be the term most widely used to describe this kind of land in gardens and public green spaces. Technically, one can make a distinction between flowering fallow land, which regrows annually, and flowering meadows that are more perennial. Indeed, the word "meadow" suggests an area of herbaceous plants that are generally perennial or semi-perennial. The word "fallow" historically has different, not to say contradictory, meanings: it can denote a piece of cultivated land awaiting sowing or a field that is deliberately left to rest uncultivated. Sometimes the word "fallow" can have negative connotations, suggesting a waste ground or abandoned land. These different terms doubtless have to do with the fact that there are many kinds of flowering meadows or fallow land, in urban and in rural contexts, sometimes with very different objectives. But regardless of what we call them or what we use them for, all these pieces of land provide a diverse range of flowers that favour beneficial insects, butterflies and pollinators, as well as small mammals such as hedgehogs, and numerous birds. Even if the ecological role of a small patch of land may seem modest, flowering meadows, fallow areas and waste ground contribute to the the ecological corridors that form a network of territory that wildlife can use to pass through urban areas, often reaching right into town centres.

1

2

3

nally simple weeds of fields and roadsides that these plants are so easy to grow in an annual flowering meadow. Their generous flowering can form great masses of brilliant colour, where the yellow of chrysanthemums, the blue of love-in-a-mists, the white of chamomile and campions and the pink of corn cockles intermingle, the whole scene shot through with countless red splashes of poppies. Depending on the effect desired, one can use a limited range of eight or ten species to create great sheets of colour, or alternatively one can expand one's range of plants to the maximum, to achieve a pointillist effect composed of a multitude of different flowers.

1. Love-in-a-mist is a species that germinates very easily in poor soil. The species that make up an annual meadow are plants which germinate fast and can form great masses of bright colour.

2. The corn cockle (*Agrostemma githago*) is an annual plant found, along with other cereal crop species such as poppies and cornflowers, in cornfields that have not been treated with herbicides.

3. As well as annual species, the semi-perennial meadow includes numerous biennial or perennial plants whose flowers do not appear until the second or third year.

spectacularly. Finally, in summer the scythed meadow becomes a great expanse of yellow, like a cornfield after the harvest. The cycle is then ready to start again, the soil being dug over once more during the course of the summer or at the beginning of autumn.

The species that make up an annual meadow are plants that germinate rapidly, adapted to an open environment. Most of them are messicole or ruderal plants. Messicole plants (from the Latin *messio*, "harvest" and -cole, derived from *colere*, "to inhabit") are the flowering plants, such as cornflowers and poppies, that coexist with cereal crops that have not been treated with herbicides. Ruderal plants (from the Latin *rudus*, *ruderis*, "rubble") are the wild flowers that grow among rubble or along roadsides, such as borage or the horned poppy. It is precisely because they were origi-

A semi-perennial meadow contains a richer range of plants. As well as annuals, it includes biennials and perennials, which will start flowering from the second year. Unlike an annual flowering meadow, which requires digging over every autumn, the semi-perennial meadow only needs to have the soil dug when the initial sowing is made, after which it looks after itself as it evolves from year to year. It thus requires less maintenance than an annual meadow: a simple scything at the beginning of summer may sometimes need to be repeated in autumn. The appearance of the meadow changes as it matures: in the first year, the flower-

ing resembles that of an annual flowering meadow, while in the following years a lessening of the spectacular spring flowering is compensated for by a greater diversity of flowers and prolonged flowering period. In a semi-perennial meadow, one can indeed achieve an interesting recurrence of summer or autumn blooming thanks to species such as mallow, wild carrot (Queen Anne's lace), lucerne, fennel, chicory and sticky fleabane, the dates of scything greatly affecting the dates at which these species flower. Although, unlike annuals, these species rarely form spectacular, uniform flowering masses, they can be very ornamental when in flower. The wonderful luminous blue of chicory, for example, is set off perfectly by the acid yellow of fennel flowers, both species flowering together at the end of summer in spite of the heat and drought. The increase in the diversity and duration of flowering is of great benefit to beneficial insects: of the different types of flowering meadow, the semi-perennial meadow certainly functions best as an ecological reserve.

The semi-perennial flowering meadow soon becomes home to other wild species which come to join the plants originally sown, and in particular grass species such as wild oats, barley, cocksfoot and various brome grasses. If the soil is too rich, the meadow tends to be invaded by vigorous species that become dominant and take up space, reducing diversity. A semi-perennial flowering meadow gives better results on poor soil. It reaches its maximum floral diversity after two or three years. If a semi-perennial meadow is grown

Achillea millefolium and wild chicory in July. Although the flowering of a semi-perennial meadow is less spectacular than that of an annual meadow, it is much more diverse so that the flowering season is longer.

dynamics of plants that do best on poor soil, for otherwise the addition of organic material every year would enrich the soil and lead to a loss of diversity. After four or five years, there is often the danger that the environment will progressively become closed, with the appearance of brambles and other woody plants which mark the first stage of the land's evolution towards forest. To maintain an open environment, ideally one should replant the semi-perennial meadow every four or five years. Digging over the soil again starts off a new cycle, with a renewed spectacle of spring flowering annual plants, after which a richer semi-perennial meadow will gradually develop.

on the same piece of land for a long time, it is preferable to remove the hay after scything in order to maintain the

Annual and semi-perennial flowering meadows are not necessarily mutually exclusive choices. When the size of the piece of land allows it, you can easily combine them

1. When a semi-perennial meadow is grown for a long time on the same piece of land, it is better to remove the hay after scything and hold back this organic matter: in poor soil the meadow maintains greater floral diversity.

2. It is possible to benefit from the respective advantages of an annual flowering meadow and a semi-perennial meadow by planting them together on the same piece of land.

in a landscape design to make the most of their respective advantages. A semi-perennial meadow could, for example, be surrounded by a large band of annual meadow. In the outer and more visible zone spectacular flowering will recur each spring, while the central area, although less colourful in spring, will maintain staggered flowerings over a longer period. In public green spaces, in order for the meadow to serve as a place of observation and discovery, the continuity of the site can be interrupted by paths and clearings where people may walk or rest, which will make the meadow directly accessible to the public. If scythed regularly, these paths and clearings will evolve towards a different range of plants, including a predominance of species that grow in flat rosettes which tolerate regular encounters with the blade of the scythe, as in a wild lawn (see page 63). Some of these species have different flowering seasons from those of the meadow plants. Daisies and dandelions, for instance, flower from the end of winter in the areas treated as wild lawn, and thus add both to the ornamental appearance of the piece of land and to the availability of sources of nectar and pollen useful to insects. The creation of mixed areas of high ecological interest, including annual meadows, semi-perennial meadows and areas of wild lawn, is thus one of the most easily implemented means of replacing lawns in urban parks with large spaces accessible to the public.

In defence of yellow

Whether they are annual or semi-perennial, flowering meadows in mediterranean climates have one thing in common that is often seen as a major drawback: in summer, after being scythed, they turn into a sea of yellow. Mediterranean gardeners sometimes have an excessively negative reaction

In the mediterranean climate, a flowering meadow becomes golden after its summer scything. Here the yellow is set off by the dark foliage of a carob tree.

to groundcover vegetation that dries out in summer. Yellow may be enjoyed as a flower colour, in for example daffodils, broom or mimosa, but it is felt to be very much less acceptable in dry lawns or meadows. Here yellow is seen as the absence of green, and the powerful cultural influence of the English garden model makes people prefer green in the garden above all other colours. There are, however, some magnificent mediterranean landscape models that focus on the visual power of expanses of yellow in summer. Take, for example, the mosaic of agricultural landscapes where the yellow-ochre land is punctuated by the contrasting dark green of cypresses and oaks and the varied greens of olives and almonds.

Mediterranean landscapes such as these can provide a model for public spaces. For example, in the south of the Iberian Peninsula the *dehesas* or *montados* are mixed cultivations where woods of widely-spaced cork oaks leave large open areas for cereal crops or pasture. It is in full summer that the beauty of the *dehesas* shows to its best advantage, the dark silhouettes of the trees contrasting with the yellow of the hills that stretch as far as the eye can see. In Sicily, on the remarkable plateau of Noto near Syracuse, one can also see fine examples of mixed cultivations, called in Italy *coltura promiscua*: in this region, fields of cereal crops, planted regularly with olives, fig trees, almonds and carobs, create a stunning picture when the entire landscape turns gold in

In June, the majestic *Genista aetnensis* flowers when the grass has already dried out on the foothills of Mount Etna in Sicily. The contrast between the woody and herbaceous layers contributes to the visual power of this landscape in which gold is the dominant colour.

the bright summer light. In the South of France, the Larzac plateau has great expanses of pasture whose changing colour throughout the seasons is highlighted by the permanent architecture of dark box and junipers. The golden pastures of Larzac become spectacular when the tight masses of *Stipa pennata* reflect the sun as they undulate in the north wind. On the slopes of Mount Etna, large wild meadows provide a backdrop for *Genista aetnensis*, a magnificent broom whose yellow flowers open in June when the grass is already completely dry, as if inviting mediterranean gardeners to reconcile the yellow colour of the flowers with the golden colour of the land.

PLANTS FOR FLOWERING MEADOWS

Some horticultural seed mixtures for flowering meadows include "improved" plants that are of little use to insects. In the large double-flowered multicoloured cornflowers, for example, the corolla is composed of a multitude of petals that replace the nectar- and pollen-producing organs. For insects they act as decoys, since the large and seemingly attractive flowers have in fact nothing to offer them. These horticultural seed mixtures fulfil a purely ornamental role, but are not suitable if one is seeking to create a flowering meadow which has an ecological purpose. Specialist seed suppliers (see the addresses given on page 230) put together mixtures for particular uses such as for fallow land with beehives or for ecological margins around fields of organic crops. The composition of such mixtures is based on the criteria according to which the species are chosen: for example, in general only local wild species are chosen when the piece of land is adjacent to a natural environment.

Species for annual flowering meadows in mediterranean climates
Agrostemma githago
Ammi majus
Borago officinalis
Centaurea cyanus
Chrysanthemum segetum
Consolida regalis
Eschscholzia californica
Glaucium flavum
Glebionis coronaria
Legousia speculum-veneris
Linum grandiflorum
Linum usitatissimum
Matricaria recutita
Nigella damascena
Onobrychis arenaria
Orlaya grandiflora
Papaver rhoeas
Phacelia tanacetifolia
Silene vulgaris
Sinapis alba
Sixalix atropurpurea
 subsp. *maritima*
Tordylium maximum
Torilis arvensis
Trifolium incarnatum
Trifolium purpureum
Tripleurospermum inodorum

Species for semi-perennial flowering meadows in mediterranean climates (to this list may be added all the species for an annual flowering meadow, ensuring a spectacular flowering in the first year)
Achillea millefolium
Bituminaria bituminosa
Catananche caerulea
Cephalaria leucantha
Cichorium intybus
Daucus carota
Echium vulgare
Foeniculum vulgare
Galium verum
Hypericum perforatum
Lathyrus tuberosus
Malva sylvestris
Medicago sativa
Melilotus officinalis
Onobrychis viciifolia
Plantago lanceolata
Rumex acetosella
Salvia sclarea
Sanguisorba minor
Sixalix atropurpurea subsp.
 maritima
Trifolium pratense
Verbascum blattaria
Verbascum phlomoides
Verbascum sinuatum
Verbascum thapsus
Vicia cracca

On the Larzac plateau in the South of France: the dark foliage of box and juniper creates a rhythmic visual counterpoint to the expanse of dry meadow in summer.

PLANTING AND MAINTAINING
THE GROUNDCOVER GARDEN

Traditional agricultural principles are of no use to the gardener who is planning to create a bed of Mediterranean groundcover plants. The levels of organic matter in the soil, the balance between clay and humus and the presence of sufficient nutrients bear no relation to the conditions these plants find in their natural habitat. The majority of groundcover plants that grow around the Mediterranean live in very poor soil (see page 25). They are adapted to an eroded environment where the combined action of fire, grazing and repeated onslaughts by wind and heavy rain has for centuries been removing the topsoil. In a dry climate, the main purpose in preparing the soil is to help root development, in order for the plant to become independent as soon as possible after planting. The factor that plays the largest part in root development is not the fertility of the substrate but the presence of oxygen in the soil.

Oxygen for roots

In Mediterranean groundcover plants the absorbent hairs at the tips of the rootlets are very numerous, for their root system is much more extensive than that of temperate-climate plants. This enables them not only to take up the moisture necessary for their survival more efficiently, but also to gain access to the nutrients available in small amounts among the stones. The ramified roots of a cistus, for example, are capable of reaching a depth of more than 4 m in the crevices of a rocky soil and will spread over a radius of almost 10 m. To improve their absorption capacity, most Mediterranean plants depend strictly on a symbiosis with mycorrhizal fungi (from the Greek *mukēs*, "fungus", and *rhiza*, "root"). These fungi, composed of a dense network of very fine filaments, are able to extract minerals present in the soil that are not very soluble, even to the point of attacking bedrock, thus helping to nourish the plant on whose roots they live. Some leguminous species, such as *Dorycnium pentaphyllum*, *Coronilla minima* and *Trifolium fragiferum*, also establish other kinds of symbiosis with specialized bacteria. These bacteria transform atmospheric nitrogen, which plants cannot use, into ammonium which can be directly assimilated by their roots. These plants are generous: they do not exploit the nitrogen in the air only for themselves but also redistribute it to the companion species that live around them in the garrigue. The decomposition of their dead leaves releases the nitrogen stored in them and returns it to the soil, while the secretion of nitrogen compounds from their roots makes nitrogen directly available to other plants.

A groundcover garden that combines cushion-shaped plants, carpeting plants and gravel paths. Methods of reducing maintenance should be considered when a groundcover garden is at the planning stage.

Facing page
Globularia alypum above the Marseilles *calanques* (creeks). The groundcover plants that grow around the Mediterranean live for the most part on stony, perfectly drained ground from which centuries of erosion have removed all the topsoil.

1. The Parc de la Tête-d'Or in Lyons. In a temperate climate, the creation of flowerbeds requires fertile soil enriched with organic matter. By contrast, in the mediterranean climate these traditional horticultural principles are not suitable for planting a bed of groundcover plants.

2. *Cistus × florentinus* 'Tramontane' thrives on the poor soil of a slope which, together with the stony soil, provides excellent drainage.

3. If you carefully unearth the roots of a leguminous plant, you will see strings of bacterial nodules arranged along the finest roots, which fertilize the soil. Shown here are the roots of a *Dorycnium pentaphyllum* from our garden.

1. *Santolina magonica* on the Levant peninsula of Mallorca. In order to survive in poor soil, most mediterranean plants depend on symbioses with mycorrhizal fungi. Composed of a dense network of very fine filaments, these fungi are able to extract barely soluble minerals present in the soil, going as far as to attack bedrock in order to help supply nutrients to their host plant.

2. This young rosemary seems to be growing without soil. It survives thanks to its long roots which penetrate deep into fissures in search of the elements they need.

3. The roots of garrigue plants find the oxygen and trace elements they need in the small pockets of soil that form in fissures between the rocks, sometimes at some distance from the crown of the plant. In the garden, groundcover plants native to the garrigue do not need fertilizers or potting compost, just excellent drainage (redrawn after Rackham & Moody, 1996).

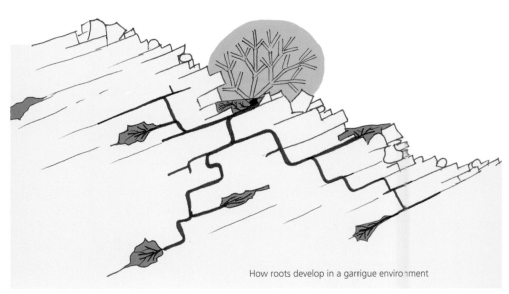

How roots develop in a garrigue environment

2

3

These symbiotic mechanisms are established naturally in the garden, as they are in nature: the spores of the mycorrhizal fungi are omnipresent in the air and in the soil. Nevertheless, the biological activity that allows Mediterranean groundcover plants to grow in poor soils depends to a great extent on the permeability of the soil, for it requires a large amount of oxygen. The bacteria and the mycorrhizal fungi on the roots of dryland plants are aerobic organisms (from the Greek *aeros*, "air", and *bios*, "life"), which means that they need oxygen to live. Root growth also depends on the presence of oxygen in the soil. Indeed, beneath the plant, root respiration is very active, with the root cells absorbing oxygen and releasing CO_2 just like all the other parts of the plant. Soil with poor permeability, which limits the availability of oxygen, slows the development of the roots. On the contrary, a well-aerated soil rapidly increases the volume of it that the roots can explore, enabling groundcover plants to resist drought better by drawing on a larger hydric reserve.

When you are making a new garden, the soil structure has often been profoundly disturbed by recent work. The worst situation is when the garden is being created around a newly built house, especially if the site is on clay soil. The passage of construction machinery, the storing of materials on soil that is sometimes waterlogged, the parking of the crane or the cement mixer: all these lead to a very serious compaction of the soil. When the time comes to plant, the gardener may be tempted simply to add potting compost or fertilizer to each planting hole to compensate for the poor state of the soil. However, if one improves the fertility of the soil around the base of each plant without decompacting the soil

of the entire bed, the rapid growth seen during the first year risks being followed by a stationary phase. The roots find it hard to move out from the comfortable nest of the planting hole, and the plant will be unable to withstand drought in the future. Before planting a bed of Mediterranean groundcover plants, the most important thing is thus to ensure that the soil structure is well enough aerated to allow the rapid growth of the roots in all directions. Decompaction of the soil and improvement of its drainage are two vital steps on which depend the good development and life span of the planting.

Soil preparation in a garden on clay

Depending on the size of the area to be planted, there are various ways of decompacting the soil. When the area is small or medium-sized, from 100 to 200m², the simplest method, if the ground is not too stony, is to dig it over with a garden fork. You begin by digging an initial hole then, working backwards, you make a series of vertical openings, each time pushing in front of you the sods dug out by the fork. When you reach the end of the row you start again with a second parallel row. This labour is time-consuming but effective: it breaks up the hardpan by creating a network of horizontal and vertical clefts or openings, about 30 cm deep, which helps the soil regain a good degree of permeability. It is not necessary to turn the sods over, you simply push them forwards with a continued movement of your arm after you have thrust the fork into the ground. This method preserves the natural strata of the soil, thus avoiding too much disturbance of its bacterial life, always greatest in the top surface layer. The decompaction process can be

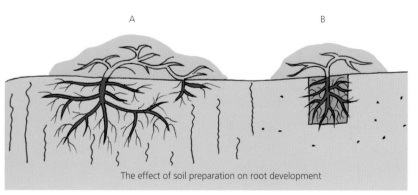

The effect of soil preparation on root development

1

2

1. Digging with a garden fork is the simplest way of decompacting the soil when the ground is not too stony. Decompaction can be followed by the addition of sand, which will improve drainage.

2. A: Soil that has been meticulously decompacted to a good depth allows roots to grow rapidly in all directions.
B: If one improves the fertility of the soil around the crown of the plant without decompacting the whole area, the rapid growth seen in the first year is followed by a check on growth. The roots have difficulty developing outside the comfortable nest of the planting hole and the plant will be unable to resist future drought.

completed by raking the soil to level the surface and removing any perennial roots present in the soil.

For large areas, decompaction can be carried out using a tractor equipped with a plough. When the layout of the areas makes access by tractor difficult, the bucket of a mini-excavator mounted on tracks can decompact inaccessible areas relatively quickly. Just as when a garden fork is used, large sods do not have to be lifted and turned, all that is needed is to move the bucket backwards and forwards once it is in the ground in order to break up the compacted layers of the soil.

Once the soil has been decompacted, drainage needs to be improved if the soil is heavy and consists largely of clay. Drainage allows excess water after heavy autumn or winter rains to run off quickly. Standing water replaces air in the soil, leading to asphyxiation of the roots which harms the growth of most Mediterranean groundcover plants. In some cases root asphyxiation can cause the death of many of the plants in the bed. The best drainage of all is a natural slope that lets water run off by gravity: a garden consisting of a series of terraces on a hillside, where the stony soil is retained by old dry-stone walls, has excellent natural drainage. When the garden doesn't have an adequate slope, try making raised beds filled with a mixture of soil and sand or gravel (for example two-thirds soil and one-third sand or gravel) to mimic a miniature hillside: this is often the best way to achieve large, perfectly drained groundcover beds.

You can improve drainage on a flat area that is intended for groundcover planting which can be walked on by adding sand to the surface. You can complete the job by laying a network of land drains buried in the soil, provided that there is a low point into which the drains can empty. After decompacting the soil, spread the sand over the entire surface, then mix it into the soil by raking or by going over it with a cultivator. The thickness of the layer of sand will depend on the heaviness of the soil. On a very clay soil, add 5 cm of sand over the whole area (i.e. 1 m³ per 20 m²) to give a draining layer, once it is mixed into the soil, of about 15 cm thick consisting of a mixture of 2/3 soil and 1/3 sand. This type of soft surface is ideal for carpeting plants that withstand pedestrian traffic because they spread by layering much more easily when they are creeping over a light surface. Adding sand also improves the life span of the plants: it reduces the compaction caused by regular foot traffic and thus maintains in the long term a well-aerated soil structure that helps the groundcover plants live for many years.

If it is not possible to improve the drainage of your clay soil, it is best not to attempt to grow groundcover plants originating from Mediterranean garrigues. Instead, the perennial species that make up wild lawns, such as clover, self-heal, yarrows, burnets, plantains or ground ivy, are relatively tolerant of soil which can sometimes become saturated with water. A small number of drought-adapted plants are able to tolerate temporary flooding, including *Achillea crithmifolia*, *Achillea nobilis*, *Phyla canescens* and *Halimione por-*

1. In this clay soil, water lies on the surface after heavy autumn rains. By taking the place of air in the soil, standing water causes root asphyxiation, harming the plants' development. Decompaction and drainage are the two most important steps for the successful planting of groundcovers.

2. Decompaction of the soil before planting a groundcover bed. Laying a path between the beds completes the drainage of this area. The next step will be to raise the level of the beds slightly by the addition of sand.

tulacoides. These species can prove very useful when, for example, you want plants to colonize the bottom of a water retention basin which is subject to occasional flooding.

Biological decompaction, an alternative to the garden fork

It is often difficult to design all the groundcover areas of the garden in one go, because decompaction of the soil and improving drainage can take a long time. It is better to proceed in stages, taking the time to prepare the soil properly in each area rather than trying to plant in poor conditions. In a large garden, you might want to leave some parts uncultivated until you have time to work on them and on these you might consider a temporary planting which will restore

the soil structure naturally by means of biological decompaction.

Biological decompaction consists of sowing a semi-perennial flowering meadow and renewing it every three or four years in order to maintain a good floral diversity. Many of the annual, biennial or perennial species grown in flowering meadows (see page 107) possess powerful root systems, capable of breaking up the soil as they penetrate deep into the ground. Wild carrots, chicories, mallows, clovers and lucernes have twisting roots that pierce through the soil like vertical drills, some of the thick roots being able to reach a depth of more than 2 m. When these roots die, they decompose through the biological activity of the soil, leaving gaps

1. The best drainage is provided by a natural slope which removes excess water by gravity: if a garden consists of a series of terraces on a hillside whose stony soil is retained by old dry-stone walls, then the natural drainage will be excellent.

2. Raised beds, which remove excess water by gravity, are an effective way to grow garrigue plants in a garden on heavy soil.

3. In uncultivated parts of a large garden, planting a temporary flowering meadow will naturally restore the soil structure by biological decompaction.

4. Careful excavation lets us see the depth to which the root of a wild carrot reaches. Wild carrots, chicories, mallows, clovers and lucernes have twisting roots that pierce through the soil like vertical boreholes.

that contribute to the natural aeration of the soil. Thus renewing a flowering meadow regularly over a period of six to eight years leads to a remarkable restructuring of the soil, re-establishing the permeability and biological activity required for future plantings. Although roots start the aeration process, it is completed by earthworms and countless tunnelling soil insects, which find the meadow a favourable environment for reproduction. In this way, long, hard work with a garden fork is replaced by the natural work of the flowering meadow. All the gardener has to do is to scythe it once a year and resow it every three or four years.

Soil preparation in a garrigue garden

If you are planting groundcovers in a garden situated in real garrigue that consists almost entirely of large stones protruding from the ground, the soil preparation procedure is very different. Drainage is not usually a problem, since water percolates between the layers of stones. The size of the stones, however, can make planting difficult. When creating a large groundcover bed composed of shrubs that grow wild in a stony environment, such as lavender, rosemary, helichrysum or euphorbia, it is possible to make an individual hole for each plant without digging over the whole area. The stones are patiently removed with a pickaxe or crowbar and as large a hole as possible is opened up, measuring about 30 × 30 × 40 cm. When the hole is filled in again, the large stones are replaced by a mixture of earth and sand, in which the young roots will develop rapidly as the plant becomes

established. The roots of these shrubs will subsequently be able to anchor themselves deeply, making the most of every fissure between the blocks of stone, just as they do naturally in the garrigue. Rocky ground is indeed riddled with a large network of fissures, expanding occasionally to form small pockets of soil, where roots can find the oxygen and mineral elements that they need.

If, however, you want to plant a carpeting groundcover on rocky ground, the best solution is to cover the entire surface with topsoil. The planting density is generally too high for it to be feasible to remove stones and open up holes for each plant. Adding a layer of 15 to 20 cm of soil, mixed with sand to ensure perfect drainage, makes planting very simple. The surface layer of imported soil allows stolons to root easily, while deep roots are soon able to seek cracks between the rocks. Another solution is to make use of the rock itself as the walkable surface and partially plant it with carpeting plants set into the fissures, just as one would do when planting the cracks between the paving stones of a terrace.

Soil preparation for flowering meadows

A flowering meadow requires a relatively small amount of work. Most of the species used are plants that were originally simply weeds that grew among cereal crops. With the development of agriculture, they spread around the Mediterranean Basin about six thousand years ago, content with the rudimentary ploughing that the first agricultural tools

1. In a garrigue garden, make the most of the rocky soil by using it as a surface that can be walked on. This rocky surface can be planted with a range of specialized plants that like living among stones, such as the *Cyclamen* and asphodels shown here.

2. In gardens with very stony soil, the stone can be used to construct retaining walls which reduce erosion and retain the soil in the cultivated areas.

1

2

were capable of. The main work consists of preparing an even seed bed at the end of summer to provide the best conditions for germination. For large areas, traditional agricultural tools are most suitable such as a disc harrow to bury the existing vegetation followed by a cultivator and then roller to prepare and smooth the seed bed.

A new flowering meadow will always include a certain number of weeds, in other words plants that exploit the upturned soil to germinate among the flowering species. To avoid too great a competition from weeds, the technique of false sowing can be used. This consists of preparing a first seed bed to allow the weeds to germinate in advance. As soon as they have germinated, the young weeds are cut down and a new seed bed created by going over the ground with a very shallow rotavator; the new bed is now ready for the flowering meadow seeds. For false sowing to be effective, the rotavator must be used with great precision, turning the soil to a depth of only 1 to 2 cm, for otherwise it will bring a new crop of weed seeds to the surface.

For small areas in a private garden, the simplest method is to work the soil with a hoe then finish off with a rake to break up the clods and smooth the surface. If the soil is not too hard, the rotavator can also be used. However, it is always better not to pass a rotavator over ground that has not been decompacted, especially if it is a clay soil: the rapid rotation of the blades risks creating a hard layer of soil, called a plough pan, which blocks the roots of the young plants. To carry out false sowing on small patches, cut down the weeds just after they have germinated with the well-sharpened edge of the hoe, before proceeding with the sowing proper. The quality of the result depends to a large extent on the species chosen (see page 115) and the date of sowing. In the mediterranean climate, the best results are obtained with sowing right at the beginning of autumn when the soil is still warm, just at the moment when the first rains arrive which will trigger germination.

1. The Essaouira region in southern Morocco. Traditional techniques for the cultivation of cereal crops encourage messicole plants such as poppies and cornflowers, with the result that the whole plain is covered in multicoloured flowers before the harvest.

2. Thin soil, barely scratched by a plough, becomes a favoured germination site for species that make up an annual flowering meadow.

PLANTING GROUNDCOVERS

How dense should a groundcover planting be? Planting density depends on both the speed at which the chosen species grows and the gardener's patience. Interestingly, although the density of planting will affect the time it takes for the cover to develop, it does not necessarily have a bearing on the final result. In our garden, for example, we have compared various different planting densities for a carpet of *Thymus ciliatus*. All of them gave the same result in the end, but the time it took for the cover to develop differed greatly. Planting at a density of one plant per square metre took three years to cover the soil, while planting at nine plants per square metre covered the soil in less than eight months. For every species mentioned in the plant directory, I note the usual planting density required to achieve a total cover in one or two years, depending on the growing conditions. According to the speed of cover desired, you can alter the planting density to suit your requirements. The planting density also depends on the type of planting envisaged: a carpet of plants or a flowering steppe, a large groundcover bed or a gravel garden.

Planting green carpets

Once the soil has been carefully prepared, groundcover carpets are quick to plant. In ground that has been deeply decompacted and lightened by the addition of sand (see the preceding chapter) it is an easy matter to make planting holes with your hands or with the help of a small trowel. Place the young plant so that the top of the rootball is just below the soil level. Then fill in the hole using the earth-sand mixture, without adding potting compost or fertilizer. To finish off, pile up the soil carefully around the young plant leaving a slight basin which will help retain its first waterings. When groundcover carpets are being planted,

PLANTING DENSITY

Gardeners often hesitate when it come to working out the relationship between planting density and planting distance. Here are some guidelines (some numbers have been rounded up):

1 plant per 4 square metres: space between plants 2 m
1 plant per square metre: space between plants 1 m
2 plants per square metre: space between plants 70 cm
4 plants per square metre: space between plants 50 cm
6 plants per square metre: space between plants 40 cm
9 plants per square metre: space between plants 33 cm
16 plants per square metre: space between plants 25 cm

There is no need to respect these planting distances down to the last centimetre, or to use string to align the young plants perfectly: the groundcovers will spread rapidly so that after a few years it is impossible to make out their initial positions.

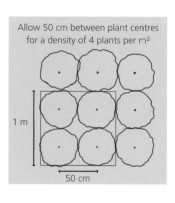

Allow 50 cm between plant centres for a density of 4 plants per m²

1 m

50 cm

Facing page
The planting technique depends on the type of groundcover envisaged. Here young plants are surrounded by broad watering basins, which make hand-watering easier during the first year.

1. You can adjust the planting density according to the speed with which you want the ground to be covered.

2. New planting of *Achillea umbellata*. During the first year regular care is needed in terms of weeding and watering to allow the young plants the best conditions in which to become established.

this watering basin should, however, not be too large or deep since it is hard to level the basin once the carpeting plants have covered the soil, which may make walking on it less comfortable.

When you finish planting, it is true that the result rarely inspires enthusiasm. Little tufts of *Frankenia*, *Thymus* or *Matricaria* look lost in the middle of bare soil and it seems as if they will never to be able to cover it. Perhaps your neighbour, who keeps a beautiful traditional lawn and has watched you carry out all the work of decompacting, drainage and planting for a result which at this stage looks so meagre, may not be able to resist a smirk as he greets you over the fence. You just have to be patient and make sure that your young plants get the regular care they need

to become established. During the first year, maintenance consists of two main tasks: regular weeding so that the early

1. A newly planted mixed lawn consists of strawberry clover, cinquefoil, daisies, bugle and self-heal. Watering basins around the young plants allow for the initial watering.

2. With a planting density of 4 plants per square metre, it will take about a year to achieve a uniform carpet of *Frankenia laevis*.

growth of the plants will not be checked by competition from weeds, and the watering to ensure that they get a good start (see the following chapter).

Planting a flowering steppe

Some groundcover plants that can tolerate foot traffic grow naturally in stony environments. This is the case with *Artemisia pedemontana* for example, which grows in the mountains of Central Spain on expanses of stony soil frequented by sheep. It is possible to reproduce these growing conditions in the garden by planting on gravel, by which I mean growing carpeting plants (often planted as a mixture of species in order to create a contrast between different types of foliage) on a thick bed of gravel. Planting on gravel has two great advantages for the gardener. First, seed germination is almost entirely suppressed by the layer of gravel so weeding is very much reduced, not only during the initial period but over the long term. Second, the mineral mulch limits water loss by direct evaporation from the surface of the soil so carpeting plants are able to withstand drought more easily because their roots find moisture more easily in soil protected by gravel.

After carefully preparing the ground as for a groundcover carpet, spread a layer of fine gravel to a thickness of about 6 cm over the whole surface. This thickness is the minimum necessary to prevent the germination of weeds. In our experience, the grade of gravel most suitable for this kind of mulch is from 8 to 12 mm. Once the gravel has been spread, lay out the plants in their pots at the chosen density. Two different densities can be used for flowering steppes: either the normal density to achieve coverage of the ground after a year, as with groundcover carpets, or a

much lower density so that ultimately patches of gravel will remain visible between the patches of carpeting vegetation. The visual effect of the latter is very different: it shows off the contrast between stone and plants, calling to mind the natural scenes one sees on countless high plateaux around the Mediterranean.

How do you plant through this layer of gravel? Move the

1. To reduce maintenance during the first year, we can "plant on gravel", in other words grow carpeting plants on a bed of gravel, which reduces the germination of weeds and conserves moisture in the soil. (Keith Yves' garden.)

2. Planting on gravel makes it possible to create large areas of flowering steppe that require little maintenance.

Planting on gravel: after meticulously decompacting the soil, spread over the whole area a layer of fine gravel about 6 cm thick. Move aside the gravel with your hand (3) and make a hole in the underlying soil deep enough to take the bottom of the rootball (4). Then put a few handfuls of fine soil around the rootball, to avoid the roots drying out at the sides through direct contact with the aerated structure of the gravel. Finish by filling in the hole and replacing the gravel all around the plant (5).

3

4

5

Planting large groundcover beds

Planting large groundcover beds composed of perennials and dry-climate shrubs is done in several stages over the course of a whole year. The first step is to plant in the traditional manner in soil that has been perfectly decompacted and drained, without adding potting compost or fertilizer to the planting hole. The second step is to create large watering basins. Although carpeting plants that are walked on can be watered by sprinklers, wetting the whole surface of the soil in order to encourage stems to root as they spread progressively over the soil, the most effective way of watering to establish a large groundcover bed is by hand, filling a broad basin created around each plant. These basins make it possible to give deep watering at widely spaced intervals during the first year. The third step is to hand-weed the bed regularly, checking the state of the basin before each watering. Finally, the last step is to fill in the watering basins at the end of the first summer as the groundcover perennials and dry-climate shrubs will need no further watering after the first year. Once the watering basins have been levelled out, it may be useful to add a thick layer of mulch to cover the surface of the soil between the plants. Depending on the plants used, this mulch may be mineral or organic (see page 153).

gravel aside with your hand and make a small hole in the underlying soil to fit the bottom of the rootball. Then surround the rootball with a few handfuls of fine soil, in order to prevent it drying out at the sides through direct contact with the aerated structure of the gravel. Finish by filling in the hole and replacing the gravel all around the plant. The carpeting vegetation will then spread by layering over the surface of the gravel.

1. The carpeting vegetation of *Thymus serpyllum* 'Elfin' spreads by the layering of its stems across the gravel surface.

2. Traditional planting of beds of dry-climate shrubs. The watering basins around each plant allow deep watering to be given at periodic intervals during the first year.

3. At the end of the first summer the watering basins are flattened out and the soil can now be covered with a layer of gravel 6 to 8 cm thick.

When large groundcover beds are being made on a professional scale, many gardeners prefer to lay down a mulch immediately after planting, in order to reduce the amount of weeding needed from the very first year. However, this almost always comes with the installation of a drip irrigation system to replace hand-watering. Indeed, the mulch makes it impossible to create the wide basins necessary for deep watering. Gardeners everywhere seem to be whole-heartedly attracted by drip irrigation systems, yet it is worth knowing that a badly used drip system can lead to many disappointments, including a deformation of the root system making the plant less drought-resistant, and a major risk of deaths due to cryptogamic diseases (see page 147). Before deciding whether a drip irrigation system is really necessary, it is worth having a close look at the water requirements of different groundcover plants in mediterranean gardens.

Planting a groundcover bed consisting of dry-climate plants requires patience: it is only at the end of the second or third year that they will reach their full potential in terms of visual interest.

ECONOMIZING ON WATER

The management of water in a groundcover garden should be worked out when the garden is at the planning stage. First, identify the water requirements of the different species, in order to create distinct watering zones that group plants according to their irrigation needs. Then reduce the area of the irrigated zones as much as possible, while at the same time optimizing the watering schedule to minimize water loss. Finally, it is sometimes possible to harvest enough water to irrigate groundcover plants by storing rainwater or grey water from the house.

The water requirements of groundcover plants

The various groundcover plants suitable for mediterranean gardens do not all have the same water requirements. Some are perfectly able to resist drought, while others need occasional or regular watering. It is not always easy to know

when and how to water, and in many cases the gardener gets it wrong, either giving too much water (which not only

Facing page
With their silver foliage, *Ballota acetabulosa* and *Senecio viravira* make a groundcover bed that is economical on water.

1. In regions with extremely dry summers, water management should be worked out at the planning stage of the garden. Grouping groundcover plants according to their water requirements makes it possible to reduce water consumption by reducing the areas that are irrigated.

2. Native to the desert regions of Northern Mexico, *Leucophyllum langmaniae* flowers in our garden at the end of summer, just when the drought is most intense. Like many plants originating from dry climates, it does not require any watering in mediterranean gardens.

2

1. Experimental patches of groundcover plants that can be used as carpeting. The various groundcover species do not all have the same water requirements: the first step towards optimizing water use in a mediterranean garden is to identify the specific needs of each species.

According to their behaviour during the summer drought, groundcover plants can be used in the different zones of the garden:

2. Native to the steppes of Asia Minor, *Salvia multicaulis* is a species that resists drought perfectly. It is spectacular during its spring flowering but becomes less attractive in summer: its foliage dries out almost completely when the plant becomes dormant.

3. *Bupleurum spinosum* is an extremely tough species, native to the Atlas Mountains of Morocco. Barely visible in spring, it becomes magnificent in summer when it is covered in acid-green flowers.

wastes water but also weakens the plants and may sometimes cause them to die) or watering them badly, giving surface irrigation which disturbs the development of the roots and makes the plant more and more susceptible to drought. The first step towards economizing on water in a groundcover garden is thus to establish the water requirements of the different species.

In our own garden we have studied the behaviour of numerous groundcover plants by submitting them to various different watering regimes and to more or less prolonged periods of dryness. The results have sometimes been surprising. For example, one of the carpeting plants reputed to be among the greediest for water, *Dichondra repens*, proved in fact to be resistant to drought. However, the plant's appearance if one doesn't water it in no way meets

the gardener's expectations: the strategy used by *Dichondra* to resist drought consists of losing all its leaves for the whole summer. The plant is able to enter into dormancy thanks to its rhizomes which serve as storage organs, and new carpeting leaves reappear with the first autumn rains. When you plant a carpet of *Dichondra*, it is usually to achieve a beautiful, even green surface all summer long that you will be able to walk on or lie on beside the swimming pool. Thus *Dichondra* has to be watered regularly, at least once a week and up to twice a week in heat waves, not because *Dichondra* itself needs water, but because the gardener has decided to use it in a way that necessitates regular irrigation. So when you consider the water needs of a groundcover plant for a mediterranean garden, examine two scenarios: first, the drought resistance of the species when it follows its natural cycle and second, the amount of water it needs if its summer appearance is to meet your expectations.

Some species can accept different watering regimes depending on the way we use them. For example, *Thymus ciliatus* can be used to make beautiful carpets, both soft and dense, if it is watered once a fortnight in summer (in the Montpellier region of France). By contrast, the very same *Thymus ciliatus* needs no watering if it is planted in a flowering steppe (see page 129). It becomes partially bare in summer and its foliage takes on a brownish violet hue, which might look odd in a single-species planting but becomes a bonus in a mixed planting since it creates an interesting contrast with grey- or silver-leaved plants such as *Centaurea bella* or *Tanacetum densum*.

Dichondra repens and *Thymus ciliatus* can be given more or less water depending on the summer appearance that is desired. However these two examples are far from being generally representative of all groundcovers. Indeed, a great many garrigue plants cannot tolerate summer watering. For example, we have attempted to use *Artemisia pedemontana*, a magnificent groundcover with silver leaves, to make a thick carpet. Since the plant tends to develop bare patches in dry periods, we tried to control this behaviour by giving it regular irrigation. The result was catastrophic: by the end of the first summer all the plants in our experimental plot had died. Like many of the plants originating from stony hillsides around the Mediterranean *Artemisia pedemontana* is vulnerable to a cryptogamic disease leading to dramatic death if one gives it water during the hot period. The plant does not have a problem with heat (after all, it grows wild in the mountains of Central Spain where summer temperatures can be very high) but it cannot tolerate the combination of heat and humidity. In regions with very hot summers it is thus not possible to use this plant in parts of the garden that are irrigated.

In the many gardens all around the Mediterranean that we have visited, Clara and I have noticed that, paradoxically, the groundcover plants most resistant to drought are rarely seen. Copious watering, which remains the current practice in most Mediterranean gardens, rapidly kills species which tolerate drought but cannot tolerate humidity during the hot period. In the plant directory (from page 167-227), I shall give all the information we have been able to amass on the drought resistance of groundcover plants, the summer appearance of their foliage, and their tolerance of irrigation during the hot season.

Phlomis lychnitis is a groundcover plant which cannot tolerate being watered during the hot period. Copious irrigation, which is still the current practice in most mediterranean gardens, causes species that resist drought very well but do not tolerate humidity in the hot season to die rapidly.

Creating different watering zones

One of the most effective ways of economizing on water in a mediterranean garden is to group plants according to their water requirements by creating different zones in the garden. This practice, called hydrozoning, has become one of the bases of the rational management of water in gardens in the South West of the United States, where steps to conserve water were initiated several decades ago. In groundcover gardens a large amount of water is often wasted by giving the same watering regime to all the plants. The species greediest for water risk going thirsty, while garrigue plants die from over-watering. By grouping plants according to their needs, we avoid giving water pointlessly to drought-resistant plants and can concentrate our irrigation on the species that need the most water.

The watering zones can be thought of as a series of concentric circles moving outwards from the house. The first zone can include the areas that require frequent irrigation, that is to say twice a week in summer. This would include the vegetable garden, the pot plants on a terrace or patio and, if possible, a small nursery area tucked away in a semi-shaded corner where the well-organized gardener can propagate in advance the groundcover plants that will be needed for future planting. Just outside this first circle, a second zone can include plants that need watering once a week in summer: for example a miniature lawn of *Zoysia tenuifolia* serving as a play area for children, or a mini-oasis of plants whose scents give added pleasure in the immediate vicinity of a terrace. Further away from the house, the third zone can include plants which tolerate drought but appreciate an

One of the most effective ways to economize on water in a mediterranean garden is to group plants according to their needs by creating separate watering zones: in this way we avoid pointlessly watering drought-resistant plants and concentrate irrigation on the zone that contains plants with the most demanding water requirements. The watering zones can be thought of as concentric circles, moving progressively away from the house.

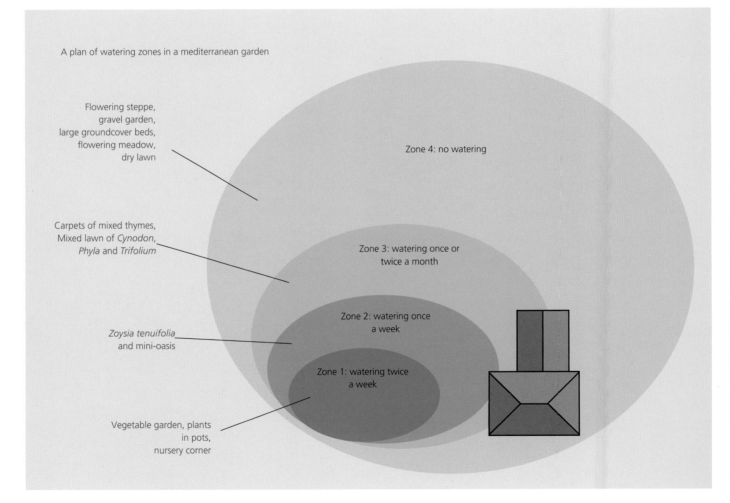

A plan of watering zones in a mediterranean garden

Flowering steppe, gravel garden, large groundcover beds, flowering meadow, dry lawn

Carpets of mixed thymes, Mixed lawn of *Cynodon*, *Phyla* and *Trifolium*

Zoysia tenuifolia and mini-oasis

Vegetable garden, plants in pots, nursery corner

Zone 4: no watering

Zone 3: watering once or twice a month

Zone 2: watering once a week

Zone 1: watering twice a week

Examples of different watering zones in a groundcover garden:

1. Close to the house, a small patch of *Zoysia tenuifolia* measuring a few dozen square metres.

2. On a medium-sized area, of about 50 to 100 m², a mixed groundcover carpet suits the intermediate watering zone where water requirements are least.

3. Different techniques can be used for areas where no irrigation is given in summer and these can be large because they require less maintenance than the other parts of the garden.

occasional watering in hot weather, once or twice a month: a mixed lawn of *Cynodon* 'Santa Ana', *Trifolium fragiferum* and *Phyla canescens* to play ball on, or a carpet of mixed thymes marking the transition to garrigue plants. The plants in this zone have the advantage of being relatively drought-resistant, even if an occasional watering gives them a more attractive appearance. If you go away for your summer holiday, there is no need for this zone to be watered: the plants will go into temporary dormancy and will green up again after a few closely spaced waterings or when the first rains of autumn arrive.

The last zone doesn't need any watering at all and can cover a far greater area than the other zones. Thanks to the diversity of species planted here, this zone permits varied and original landscaping approaches. Areas walked on a lot can be planted as flowering steppes, where the gravel covering the soil serves as a support for foot traffic and where the range of carpeting plants and bulbs creates a landscape that changes over the seasons. Continuing from the flowering steppe, a gravel garden can be home to cushion- or ball-shaped plants, highlighted by perennials that flower profusely in spring. Planted at a low density, the plants that form the structure of a gravel garden can have small paths through them, thus extending the walkable areas of the dry garden. To fill areas that are hard to access, large beds of groundcover plants, whose vigorous vegetation covers the soil completely, can establish a visual rhythm by accentuating the sense of depth through the succession of layers of plants with different heights. Between these taller beds, clearings of wild lawn, green from autumn to the end of spring and golden in summer, create flat expanses that are

This page and next page

Thanks to the diversity of species that resist drought in the wild, there are many striking landscaping options for parts of the garden that will not be irrigated.

Hyparrhenia hirta, a grass that is common in the warm regions of the Mediterranean Basin, creates a golden summer scene that contrasts with the deep blue Tyrrhenian Sea in the Aeolian islands, north of Sicily.

PLANTING AND MAINTAINING THE GROUNDCOVER GARDEN

restful to the eye. Finally, to complete the plant palette of this unirrigated zone of the garden, a flowering meadow, covered in flowers in spring and baked by the sun after scything in early summer, inhabited by butterflies, birds and beneficial insects, can serve as a place of adventure and discovery for children.

When and how to water

Regardless of the watering zone, we must make a distinction between the initial watering and the long-term watering of groundcover plants. During their first year, the purpose of watering is to help the plants get off to a good start and become established. For carpeting groundcovers, the frequency of this initial watering should be about once a week during the first summer: this regime makes rapid coverage possible and hence limits the amount of weeding needed. The initial irrigation of carpeting groundcovers can be done using sprinklers because wetting the entire surface encourages layering, the stems rooting as they spread over the soil. For irrigating small areas of carpeting plants, a movable sprinkler of the kind that can be found in all hardware stores is perfectly suitable.

As soon as the carpeting plants have completely covered the soil, the watering regime should be adjusted according to the plants: each species has different water requirements. The regime can also be adjusted depending both on the type of planting (a uniform carpet, or a mixed carpet less

In full summer, when the carpeting cistuses are already baked dry, phillyreas and lentisks retain their handsome shiny green foliage as if they were watered every day in this wild landscape at Cape Creus, in Spanish Catalonia.

demanding of water) and on its desired appearance in summer. When decreasing irrigation, the change must always be in its frequency and not in the duration of each application of the sprinkler. Whether one waters once a month or once a week, the quantity of water given each time must always be enough to wet the soil deeply. The most useful gadget when one is watering by sprinkler is a graduated rain meter, for it allows us to adjust the duration of the sprinkling by measuring the amount of water that equals a good watering. Each graduation on the rain meter is the equivalent of 1 mm of rain, in other words 1 litre of water per square metre. For example, on a clay soil lightened by the addition of sand during the preparation phase, each watering by the sprinkler should give from 12 to 15 litres of water per square metre in order to wet the soil to a sufficient depth.

Once the carpeting plants are well established, we can replace sprinkler irrigation by simple gravity-fed irrigation. In our garden, we don't use a sprinkler system to water the small patch of *Zoysia tenuifolia* adjoining our terrace. In summer, when the carpet of *Zoysia* starts to show signs of hydric stress (the leaves curl inwards and become needle-like and the *Zoysia* takes on a slightly grey hue), I place a hose on the soil to trickle gently, then move it a little further on when several square metres have been well flooded.

The division of the garden into watering zones requires differentiated irrigation techniques. Sprinklers are well suited to densely planted carpets. On the contrary, they are unsuitable for the initial watering of dry-climate groundcover plants with a spreading habit, such as prostrate rosemary

Although a sprinkler system can be useful for watering carpets of plants, it is not suitable for the first stage of irrigation needed to establish beds of dry-climate perennials and shrubs.

or cistus, which are planted at a low density. If the entire surface between the plants is pointlessly wetted, both the germination of weeds and water loss through direct evaporation from the soil are increased. Many gardeners then give in to the temptation of drip systems, which can in some cases unfortunately do more harm than good.

A drip irrigation system is useful to water a section of the garden regularly over the long term. In the vegetable garden, for instance, furrow irrigation can be replaced by a drip system that will be used all summer, year after year. The best models have integrated drip outlets relatively resistant to clogging; they can even be buried, so that sometimes one can water carpeting plants or green roofs "from below". Care should be taken to position the drippers in a tight network (for example one dripper every 30 cm in parallel lines 30 cm apart) in order to wet all the soil thoroughly. If the drippers are too far apart, the alternation of damp patches and dry patches limits the volume of soil available for the roots to explore, and the plants' drought resistance between each watering is consequently reduced.

Drip systems are less suitable for the initial watering of dry-climate groundcover plants. For these plants, the main purpose of the initial watering is to encourage the development of the root system so that the plants can survive on their own as rapidly as possible. Yet most gardeners instinctively place a drip outlet at the base of each plant. Roots are lazy, and a dripper at the base of the plant has the opposite effect from what was intended – instead of encouraging the roots to develop in all directions, it concentrates them in a restricted area, the size of the small plug of moisture that forms beneath the dripper. As it is usually applied, drip irrigation has a double impact: a positive psychological impact on the gardener and a negative impact on the plants. When after a few years the gardener decides that it is time to stop irrigation, a disagreeable surprise lies in store as his plants die one after the other. Thanks to the artificial support during their early years, they have lost their principal strategy for resisting drought: the depth of their root system.

To encourage the early development of roots, you need to install a network of drippers that will create a continuous

moist zone below the surface of the soil (drip outlets every 50 cm in lines spaced 50 cm apart). This type of installation, more laborious to put in place than a simple dripper at the base of each plant, can sometimes be justified when planting is on a professional scale, or when the lie of the land makes hand-watering difficult, for example on steep slopes, or when a biodegradable geotextile has been used to reduce maintenance. But in a private garden a drip irrigation system is rarely justifiable. We need to remember that dry-climate plants should be watered only during their first year: so the entire drip system is going to be removed after having been used only four or five times over a period of a few months.

Instead of a drip system, hand-watering is the easiest means of giving the initial irrigation to dry-climate groundcovers. If the planting has been carried out in good conditions in early autumn, the broad watering basins created around each plant or group of plants will need to be filled about once a month during the first summer. If the planting has been done in spring, which is less favourable from the point of view of water management, the initial watering will need to be more frequent, about once every ten to fifteen days. Each watering basin, measuring about 60 cm in width and 20 cm in depth, should be able to hold 20 to 30 litres of water each time. This large amount of water creates a patch of humidity beneath the rootball, encouraging the roots to grow downwards and helping the plant to become established. At the end of the first summer the watering basins

If wrongly used, a drip irrigation system can do more harm than good: instead of encouraging the roots to develop in all directions, it causes them to develop in a restricted area the size of the plug of moisture that forms beneath the drip outlet.

1

1. An alternative to drip irrigation is traditional watering, which involves filling large watering basins around the plants. This is the easiest way of giving initial irrigation to dry-climate groundcovers.

2. When planning a groundcover garden, it is useful to calculate the water consumption per watering zone before deciding on the areas that each zone will cover. For example, in the Montpellier region of France, a 50 m² area of *Cynodon* 'Santa Ana' consumes an average of about 3,000 litres of water per year, provided one accepts a partial yellowing of its foliage at the end of summer.

3. If you use a cistern with an adequate capacity, stored rainwater makes it possible to cover the water needs of small areas of groundcover carpet in mediterranean gardens. Cistern-building techniques, often remarkably sophisticated, form part of the history of Mediterranean gardens. The cistern of the Alcazar garden in Seville is shown here.

can be flattened out: the dry-climate plants will never need to be watered again.

Harvesting water for the garden

By creating watering zones in the garden, we are able to see more easily which zones use a lot of water and which are economical in their water consumption. To help decide on the areas that each zone will cover, it is useful to estimate water consumption by zone. For example groundcover carpets and warm season grasses like *Zoysia tenuifolia* require approximately 15 litres per square metre at each watering. Thus for an area of *Zoysia tenuifolia* measuring 15 m², the water consumption will be about 15 × 15 = 225 litres of water at each watering. In the Montpellier region of France, to keep a carpet of *Zoysia tenuifolia* green one must count on watering it about ten times during the course of the summer. Thus the average annual consumption for an area of 15 m² reaches 2,250 litres.

A similar calculation can be made for watering zones where watering is less frequent. The water consumption amounts to about 3,000 litres if one waters an area of 50 m² of *Cynodon* 'Santa Ana' four times during the summer, which is enough to keep it reasonably green. By comparison, 50 m² of conventional lawn consumes about 50,000 litres of water per year (1,000 litres of water per square metre per year) in the Montpellier region of France.

The scale of water consumption by lawn alternatives may encourage you to consider storing rainwater to irrigate the garden. Although in some northern European countries this practice is common, few gardeners harvest rainwater in mediterranean regions. Nevertheless, it is perfectly possible to water small areas of lawn alternatives in a garden and become self-sufficient as regards water consumption. In regions with an annual rainfall of 500 mm per year, a roof with a surface area of 100 m² allows one to harvest about 50,000 litres of water. The problem is thus not so much the availability of water over the year but its storage, given the fact that generally it does not rain during the period when the garden needs water.

3

When building a new house, the cost of installing a rainwater harvesting system is modest compared to the overall construction cost. Many models are available on the market, including tanks to be buried underground and flexible tanks to be placed in the cavity under the house or beneath a wooden deck. Although they are more complicated to set up, there are other solutions that involve saving and filtering grey water from the house. The creation of watering zones in the garden and the calculation of water consumption per zone may thus prompt you to reflect more widely on the water management of your mediterranean property as you consider planting lawn alternatives.

A blue tree frog (*Hyla meridionalis*) walks over a carpet of *Thymus ciliatus* in our garden. The search for lawn alternatives forms part of a wider reflection on water management in mediterranean habitats.

Reducing the maintenance in a garden requires a broad overview that includes economizing on water use but also reducing all inputs – herbicides, fertilizers, fungicides and insecticides. This policy is based on a new approach to the management of diseases, harmful insects and weeding. Here are a few examples to illustrate how the evolution of gardening practices allows us to solve the principal maintenance problems encountered in groundcover gardens.

Management of diseases

It is often the gardener himself who creates the growing conditions that favour disease in groundcover plants without being aware of it. Watering in the hot season, excessive use of fertilizers, single-species planting or the choice of an unsuitable mulch are often the start of health problems in a mediterranean garden. It is hard to combat diseases in groundcover plant once established and better to prevent them occurring in the first place by changing the cultivation conditions that give rise to them. For example, many garrigue plants are vulnerable to various fungi and pathogenic

Facing page
Hanging from fine threads, among a colony of yellow aphids, the eggs of the lacewing will hatch into formidable predatory larvae.

1. A shield bug (*Graphosoma semipunctatum*) on a fruit of *Sixalix atropurpurea* subsp. *maritima*, a "weed" which acts as a host plant for numerous insects. Reducing maintenance is part of an overall garden policy that includes abandoning herbicides and insecticides.

2. *Euphorbia rigida* seeds itself in our garden among different lavender species. Gardening practices can limit the problem of diseases, for example by planting a great diversity of species in a groundcover garden.

1. A classic sight in mediterranean gardens where drip irrigation is used: a cistus is dying due to *Phytophthora*. Frequent watering in the hot season and organic mulches create the ideal conditions for the rapid spread of *Phytophthora*.

2. An inorganic mulch creates a well-drained surface that dries out quickly, which prevents the spread of *Phytophthora* spores.

3. *Hypericum balearicum* in its natural environment on the peaks of the Sierra de Tramuntana in the Balearic Islands. The stony or rocky soil does not favour the development of cryptogamic diseases.

organisms when grown in gardens. These diseases develop in precisely the conditions of heat and humidity that are found in gardens irrigated in summer. The example of *Phytophthora* is worth analysing, for it is without doubt the disease that causes the most damage to large groundcover plantings in mediterranean-climate regions.

Phytophthora cinnamomi is a disease responsible for the death of plants such as rosemary, santolina, lavender, cistus, sage and heather. It causes the base of the stem to rot, preventing the circulation of the sap and making the plant suddenly wilt. *Phytophthora* is active when the soil temperature is high, around 24 to 28 °C, which corresponds to the summer temperature of the soil beneath the foliage of groundcover plants. The spores attack plants by penetrating at crown level before moving to the roots. *Phytophthora* needs water to spread, for its flagelliform spores "swim" through the upper layers of the soil when it is damp. In a hot climate, this disease spreads very easily in parts of the garden that receive regular irrigation in summer, especially if the soil is covered by an organic mulch that retains moisture.

Phytophthora spreads even more easily in monocultures, for example in a bed planted exclusively with santolina or lavender. If these plants are given frequent irrigation, whether by sprinklers or drips, they have a slim chance of survival. Then, when the plants begin to die it is all too easy to make a wrong diagnosis, for *Phytophthora* sets a trap for the novice gardener. A symptom of the disease is the drying-out of the leaves, which suggests that the plant is thirsty, but by then giving it more water the well-intentioned gardener hastens the death of his groundcover plants just as surely as if he had applied a herbicide to them one by one.

Fortunately, the spread of *Phytophthora* can easily be avoided in a mediterranean garden by adopting the following gardening practices:

- plant species vulnerable to *Phytophthora* in sectors of the garden that are not irrigated;

- preferably plant species vulnerable to *Phytophthora* in autumn: in this way, the amount of watering needed during the first summer will be reduced as the roots will already have had time to become established during the autumn and winter;

- while plants are becoming established, follow a regime of deep watering given at widely spaced intervals, so that the soil dries out completely between each watering. A traditional watering basin around each plant makes it easier to give this kind of deep watering;

- avoid organic mulches (pine bark, compost, mowings, shredded branches), which retain moisture around the base of the plants and favour the spread of *Phytophthora*;

- choose mineral mulches (crushed gravel, schist, pozzolana) whose well-draining surfaces dry out quickly, thus interrupting the spread of the flagelliform spores;

- never plant large monocultural beds of a species vulnerable to *Phytophthora*. I shall note the vulnerability of the different species of groundcover plants to *Phytophthora*, as well as to other diseases, in the plant directory (from page 167-227).

Management of pests

As with diseases, it is the cultivation conditions of groundcover plants that determine whether insect pests will simply make passing appearances or become a major recurring problem. Mealybugs and aphids are two examples of pests that are easy to control simply by adjusting our gardening practices.

The mealybug, *Icerya purchasi*, may sometimes infest groundcover plants with a spreading habit such as cistus as well as *Phlomis* and salvias. These plants are more vulnerable to mealybug attacks when excessive irrigation and overly rich soil make their tissues artificially turgid in summer, just when the mealybugs are most active. Their young larvae, almost invisible to the naked eye, are mobile and move from one plant to another, especially in large beds planted with a single species. The adult females, on the contrary, stay put: they cling to a branch and lay several hundred minuscule eggs in a special organ, the ovisac, which forms a cottony

pocket attached to their bodies. Protected as they are by an impermeable mass of waxy filaments, mealybugs are hard to eradicate with chemical products: one would have to use extremely powerful insecticides to limit their proliferation.

One of the negative side effects of anti-mealybug products is that they decimate the populations of a beneficial insect, *Rodolia cardinalis*. This is a bug that gardeners never notice because of its dark colour and its minute size, barely bigger than a pinhead. In spite of its near-invisibility, *Rodolia cardinalis* is remarkably effective at fighting *Icerya purchasi*: its larvae greedily eat the eggs and the different larval stages of mealybugs. *Rodolia cardinalis* was initially introduced as a biological agent in citrus orchards and is now present all around the Mediterranean Basin. However, the size of its population varies enormously according to the environment. In a garden that is frequently treated with chemicals, populations of *Rodolia cardinalis* are small or non-existent; by contrast, in gardens where no chemical treatment is ever applied, *Rodolia cardinalis* can establish itself and go in active search of plants infested with the bugs that are necessary for its reproduction.

Aphids are another example of an insect pest that can invade groundcovers such as *Frankenia laevis* and *Matricaria tchihatchewii* or beds of artemisias. When conditions are favourable the aphid population can increase spectacularly. At the height of the season, reproduction is by parthenogenesis: like so many clones, the young aphids are formed

directly in the female's body, each adult female producing more than fifty new aphids in a fortnight. Because of their large numbers, aphids can weaken groundcover plants by sucking sap through their mouthpieces. They are obliged to take in a large quantity of sap in order to extract from it the proteins they need. They excrete through their anuses the excess sugary liquid, which forms honeydew that sticks to the leaves. On the honeydew a black powdery fungus develops, sooty mould, which asphyxiates the leaves and reduces photosynthesis.

Aphids are far easier to deal with than mealybugs, for they are controlled by a large number of beneficial creatures. Hoverfly larvae, for example, are formidable predators of aphids. They look like little transparent caterpillars and move over leaves with their mouthparts questing here and there. When they find their prey, they seize it brutally and suck out all the content of its body, before expelling the empty husk of its body backwards. A population of aphids declines very rapidly once it has been spotted by hoverflies. A female hoverfly can lay between 500 and 1,000 small white eggs among the aphids, which very quickly hatch into larvae. Each larva eats between 300 and 500 aphids: thus in one generation the hungry offspring of a single hoverfly can consume more than 100,000 aphids.

As soon as one learns to observe them, one realizes how abundant hoverflies are in a garden. Although they look like wasps in order to trick birds of prey, they are as harmless as

1. A feast on a young shoot of the common sage: three plump larvae of the ladybird *Rodolia cardinalis* are eating the cottony remains of a mealybug.

2. The birth of a ladybird. A young *Rodolia cardinalis* emerges, tearing through its pupal shell on a fallen cistus leaf. The size of *Rodolia* populations varies widely since this species is very sensitive to insecticides.

HAIRS AND CORNICLES

The anatomy of an aphid reveals the complexity of the interactions that take place deep in our groundcover plantings between pests and their natural predators. Aphids have two tubes or cornicles on their backs, angled forwards. These cornicles secrete a warning pheromone which alerts other aphids in the vicinity to the presence of a predator. Then, if it comes under direct attack, the aphid uses its cornicles to project on to its foe tiny drops of a sticky wax that dries in seconds, obliging the predator to stop to clean itself and thus giving a brief respite to the aphid and its fellows. However, the secretions from the

aphid's cornicles also act as olfactory signposts which guide hoverflies or ladybirds, directing them straight to the colonies of aphids where their predatory larvae will wreak havoc. To protect themselves from predatory larvae, some species of aphid take refuge on leaves covered with hairs that will hurt the larva's tender skin, such as the hooked hairs on the leaves of *Helminthotheca echioides*, shown here. Thus there are other specialized predators, like the tiny parasitical wasp, which lay their eggs directly into the bodies of their prey, so that their larvae are sheltered as they develop.

A seven-spotted ladybird (*Coccinella septempunctata*) feeds on nectar on a clover flower. By incorporating flowers rich in nectar and pollen into groundcover beds, the gardener encourages populations of beneficial insects which naturally reduce attacks by pests.

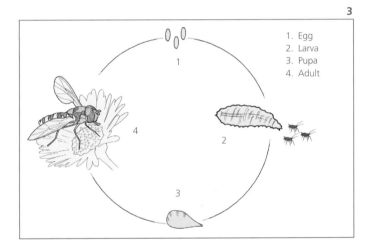

		1. Egg
		2. Larva
		3. Pupa
		4. Adult

1. A female hoverfly (*Episyrphus balteatus*) curves its abdomen to deposit an egg on a shoot of *Matricaria tchihatchewii*. The greenfly which in spring infest the carpet of *Matricaria* are hard to spot because they hide in the leaf axils. The hoverfly is guided by the smell of the greenfly, its short antennae acting as olfactory receptors.

2. Momentarily sated, a hoverfly larva takes a rest: it has eaten all the aphids within reach. Its body is strewn with the remains of the aphids whose insides it has sucked out.

3. The diet of a hoverfly (*Episyrphus balteatus*). Like many beneficial insects, adult hoverflies feed on pollen and nectar, while their carnivorous larvae eat only aphids.

flies. One can recognize them by their ability to hover, which allows them to have a good look at a flower before deciding to land on it and feed. It is here that the gardener can intervene to encourage hoverflies through the management of the garden. Unlike their larvae, adult hoverflies do not eat aphids but feed exclusively on the pollen and nectar of the flowers they find in the garden. The most effective relay plants for attracting hoverflies are "weeds" such as dandelions, daisies, chicories, poppies, yarrow and wild carrots. Integrating these relay plants at the planning stage of a groundcover garden, for instance in wild lawns or flowering meadows, is a very effective way of encouraging hoverfly populations. These flowers also encourage many other beneficial insects such as lacewings, ladybirds, the minute midges belonging to the Cecidomyiidae family and the tiny parasitic wasps that lay their eggs directly into the aphids' bodies.

Here are some gardening practices which allow us to control mealybug, aphids and other plant pests like mites and leafhoppers:

- Avoid planting single-species groundcovers which facilitate the spread of pests;

- Group together plants that are prone to pests in a part of the garden that is not irrigated to avoid artificially turgid tissues that attract piercing and sucking insects;

- When planning the garden, integrate relay plants rich in nectar and pollen that will serve as food for adult beneficial insects (see the list on page 153);

- Improve the survival of beneficial insect populations by providing places in the garden where they may over-winter, such as woodpiles, heaps of dead leaves, bundles of branches, piles of stones and dry-stone walls;

- Avoid the use of insecticides, which are counterproductive through two vicious circles: first, chemical treatments harm the natural predators of the pests, with the result that future generations of the pest are more plentiful; and second, repeated chemical treatments cause the pest to develop resistance to them, which means that more different products must be used, with an even greater impact on beneficial insects.

Weeds and 'good' plants

For many years now Clara and I have been studying the interactions between groundcover plants and beneficial insects in our garden. This has caused us to take a new look at weeds. Some plants generally considered as weeds are in fact the gardener's best allies: they form a vital link in the complex food chains which are the key to a self-regulating garden, where the populations of pests and predators are controlled naturally. Our gardening experience has led us progressively to understand that there is really no such thing as a weed or a 'good' plant – it depends entirely on when and where the plant grows in the garden. To reduce maintenance in a groundcover garden, the gardener thus has every incentive to re-examine the scale of values that distinguishes weeds from 'good' plants.

This reevaluation allows us to modulate our negative attitude towards plants that are often seen as real pests, whether native or exotic. For example, among the native weeds that most gardeners do battle with, bindweed is host to a tiny black ladybird, hard to spot if one doesn't know it, belonging to the genus *Scymnus*. The larvae of this ladybird are particularly good at controlling aphids because they are covered with a curious waxy coating that protects them from their own predators. Among the exotic species that have received a consistently bad press, narrow-leaved ragwort (*Senecio inaequidens*) was stigmatised as an invasive plant in the South of France before it suddenly began to disappear even faster than it had invaded. It is an example of an ambivalent "weed". Narrow-leaved ragwort is a noxious plant when it grows among grass cut for hay since it is toxic to cattle and horses. Yet it is an exceptional host for insects,

A long hoverfly (*Sphaerophoria scripta*) expertly licks the nectar of *Torilis arvensis*, a "weed" which we deliberately allow to self-seed in a controlled way in the large groundcover beds in our garden.

attracting more than 60 species including very dense colonies of a black aphid, *Aphis jacobaea*. Indeed, this aphid has choked off its host's invasive propensity so thoroughly that narrow-leaved ragwort is in the process of disappearing from some regions of southern France, illustrating how a plant considered invasive at one moment can in the space of a few years become locally rare. From the point of view of gardeners and organic farmers, narrow-leaved ragwort has the advantage of providing an abundant source of nectar and pollen to beneficial insects in late autumn. For our own part, we are happy to keep a few specimens of this much disliked plant in our garden, since it is particularly useful as a late source of food to help the population of hoverflies face the winter cold.

The division of the garden into many complementary groundcover sectors composed of various species enables us to take different approaches as far as weeds are concerned. The same species can be undesirable in one place but just what we want in another part of the garden. A large tuft of dandelion that appears in the middle of an immaculate carpet of *Frankenia laevis* is obviously out of place. By contrast, a wild lawn decorated with dandelions provides a sumptuous banquet for beneficial insects: the dandelions are not only pretty but extremely useful. In the same way, the self-sown fennel, mallow or wild carrot (Queen Anne's lace) that invade a new groundcover bed create competition for water and light and thus make it harder for the new planting to become established. Yet, on the other hand, these same fennels, mallows and wild carrots are particularly welcome in a

Dividing the garden into distinct groundcover areas allows us to recalibrate our value judgements on "good" and "bad" weeds. A wild lawn decorated with dandelions serves as a sumptuous banquet for beneficial insects.

flowering meadow, where their summer flowers fill one of the nectar and pollen production slots over the seasons.

Weeding and mulching

How to handle weeding is an important factor to be borne in mind when planning a groundcover garden. For a given area, different types of groundcover will require very dif-

ferent amounts of time spent on weeding. When deciding what kind of groundcover to use in the different parts of the garden, the gardener must carefully take into account the time needed for maintenance. For example, scrupulous weeding of a uniform green carpet takes a considerable amount of time. This groundcover solution, although very attractive visually, is thus suitable only for small areas if weeding is not to be an insurmountable constraint. For larger areas, 100 m² or more, a mixed carpet is preferable as the varied foliage colours mask the presence of weeds to some extent so that weeding does not have to be so regular. Thanks to their mineral mulch, which provides a surface that can be walked on as well as limiting the germination of weeds, flowering steppes need less weeding and can thus be used for even larger areas. As for wild lawns, they don't need any weeding at all, given that they are entirely composed of "weeds". They can be used for unlimited areas, the only constraint being the occasional mowing required.

The groundcover solutions unsuitable for foot traffic are those that require the least maintenance: once established, they need no mowing and almost no weeding. When planning a garden, it is thus important to pay close attention to the degree of foot traffic in various zones. In areas where there will be little or no foot traffic, it is best to go for groundcovers that require the least maintenance, as for example large beds of evergreen plants or gravel gardens. In a gravel garden planted with a range of cushion- or ball-shaped plants completed with emerging perennials and bulbs, the thickness of the layer of gravel will almost completely eliminate the need to weed.

In large groundcover beds the planting is usually not very dense, since most of the plants used in this type of bed have a sizeable lateral spread. Depending on the species, the planting density can be one plant per square metre (for example for *Phlomis × cytherea*) or one plant per four square metres (for example for the more rampant species of rosemary). The lower the planting density, the more maintenance will be needed during the first two or three years. Until the plants have entirely covered the surface of the soil, they may face strong competition from weeds, particularly in autumn and spring. If the bed is not too large, it can

---

FLOWERS AS A FOOD SOURCE FOR BENEFICIAL INSECTS

Here is a list – by no means exhaustive – of perennial plants, often considered weeds, whose flowers, rich in nectar and pollen, encourage populations of beneficial insects in the garden (hoverflies, lacewings, ladybirds, shield bugs, gall midges, tiny parasitic wasps). When planning a groundcover garden, these species can be included in areas of wild lawn or flowering meadows.

Achillea millefolium, and
  all other *Achillea* species
Agrostemma githago
Ajuga reptans
Ammi majus
Anthemis tinctoria
Bellis perennis
Borago officinalis
Calendula officinalis
Centaurea cyanus
Cichorium intybus
Convolvulus arvensis
Crepis vesicaria subsp.
  taraxacifolia
Daucus carota
Dittrichia viscosa
Echium vulgare
Erigeron canadensis
Erigeron karvinskianus
Euphorbia cyparissias and
  all other *Euphorbia*
  species
Foeniculum vulgare
Helminthotheca echioides

Lamium purpureum
Lobularia maritima
Lotus corniculatus
Malva sylvestris
Medicago lupulina
Melilotus albus
Melilotus officinalis
Papaver rhoeas
Parietaria officinalis
Phacelia tanacetifolia
Pilosella officinarum
Plantago coronopus
Senecio inaequidens
Sinapis alba
Sixalix atropurpurea subsp.
  maritima
Sonchus sp.
Taraxacum officinale
Torilis arvensis
Trifolium repens
Tripleurospermum
  inodorum
Urospermum dalechampii
Verbascum thapsus

Keep in mind
maintenance
requirements when
planning your choice
of groundcovers for
various parts of the
garden:

1. Because of the
meticulous weeding
that they require,
uniform carpets of
plants are suitable only
for small areas.

2. A gravel garden
or beds of evergreen
plants are suitable
for large areas since
they require minimal
maintenance once
established.

be hand-weeded regularly during the first years, until the developing plant cover makes it no longer necessary.

When large groundcover beds are being planted in public spaces, a biodegradable geotextile or a thick layer of organic mulch, applied immediately after planting, is often used to reduce maintenance. However, organic mulches require great vigilance as regards the watering given while the plants are becoming established. Too frequent irrigation risks favouring diseases, such as *Phytophthora*, which benefit from the moisture retained by the geotextile or the layer of organic material to spread from plant to plant. As an alternative, the spaces between the young plants can be managed, in the same way as a gravel garden, by covering the soil with a free-draining mineral mulch, which will not promote the spread of diseases. This mulch can be applied at the end of the first year, when the watering basins are no longer necessary. Or it can be applied at planting time if drip irrigation is being used instead of watering basins, although in this case precautions must be taken to avoid the problems that can be linked to this type of irrigation (see page 141).

Unlike the mulch in a gravel garden, the mineral mulch used in a large groundcover bed serves only a temporary purpose: after a few years, when the plants have entirely covered the soil, the mulch will gradually be overlaid by a thick litter of fallen leaves. For even evergreen plants shed some of their old leaves every year. In some species such

as cistus, *Phlomis* and rosemary, the decomposition of their fallen leaves releases into the soil chemicals that prevent the germination of weeds (see page 26). The threefold action of the initial mulch, the spread of the evergreen plants over the ground and the formation of a leaf litter with anti-germination properties frees the gardener completely from the arduous task of combating weeds.

In our garden we have studied the thicknesses and grades of gravel most suitable for mulch. Gravel mixtures that contain fine particles are to be avoided. A mixture of sand and gravel with a grade of between 0 and 30 mm traps organic matter and gradually turns the mulch into a seedbed for germinating weeds. However, gravel with a grade of 5 mm or more filters the dust brought by the wind and makes the germination of weeds much more difficult. Hence the grade of gravel to be used as mulch should be between about 5 and 25 mm. In our own garden we use crushed gravel with a grade of 8 to 12 mm, which gives excellent results in terms of reducing maintenance for large areas. In order to be effective, a mineral mulch needs to be at least 6 to 8 cm thick. Finally, your choice between crushed gravel (with sharp angles) or rounded gravel (whose angles have been smoothed down, usually because it comes from a riverbed) depends on what effect you wish to create, and on what local suppliers can provide. It is worth noting that crushed gravel remains in place better on sloping beds. However, small-grade rounded gravel is more comfortable to walk on barefoot, for example in a gravel garden or flowering steppe

situated near a terrace or swimming pool.

Undesirable perennials

Only weeds that multiply by seed are suppressed by mulches. Some perennial plants with an invasive tendency spread by means of powerful underground rhizomes that make their way through the mulch without difficulty, as for example couch grass, bindweed and hoary cress, *Lepidium draba*. These species are hard to get rid of, because if you cut them down they are able to sprout again thanks to their rhizomes, often very deep, which act as storage organs. Although there is no miracle cure, there are various options which allow one to manage these perennials when creating a groundcover garden.

• Before thinking of planting, exhaust the reserves held in the rhizomes by covering the soil with opaque matting in order to block photosynthesis. We have tried this method in our experimental garden, which at the beginning was a whole field of couch grass and bindweed, and it proved very effective. But the drawback for gardeners in a hurry is that you have to leave the soil covered for at least two years, the time it takes for the reserves in the rhizomes to be exhausted, in order to be sure that the perennial plant will not start off again.

• Grow a temporary flowering meadow on the land, which will prepare the soil for the final planting. After thoroughly decompacting and raking the soil in summer to remove all accessible rhizomes, sow an annual flowering meadow for several years in succession. Although it will not completely eliminate perennials like couch grass, this practice will substantially reduce their vigour: subsequently you can concentrate your efforts on small patches of them (for example by covering them with matting).

• Prepare the soil in the traditional way (decompacting, raking over) without bothering about the presence of perennial weeds, then plant a large groundcover bed of shrubs and sub-shrubs whose vegetation will in time completely cover the soil, preventing the photosynthesis of the weeds just as matting does. During the initial period, it will be necessary to clear the soil around the base of the plants in order to keep competition down, especially if the undesirable perennials are twining plants like bindweed. This solution is effective provided that the groundcover bed consists of strongly growing plants capable of completely smothering the vegetation beneath them (cistus, rosemary, ballota, *Phlomis*, lentisk, myrtle etc.).

• Alter your perspective: instead of trying to get rid of the perennial, incorporate it into your groundcover. For example in the case of couch grass, prepare the soil (in order to reduce competition temporarily), then plant *Trifolium fragiferum* (which will fertilize the couch grass by its nitrogen-fixing nodules), *Phyla canescens* (which has ornamental summer flowers) and *Achillea crithmifolia* (which keeps its leaves in winter when the *Phyla* and

1. An inorganic mulch suppresses weed germination while at the same time encouraging the self-seeding of many species that like stony soils such as *Asphodeline lutea*.

2. One way of reducing invasion by perennials such as dandelion is to sow an annual flowering meadow for several years running.

the couch grass are dormant). In time, this type of mixed planting will become a robust lawn, suitable for children to use for ball games, for example, which requires little maintenance and can be watered or not depending on how you want it to look in summer.

Clipping groundcover plants

Apart from weeding small areas of carpeting plants, occasionally mowing wild lawns and annual scything of flowering meadows, the main maintenance task in groundcover gardens is clipping. We have chosen to clip the plants in our own garden after flowering (full summer for most species) in order to restore the structure of their evergreen foliage quickly. We clip lightly to remove the spent flower heads and shorten the tips of the stems to encourage branching new growth in autumn. This clipping improves the quality of the groundcover bed, for the more branching a plant is, the denser its foliage and the greater its ability to cover the ground.

Nevertheless, we clip selectively, based on a close observation of the behaviour of each species. The faded flowers of some plants continue to be ornamental for a long time, as for example the elegant whorled inflorescences of *Salvia* 'Allen Chickering' or the delicate round ones of *Scabiosa minoana*. For other species, like *Atriplex canescens*, it is the supple silhouette of the unclipped plant that is decorative. We put off clipping these plants for as long as possible, or sometimes we don't clip them at all. The succession of clipped and unclipped plants provides visual contrasts that contribute to the ornamental appearance of a groundcover bed after the great explosion of spring flowers is over. Finally, some species such as myrtle, lentisk and wild olive lend themselves particularly well to very frequent clipping. In the mountains of southern Europe these plants may be grazed on by goats almost every day, which sometimes gives them extraordinary shapes like living sculptures. By copying goats, the gardener can also sculpt his or her evergreen plants, creating free and imaginative topiary forms.

Vegetation sculpted by goats on the island of Amorgos in the Cyclades. By imitating the action of goats, the gardener can also sculpt evergreen plants here and there in free and imaginative topiary.

GARDEN ESCAPEES: THE PROBLEM OF INVASIVE PLANTS

As you consider alternative options to the lawn you may also start wondering about the problem of invasive plants. Indeed the plants most useful for covering the ground in gardens are often fast-growing species, so well adapted to the local conditions of soil and climate that they thrive easily without needing any intervention on the part of the gardener. Because of these very qualities, some groundcover plants from other parts of the world may sometimes possess the potential to become invasive if they manage to escape from gardens into natural or semi-natural environments.

The many scientific publications on the subject of invasive plants present differing, if not contradictory, opinions. The problem of invasive plants easily gives rise to emotional reactions and discussions of the subject are often unproductive, since the different positions taken are frequently biased by partial reading of the available data. Few gardeners have the wherewithal to make a considered judgment on whether or not to use groundcover plants held to be invasive. My purpose here is not to recommend any particular approach to be followed by all gardeners. Instead I want to offer a few guidelines that will help mediterranean gardeners formulate their own thoughts on the subject.

The reading list suggested in the notes at the end of this chapter may also help gardeners and landscape managers who want to deepen their knowledge of this subject, which is likely to become increasingly important in the years to come. I invite gardeners to think for themselves about invasive plants. It is a question that does not simply concern

those working in the fields of botany, biology and ecology, but that requires a multidisciplinary approach, also bringing in history, geography, sociology and philosophy. It is possible that, by virtue of their very diversity, gardeners may be able to shed some light on this complex subject, views on which are currently evolving.

For mediterranean gardeners, the question of invasive groundcover plants requires two levels of vigilance:

• The first level of vigilance concerns the risks associated with using invasive plants that can have a negative impact when they spread to natural or semi-natural environments;

• The second level concerns the risk of overdoing it when lists of potentially invasive plants, considered undesirable in gardens and public spaces, are drawn up. This proves to be counterproductive because by detracting from the rigour with which such lists should be established, it makes it even harder to mobilize gardeners and landscape professionals on this sensitive subject.

What is an invasive plant?

Even the definition of an invasive plant is the subject of much debate in the scientific community. One of the most frequently repeated definitions is the following: it is an exotic plant introduced by man into a new territory where it is capable of reproducing, naturalizing and spreading to form large independent populations[1]. For example, Hottentot figs (*Carpobrotus acinaciformis*, *Carpobrotus edulis* and

Facing page
Eschscholzia californica is a plant that sometimes migrates to near where it was planted. The problem of invasive plants is complex: it requires a global approach, taking into account both the positive and the negative aspects of using plants considered to be invasive.

1. Pampas grass (*Cortaderia selloana*) *has become* naturalized in the damp areas of the Camargue in the South of France, and indeed in other mediterranean-climate regions. Some exotic plants can be difficult to manage when they are equipped to escape from the garden and spread to natural or semi-natural environments.

2. An *Opuntia* dominates a cliff in the Cinque Terre region of Italy. Few gardeners possess the information required to take considered decisions on whether or not to use plants held to be invasive in their gardens.

their hybrids) are groundcover plants native to the Cape of South Africa, which were introduced into the lands around the Mediterranean in the 19th century to stabilize slopes near the sea. Apart from their rapid spread by stolons, Hottentot figs also propagate themselves by seed, carried by rats and rabbits that feed on their fruit, and also, in a secondary dissemination from the rodents' droppings, by harvester ants. Perfectly adapted to tough coastal conditions, the Hottentot fig has become invasive in numerous environments such as seaside rocks, dunes and back dunes. In some cases, it forms huge single-species populations that may supplant rare species growing in particular environments.

Other invasive plants can have an impact on economic activities or on human health. *Oxalis pes-caprae*, for example, is a perennial with yellow flowers that spreads by means of small bulbils. These bulbils, carried in the soil collected on tractor tyres or agricultural tools, are capable of spreading on a large scale in agricultural areas. In the islands of the southern and eastern Mediterranean, the invasion of market gardens and cultivated fields by this oxalis creates real problems for farmers. A different problem is seen in the allergies affecting a significant part of the population that are caused by the rapid spread of wormseed, *Ambrosia artemisiifolia*, in disturbed soil in the Rhone valley.

Some invasive plants can thus have real negative impacts. Quite reasonably, many initiatives aim at encouraging gardeners to stop growing these species, because the increase in points of introduction represented by gardens is one of the factors that play a large part in the invasion process. However, the impact on the public of many other invasive plants is mainly psychological rather than social, economic or ecological[2]. There has thus been a great conflation of the few invasive plants, which under certain conditions can prove truly harmful, with the large majority of non-indigenous species that are able to spread in a natural environment without causing damage. Mark Williamson and Alastair Fitter, biologists at the University of York, cite the so-called "10% rule". According to this rule, which is of course very much an approximation, of 1,000 introduced exotic plants, 10% will be capable of naturalizing; of these 100 naturalized plants, 10% will be capable of becoming invasive[3]; and finally of these 10 invasive plants, only a single one will have a major negative impact on the biodiversity or functioning of an ecosystem[4].

The conflation of an invasive plant with a harmful plant has unfortunately been reinforced by the excessive focus of the media on the problem of invasive plants. This media coverage, playing on sensationalism and sometimes employing military[5] terminology, often uses anxiety-provoking language, which strikes home all the harder since it resonates with the fears and fantasies buried deep in our collective unconscious. In the words of Jacques Tassin, an ecologist working at CIRAD, the French agricultural research centre at Montpellier, "more and more voices are being raised to denounce the whiff of natural xenophobia, of exacerbated

1. Perfectly adapted to coastal conditions, the Hottentot Fig (*Carpobrotus* sp.) has become invasive on rocks by the sea and coastal dunes in some mediterranean regions. They sometimes form vast stretches which may supplant rare species growing in these particular environments.

2. The invasion of *Oxalis pes-caprae* into the market gardens on islands in the Southern and Eastern Mediterranean can cause a real problem to farmers.

1

2

protectionism and of displaced racism transmitted by the clichés that the media trade in, which evoke the idea of illegal immigration, or even prejudice against those who look different[6]".

In order for gardeners to engage in positive action aimed at limiting the use of groundcover plants which may turn out to be damaging we must thus begin by straightening out the tangle of unfounded fears which cloud our perception of the problem of invasive plants. These fears arise from several misconceptions which are worth analysing briefly.

Confusion regarding the impacts of the different kinds of biological invasions

Biological invasions are recognized as one of the causes of loss of biodiversity on the global level. However, using this assertion to sensitize public opinion on the specific problem of invasive plants, as conservation professionals are sometimes tempted to do, simply spreads alarmist talk that bears little relation to reality. In fact the three different kinds of biological invasion (predatory animals, pathogens, invasive plants) have entirely distinct fields of potential impact, since they are based on ecological processes that are not comparable. Predatory animals can have a terrible impact. Often cited is the example of the Guam snake, *Boiga irregularis*, which has become a worldwide example showcasing the potential impacts of biological invasions. This tree-dwelling snake is native to Australia and was introduced to Guam, a small Pacific island in the Mariana archipelago east of the Philippines. It rapidly led to the disappearance of nine out of the eleven bird species indigenous to Guam, making it impossible for them to breed by systematically attacking their nestlings in the trees. Biological invasions in the form of pathogenic agents have an even more terrible impact. Here one can cite the example of *Phytophthora cinnamomi*, a fungal pathogen introduced into Australia in about 1870 which today threatens hundreds of plant species in West

Australia, particularly members of the Protaceae family like some species of the genus *Banksia*, with a chain effect on the associated fauna.

Predators and pathogens are the main causes of the reduction in biodiversity brought about by biological invasions. As the ecologist Mark Davis remind us, invasive plants act on a radically different trophic level (from the Greek *trophē*, "food") and, in the majority of cases, have only a weak negative impact, or even no impact, on the indigenous flora and ecosystems[7]. Most often, these invasive plants quite simply merge into the existing vegetation, contributing in the same way as indigenous plants to the production of goods and services that characterizes the functioning of an ecosystem. According to the biologist Hervé Le Guyader, the idea that an exotic plant necessarily has a negative impact by its presence alone rests on two false premises: that environments are "in equilibrium" and that they are species-saturated[8]. The systematic stigmatization of invasive plants arises from a fixed view of nature conservation, which is ill-suited to the need for conservation of biodiversity that takes into account the dynamic evolution of ecosystems. The spreading of an exotic species may have a negative impact, just as it may on the contrary have beneficial effects, for example by establishing positive mutual interactions between other plant or animal species[9]. Even if in the global context it can be seen as part of the homogenization of landscapes, linked to a massive disturbance of habitats[10], on the local scale the arrival of a new plant most frequently corresponds to an increase rather than a decrease of the richness of species[11].

There is thus often an element of prejudice in the negative way we see invasive plants. This prejudice establishes *a priori* a cause and effect connection between the presence of an invasive plant in a disturbed environment and the reduction in biodiversity that can be seen in the same environment[12]. However, it is the disturbance of the environment caused by

1. *Medicago arborea*, native to the Eastern Mediterranean, colonizes disturbed soil along the coast of the Côte d'Azur. So should we consider it a harmful plant here simply because it is not indigenous? Thanks to the nitrogen-fixing nodules on its roots, *Medicago* makes it possible to revegetate areas that have been severely degraded by human activity.

2. *Erigeron karvinskianus* is often stigmatized as an invasive plant since it self-seeds easily in old walls near houses. Some invasive plants are indeed really harmful, but the great majority of non-native plant species which escape from gardens do not in fact do any damage.

3. The bearded iris is sometimes included in the list of plants that are invasive in South-West Europe. Over-stating the case as regards invasive plants can be counterproductive: it blurs the perception of what is at stake and makes it harder to take rational decisions.

human activity that is usually principally responsible for the reduction in biodiversity, and not the concomitant appearance of an invasive plant that exploits this disturbance to spread itself[13]. In an image suggested by Robert Barbault and Anne Teyssèdre, of the French Muséum d'histoire naturelle, in most cases invasive plants are only the passengers and not the locomotive of the train that is the modification of ecosystems and landscapes[14].

Nevertheless, it is impossible to make generalizations one way or the other. One of the perverse aspects of the debate on invasive plants is that it tends to focus on extreme positions, as if one had to be either for or against invasive plants. But invasive plants are neither good nor bad in themselves[15]. A new trend is currently emerging in the scientific literature: it proposes that an invasive plant should no longer be looked at only from the angle of its negative impacts in a given environment, but that ways of managing it should be promoted which take into account a global analysis of all the advantages and disadvantages involved in the different uses of the plant. We thus need to be extremely cautious in our judgments on invasive plants, avoiding any summary generalizations. Case by case investigation alone should guide decisions on restricting the use of certain plants in our gardens.

Senecio inaequidens is an invasive plant which spreads along roads and tracks and in disturbed soil. The spread of an exotic species can have a negative impact, just as on the contrary it can have beneficial effects, for example by establishing mutually positive interactions with other plant or animal species. Here a hoverfly (*Episyrphus balteatus*) benefits from the abundant source of pollen which the *Senecio* provides. The hoverfly may lay its eggs directly among the colony of black aphids (*Aphis jacobae*) that live on the *Senecio*.

Confusion regarding environments and geographic regions

A major part of the scientific literature on invasive plants concerns parts of the world where the problem is particularly noticeable, such as Australia, South Africa, New Zealand and islands like Réunion and Hawaii. Yet the management of exotic plants cannot be the same in different regions of the world and in different environments, because what is at stake is not the same. The problem of invasive plants, as of biological invasions in general, is for example more serious on islands and in lakeside environments, where species have evolved in isolation and have thus faced reduced pressure from competition[16]. In the same way, some regions of the world have a longer history of introduced and intermingled flora, while others, having remained isolated for a long time, are much more vulnerable to invasion. The South African *fynbos* invaded by pines that disturb the equilibium of water resources and the forests of Tahiti overrun by *Miconia calvescens* whose dense cover weakens the native vegetation are among the famous examples of particularly damaging invasions in regions where until relatively recently there was little intermingling of flora. The Mediterranean Basin has a status of its own: the composition of the flora of the Mediterranean countries has been profoundly shaped for several millennia by human activity. Proposals aimed at encouraging the control and systematic eradication of invasive plants are thus less applicable here than elsewhere. Let us recall that in south-west Europe plants as diverse as the poppies that bejewel cornfields, the vetches that grow along the sides of roads and the chestnut trees that fill valleys in the Cévennes are all exotic plants, introduced by man, and so are all nothing more nor less than invasives. The date of 1492, often suggested as marking the beginning of the intermingling of floras, is sometimes used to distinguish "good" invasive plants which one may consider to have been assimilated into the native flora from "bad" invasive plants introduced more recently. This date, however, has no basis in the specific context of the Mediterranean Basin, where the intermingling of floras goes back to very ancient times. The exchanges between civilizations around the Mediterranean led to a significant permeability between floras, to the point where it is often hard to know what is indigenous and what is not: there are no biological

1. A field of poppies in the Luberon, France. Like many of the heritage plants in our landscapes, the poppy was originally an exotic plant.

2. The lucerne that grows on roadsides in the South of France is an exotic plant. The composition of the flora of Mediterranean landscapes has been profoundly altered by human activity over many millennia. In the historical context of the Mediterranean Basin, the spreading of a new plant often disturbs our cultural or aesthetic sensibilities more than it disturbs the landscape itself.

3. A Roman bridge near Cyrrhus in Syrian Kurdistan indicates the path of the ancient Roman road that linked Antioch to the caravan routes of the Silk Road. For millennia exchanges between the civilizations around the Mediterranean led to an intermingling of floras, to the point where it is often difficult to know which plants are indigenous and which are not.

1

1. Analysis of their mode of dissemination is an important step in determining the restrictions to be recommended as regards the use of plants that have a negative impact. *Pennisetum villosum* and *Oxalis pes-caprae* are both able to spread over long distances, the former by the wind which disperses its seeds and the latter by its bulbils which are carried on agricultural implements.

2. Lippia (*Phyla canescens*) planted on a green roof of a service building at the Alhambra in Granada. Lippia is a potentially invasive plant which affects grazing in specific environments, namely salt meadows subject to temporary flooding. Outside the flood zone, lippia does not escape from gardens since its seeds are not dispersed over a long distance. It deserves a place in the garden because of its remarkable qualities: it allows a reduced consumption of water, fertilizer and pesticides.

characteristics that allow one to distinguish between native and non-native species [17].

Although we sometimes forget it, most of the traditional plants in our landscape are of exotic origin: the vine, the almond, the pomegranate, the cultivated olive tree, the mulberry, the fig, the cypress, the plane tree. The particular historical background of the Mediterranean Basin thus suggests that we should treat with great reservations any recommendations on combating the invasive plants which are disturbing the "integrity" of our landscapes. In many cases, the spreading of a new plant disturbs our cultural and aesthetic perceptions of the landscape more than it disturbs the landscape itself [18]. To avoid falling into the trap of letting a knee jerk sense of identity sometimes cloud our thoughts about invasive plants [19], it is better to judge a plant by its behaviour and not by its origins or date of arrival.

Confusion regarding the terminology

A third subject of confusion is the terminology used when we speak of invasive species. It is never a species that is invasive, but only a population of the species that may prove invasive at a given moment and in a given place [20]. This clarification is of fundamental importance to gardeners. It means that a species may have an invasive population, causing negative impacts, in one specific environment, while other populations of the same species may provide important benefits in another place. In this way, an invasive plant may have both major positive advantages in the garden (for example lippia can be used to replace a lawn and thus

reduce water use, fertilizers and pesticides), and at the same time negative impacts (the very same lippia is harmful to grazing in the salt flood meadows of south-west Australia or the lower valley of the River Aude in southern France). The risk that it could spread from one environment to the other, depending among other things on its mode of dissemination over shorter or longer distances, will thus be a key factor in assessing an invasive groundcover plant.

How should we apply these thoughts in practice? The lists of invasive plants produced by the conservation agencies of southern Europe don't help gardeners much since they are often confusing. If we consult the official website of DAISIE (European Invasive Alien Species Gateway) to find exotic species that are potentially invasive in Europe, looking for information on Spain and Portugal, we get a long list of plants that includes, for example, the cornflower (*Centaurea cyanus*) the Algerian iris (*Iris unguicularis*) and the caper (*Capparis spinosa*). So should we pull out all our cornflowers and capers? In Portugal the law on invasive plants provides for a fine of up to 600,000 escudos (the equivalent today of about 3,000 euros) for anyone contributing, including indirectly from ornamental plantings, to the involuntary dissemination into nature of species like clary sage (*Salvia sclarea*), santolina (*Santolina chamaecyparissus*) or bearded iris (*Iris × germanica)* [21]. Do we have to get rid of all the irises that combat erosion on our slopes? In France the groundcover *Stenotaphrum secundatum* is considered to be an invasive plant, whereas in Spain, on the contrary, its planting is strongly encouraged to create "gardens free of invasives" [22].

2

Must we dig up our *Stenotaphrum* in Perpignan and go across the border to plant it in Barcelona? It is often difficult to find one's way among the mass of recommendations, sometimes contradictory, given by different authorities.

To help mediterranean gardeners adopt a reasoned approach to invasive plants, we have established with James Aronson, an ecologist at the Centre d'écologie fonctionnelle et évolutive of Montpellier, a protocol to help decide on the categorization of invasive plants by restriction of their use to be recommended for gardens and public green spaces in the Mediterranean region[23]. This protocol takes into account the following criteria for assessment:

- the future negative impacts of the plant;
- the future positive impacts of the plant;
- the environment in which it is invasive;
- the mode of reproduction that allows or does not allow the plant to escape from gardens and reach the environment in which it is invasive.

This decision-assisting protocol is included as an appendix, with examples of the categorization of potentially invasive groundcover plants by restriction of their use in gardens and public green spaces (see page 232).

In this book, the restrictions that I recommend for the use of invasive groundcover plants are based on an analysis of the data available for each plant as I write (December 2010). There is nothing definitive about them: new information might alter the categorization of the various species. We constantly review this categorization in order to decide, for example, which are the groundcover plants held to be invasive that we continue to grow in our nursery, and which are those that we have decided not to grow. In our daily investigations aimed at introducing new groundcover plants of potential interest as lawn alternatives, this approach to the categorization of invasive plants is reinforced by a precautionary principle that might also inspire other nurseries or collector-gardeners. We study attentively the lists of invasive plants all over the world in order to avoid introducing into our own region any exotic plant which fulfils these three criteria: it is recognized as being invasive in a climate zone similar to our own; it is recognized as having a negative impact on the environments where it is invasive; it has a mode of long-distance dissemination that carries a serious risk of its spreading beyond the garden.

Notes

1. Richardson D. M., Pysek F. D., Rejmanek M., Barbour M. G., Panetta F. D. & West C. J., 2000. Naturalization and invasion of alien plants: concepts and definitions. *Divers. Distrib.*, 6: p. 93-107.
2. Davis M. A., 2009. *Invasion Biology.* Oxford University Press, Oxford, 244 pages.
3. Williamson M. & Fitter A., 1996. The varying success of invaders. *Ecology*, 77: pp. 1661-1666.
4. Richardson *et al.*, 2000, *op. cit.*
5. Larson B., 2005. The war of the roses: demilitarizing invasion biology. *Front Ecol. Environ.*, 3(9): pp. 495-500.
6. Tassin J., 2010. *Plantes et animaux venus d'ailleurs : une brève histoire des invasions biologiques.* Editions Orphie, Chevagny-sur-Guye, p. 101.
7. Davis M. A., 2003. Biotic globalization: does competition from introduced species threaten biodiversity? *BioScience*, 53 (5): p. 481-490.
8. Le Guyader H., 2008. La biodiversité : un concept flou ou une réalité scientifique ? *Courrier de l'environnement de l'INRA*, 55: pp. 7-25.
9. Low T., 2003. *The New Nature – Winners and Losers in Wild Australia.* Viking, Ringwood, Australia, 390 pages.
10. Marris E., 2009. Ragamuffin Earth. *Nature*, 460 (7254): pp. 450-453.
11. Sax D. F. & Gaines S. D., 2003. Species diversity: from global decreases to local increases. *Trends Ecol. Evol.*, 18 (11): pp. 561-566.
12. Tassin J., 2010, *op. cit.*
13. Teyssèdre A. & Barbault R., 2009. Invasions d'espèces : cause ou conséquence de la perturbation des écosystèmes ? *Pour la science,* 376: pp. 22-25.
14. Barbault R. & Teyssèdre A., 2009. La victime était le coupable ! *Dossier pour la science,* 65: pp. 56-61.
15. Slobodkin L. B., 2001. The good, the bad and the reified. *Evolutionary Ecology Research,* 3: pp. 1-13.
16. Pascal M., Lorvelec O. & Vigne J.-D., 2006. *Invasions biologiques et extinctions : 11 000 ans d'histoire des Vertébrés en France.* Coédition Belin-Quae, Paris, 350 pages.
17. Thompson K., Hodgson J. G. & Rich C. G., 1995. Native and alien plants: more of the same? *Ecography*, 18: p. 390-402.
18. Sagoff M., 2005. Do non-native species threaten the natural environment? *J. Agr. Environ. Ethics*, 18: pp. 215-236.
19. Coates P. A., 2006. *American Perceptions of Immigrant and Invasive Species. Strangers on the Land.* University of California Press, Berkeley, 272 pages.
20. Colautti R. & MacIsaac H., 2004. A neutral terminology to define 'invasive' species. *Divers. Distrib.*, 10: pp. 135-141.
21. Decreto-Lei n° 565/99 du 21 décembre 1999.
22. Pere Fraga i Arguimbau V., 2009. *Jardinería mediterránea sin especies invasoras.* Publicaciones biodiversidad, Generalitat Valenciana, Consellería de Media Ambiente, Agua, Urbanismo y Vivienda, Valence, 208 pages.
23. Filippi O. & Aronson J., 2010. Plantes invasives en région méditerranéenne : quelles restrictions d'utilisation préconiser pour les jardins et les espaces verts ? *Ecologia mediterranea*, 36 (2): pp. 31-54.

A-Z OF GROUNDCOVER PLANTS
FOR DRY GARDENS

The plant descriptions contain the following:

– the botanical name of each plant and the common name where one exists. To find plants by their common names, see the index at the end of the book.

– practical information: place of origin, height and spread, position, hardiness. This information comes from our observations of plants in gardens in the Montpellier region of the South of France. It should be adjusted according to the climate conditions in your own area.

– a drought resistance code, using a scale from 1 to 6: 1 denotes plants with the least resistance to drought, while 6 denotes those most resistant. Drought depends not only on the climate but also on the specific conditions prevailing in each garden (type and depth of soil, wind, orientation). The code used here thus does not indicate an absolute resistance to drought but rather allows you to compare the relative behaviour of groundcover plants when you are selecting them for a particular watering zone in the garden (see also *The Dry Gardening Handbook*, Thames and Hudson, 2008).

– a description of the foliage and flowers, together with advice on maintenance and suggested associations with other plants. The plant's appearance in dry periods and its tolerance of irrigation are also noted. Soil requirements are specified at the end of each description. All the plants selected tolerate both alkaline and acid soils.

– the usual planting density depending on the different uses of the groundcover plants.

– advice on propagation, with simple techniques that amateur gardeners can easily put into practice in their own gardens.

In addition to the main species which are described in full, further species or cultivars, described more briefly, are marked with a bullet point.

The list of species given here is certainly not exhaustive. I invite every gardener to expand the range of groundcover plants to create original lawn alternatives, adapted to the local soil and climate conditions.

Facing page
Euphorbia rigida is at its best at the end of its flowering: for a few weeks its bracts take on a bright red colour which lights up the groundcover garden in June.

Achillea (Asteraceae)

There are more than 100 species of *Achillea*, or yarrow, most of them native to southern Europe and Asia Minor. They are particularly useful in mediterranean gardens since they can be used for many different groundcover alternatives to a lawn: green carpets (*Achillea tomentosa*), mixed flowering carpets (*Achillea crithmifolia*), wild lawns (*Achillea millefolium*), flowering steppes (*Achillea odorata*), gravel gardens (*Achillea coarctata*) and as pioneer plants that help to combat erosion on slopes (*Achillea nobilis*). Their flowers, rich in pollen, attract numerous beneficial insects such as ladybirds.

Achillea coarctata

Origin: Balkan peninsula, Turkey. **Height of foliage**: 2 to 15 cm depending on cultivation conditions and degree of foot traffic; **Height when in flower**: 30 cm or more; **Spread**: 60 cm or more; **Position**: sun; **Hardiness**: –15 °C and below; **Drought resistance code**: 3.

An evergreen or semi-evergreen perennial with silver-grey finely-cut leaves. The plant spreads by means of its rhizomes and forms elegant downy rosettes that colonize the soil, creeping between neighbouring plants. The bright yellow flowers are arranged in very dense corymbs. Flowering is spectacular in May-June, then is repeated on and off in autumn. In the driest parts of the garden the plant is dormant in summer, losing some of its leaves. In parts of the garden that receive occasional irrigation, the leaves last well throughout the year and flowering may continue for the whole summer, especially if one takes care to remove the dead heads. In our gravel garden we like to combine the luminous flowers of *Achillea coarctata*

with blue-flowered plants such as *Salvia chamaedryoides*, *Perovskia* 'Blue Spire' and *Lavandula* × *chaytorae*. This achillea can also be used in flowering steppes, since its rosettes withstand occasional foot traffic (used like this it is lower-growing and more compact). *Achillea coarctata* requires well-drained soil. It is a tough groundcover plant, easily grown and long-lived. Planting density: 4 per square metre.
Propagation by division in autumn or by cuttings in March, before flowering.

Achillea crithmifolia

Origin: Balkan peninsula, Turkey; **Height of foliage**: 2 to 10 cm depending on cultivation conditions and degree of foot traffic; **Height when in flower**: 20 cm (sometimes more in damp soil); **Spread**: 50 cm to 1 m; **Position**: sun or semi-shade; **Hardiness**: –15 °C and below; **Drought resistance code**: 2.5.

A perennial with rosettes of evergreen grey-green leaves which are downy and finely cut. The plant rapidly colonizes the available soil surface due to the vigour of its rhizomes. The creamy-white flowers appear in June-July. This achillea, which is one of the best lawn alternatives, can be used in various ways:
– as a vigorous carpet that can be walked on, covering the soil throughout the year. Cultivation requirements: watering once a week in summer and mowing about once a month. This carpet needs little weeding since its aromatic leaves release chemical substances that inhibit the germination of weeds (allelopathy);
– mixed with *Phyla canescens*. Cultivation conditions: watering every two or three weeks in summer, mowing three or four

When it is good and dense, a carpet of *Achillea crithmifolia* needs little maintenance: the aromatic leaves release chemical substances that limit competition by inhibiting the germination of weeds.

times a year in order to cut off the dead flowers and limit the growth of weeds. This achillea becomes partially dormant in summer when the *Phyla* covers the entire surface and, vice versa, the achillea regains its foliage vigorously in winter when the *Phyla* loses all its leaves. This mixture can serve as the basis for a very ornamental mixed planting, suitable for foot traffic, that includes many other carpeting species (thymes, *Frankenia*, *Matricaria*, etc.);
– in a large wild lawn suitable for foot traffic, planted with four very vigorous species: *Achillea crithmifolia*, *Cynodon* 'Santa Ana', *Trifolium fragiferum* and *Phyla canescens*. The *Cynodon* and the *Phyla* give summer groundcover thanks to their drought resistance, while the *Trifolium* and the achillea offer a better appearance in winter when the other two species are dormant. Watering varies according to the appearance desired but this mixture tolerates drought once established. Mowing once or twice a year to limit weeds;
– in mixed planting on a flowering steppe, requiring neither watering nor mowing. In this case the achillea loses all its leaves in summer. The winter rosettes, by contrast, offer an interesting pointillist-style cover of the gravel surface in the midst of the other groundcover plants used on the steppe.
In our unirrigated garden, *Achillea crithmifolia* does not flower abundantly: we use this achillea mainly for the remarkable groundcover qualities of its foliage. However, in damper gardens we have noticed that its behaviour is quite different: the flowering is more generous, the foliage remains dense in summer, and both it and the flowering stems are markedly taller. *Achillea crithmifolia* is

Achillea coarctata spreads by means of its rhizomes and slips between neighbouring plants. Here it spreads through a bed of white-flowered lavenders.

A mixture of *Achillea crithmifolia* and *Phyla canescens* is one of the best solutions for covering the ground in parts of the garden that are subject to foot traffic.

Achillea nobilis is a pioneer plant that spreads rapidly by means of its invasive rhizomes. It colonizes a wild part of our garden with *Centranthus ruber*, *Medicago arborea*, *Achillea coarctata* and *Dorycnium hirsutum*.

unfussy as regards type of soil. Planting density: 4 per square metre if one wants achieve a single-species carpet rapidly.

Propagation is easy by division or cuttings, at all times of year except summer.

Achillea nobilis

Origin: Southern Europe, Asia Minor; **Height of foliage**: 10 to 15 cm; **Height when in flower**: 30 to 40 cm; **Spread**: 1 m and more; **Position**: sun or semi-shade; **Hardiness:** –15 °C and below; **Drought resistance code**: 3.

An incredibly vigorous plant! Evergreen, aromatic, finely-cut grey-green leaves. The plant spreads by means of its powerful rhizomes, which give it a rapidity of growth and a lateral spread that are often spectacular. The cream-coloured flowers are very abundant, covering the entire plant in May-June. After flowering the plant becomes dormant and the foliage partially dries out. It is possible at this point to get rid of the brown mass of dead flowers by clipping with secateurs or by strimming, depending on the area covered. We have found that the rosettes bearing dead flowers are easily pulled out by hand: in early summer we rapidly tidy up the patch of *Achillea nobilis* in our garden by summarily pulling out all the dry inflorescences, which seems to multiply the colonizing power of the rhizomes tenfold. In the South of France, this species is found growing wild above the ditches that run along roads, where it forms impressive patches of flowers in late spring. The leaves give off chemical substances that limit competition from weeds (allelopathy). *Achillea nobilis* can be planted in

The flowers of *Achillea nobilis*, rich in pollen, are appreciated by numerous insects. Here the silky bodies of two longhorns (*Stenopterus rufus*) are covered in pollen during their amorous embrace.

large areas of wild garden, where its flowers, rich in pollen, are appreciated by numerous insects. It can also be used to stabilize slopes. For example, to limit erosion it can be planted together with *Potentilla reptans* and *Malvastrum lateritium*, two other species with spectacular growth rates that stabilize slopes by layering. *Achillea nobilis* is unfussy as regards soil type. Planting density: 1 or 2 per square metre.

Propagation is easy by division or cuttings at any time of year except summer.

Achillea tomentosa

Origin: Southern Europe, Western Asia; **Height of foliage**: 2 to 5 cm; **Height when in flower**: 15 cm; **Spread**: 30 cm; **Position**: sun; **Hardiness**: −15 °C and below; **Drought resistance code**: 3.

A perennial with small evergreen leaves, very finely cut. The appearance of the foliage changes over the seasons: in winter the leaves are not very downy and their green epidermis can be seen. At the end of spring and in early summer they are covered in a thick fleece of downy hairs, which transforms the plant into a remarkable silver-grey carpet. The flowers, a fine luminous yellow, open in May-June. In periods of great drought, the foliage may be partially lost as the plant becomes dormant. This achillea gradually spreads by suckering and layering, forming a compact carpet that can withstand moderate foot traffic. If watered occasionally, it will create, over a small area, a beautiful and uniform carpet that remains dense throughout the year. In spite of the thinness of its carpet, the plant is not very vulnerable to competition from weeds since its leaves release chemical substances which inhibit their germination (allelopathy). *Achillea tomentosa*

requires a light, well-drained soil. In our garden it is particularly happy in areas where we have planted it on a bed of gravel. Planting density: 9 per square metre.

Propagation by division or cuttings, at the end of winter.

Achillea umbellata

Origin: mountains of Central and Southern Greece; **Height of foliage**: 10 to 15 cm; **Height when in flower**: 25 cm; **Spread**: 30 to 40 cm; **Position**: sun; **Hardiness**: −15 °C and below; **Drought resistance code**: 4.

A perennial with evergreen or semi-evergreen leaves with toothed edges. The foliage, silver-grey in winter, becomes almost white in the dry period of summer: it has the most luminous foliage of all our collection of silver-leaved plants. The plant spreads gradually by suckering and layering, forming a very regular spreading cushion. The pure white flowers, produced in abundance, appear in April-May on short flowering stems. A clipping after the plant has flowered is useful: it enables the foliage to be refurbished rapidly, to form a fine cushion during the summer. *Achillea umbellata* grows in rocky soil on mountains, for example on Mount Parnon in the southern Peloponnese. In the garden it likes poor and stony soils, with perfect drainage, which provide conditions similar to those it finds in the wild. It is a plant that cannot tolerate summer watering: it gives the best result in parts of the garden that receive no irrigation, for example in flowering steppes or gravel gardens. Planting density: 9 per square metre.

Propagation by division or cuttings, at the end of winter.

Achillea millefolium can be used in different situations: when it is mown it can be one of the constituents of a wild lawn and if it is left to flower it can belong in a semi-perennial flowering meadow.

The white flowers of *Achillea umbellata* marry well with the pink flowers of *Centaurea bella*. These two species like soil with perfect drainage.

• ***Achillea millefolium*** is an undemanding plant, adaptable to many different situations. With regular watering and an occasional mowing, it can be used, for example, as a uniform carpet. In this case, pot-grown plants are usually planted. However, it is most valuable in semi-perennial flowering meadows: its flowers are rich in pollen and provide food to numerous beneficial insects. In this case it can be sown directly *in situ* together with the other annual and perennial species that make up the meadow (see page 115). Origin: Europe, Asia Minor. Hardiness: −15 °C and below. Drought resistance code: 2.5. Planting density in pots: 4 per square metre.

• ***Achillea odorata*** forms a dense carpet that withstands foot traffic and requires little maintenance: the leaves release chemical substances that limit competition by inhibiting the germination of weeds (allelopathy). The creamy-white flowers, borne on upright flowering stems, appear from May to July. *Achillea odorata* grows naturally on the Larzac plateau, very near where we live, on grazed stony expanses: it is an excellent lawn alternative, whether as a uniform carpet, mixed in a carpet of thymes, or in flowering steppes that resemble its natural habitat. In parts of the garden that are not irrigated the plant may lose some of its leaves when it becomes dormant at the end of summer. Origin: the South of France, Spain, North Africa. Hardiness: −15 °C and below. Drought resistance code: 4. Planting density: 4 per square metre.

• ***Agrostemma githago***, or corn cockle, is an annual plant whose pink flowers, rich in nectar, attract beneficial insects like hoverflies. Although once thought of as a weed in cornfields (its seeds could render flour toxic), it is now considered to be a heritage plant and is protected in some regions. It is highly ornamental and easy to grow in annual flowering meadows. Sow seed in early autumn for flowering from May to June. Probable origin: Middle East.

• ***Ajuga reptans***, or bugle, is a perennial with dark green evergreen leaves, which spreads by means of its numerous stolons. It very easily colorizes wild lawns that are irrigated ocasionaly, in soil that is moist but well drained, preferably in shade or

Allium neapolitanum naturalizes easily in wild lawns.

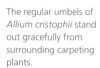

The regular umbels of *Allium cristophii* stand out gracefully from surrounding carpeting plants.

semi-shade. Its spikes of blue flowers, very much frequented by bees, appear in May-June. Origin: Europe, North Africa, Western Asia. Hardiness: −15 °C and below. Drought resistance code: 2. Planting density: 6 per square metre.

• ***Allium***: several species of garlic are useful for creating colourful patches between groundcover plants. *Allium moly* (with yellow flowers, spring-flowering) and *Allium tuberosum* (white flowers, summer-flowering) are species that can briefly brighten flowering steppes. The spectacular umbels of *Allium cristophii* (mauve flowers in May) rise from the middle of silver cushions in a gravel garden. *Allium neapolitanum* (white flowers in March-April) naturalizes easily in wild lawns.

Ampelodesmos mauritanicus (Poaceae)

Origin: Western Mediterranean Basin; **Height of foliage**: 80 cm to 1 m; **Height when in flower**: 2 to 3 m; **Spread**: 80 cm to 1 m; **Position**: sun, shade or semi-shade; **Hardiness**: −12 to −15 °C; **Drought resistance code**: 5.

A grass that forms a vigorous clump whose long evergreen leaves have a fountaining habit. The leaves remain green in both summer and winter. The large yellow-green inflorescences, borne on long airy stems, appear in May-June. In summer they turn a golden colour and remain ornamental until the end of autumn. In some areas of Morocco (the Béni-Snassen mountains) or in the Balearics (the Sierra de Tramuntana), *Ampelodesmos* forms great swathes of groundcover that dominate the landscape. This plant is extremely tough and adaptable

and does equally well in full sun and in the heavy shade of Aleppo pines, where it is able to withstand the dryness caused by the competing tree roots. Its initial growth is slow but it is very long-lived. In our garden we have planted it in a groundcover bed consisting of *Phlomis* and *Teucrium fruticans*, between which its large golden inflorescences emerge throughout the summer. *Ampelodesmos mauritanicus* is unfussy as regards soil. It withstands salt spray by the sea. Planting density: 1 per square metre. *Propagation by division in autumn or by seed in spring.*

• ***Anemone coronaria*** and ***Anemone hortensis*** are bulbous plants which colonize wild lawns. The flowers are followed by silky seeds dispersed by the wind (the name *Anemone* derives from the Greek *anemos*, "wind"). To get a sense of the potential beauty of a wild lawn, I suggest that you visit the botanic garden of the Villa Thuret, at Antibes, during the month of March. Here you can admire a vast lawn where the dense profusion of flowering *Anemone hortensis* creates one of the most beautiful late-winter groundcover scenes we have ever seen in the South of France. Origin: Southern Europe, Asia Minor. Hardiness: −12 to −15 °C. Drought resistance code: 4. Planting density: 9 per square metre.

• ***Antirrhinum hispanicum*** is a perennial with small grey-green silky leaves. In April-May the plant is covered in velvety flowers, pale pink with a yellow throat. It forms a regular cushion, very attractive in gravel gardens, in dry-stone walls or at the sides of paths and steps. It likes poor, stony or sandy soils with perfect drainage. The plant is relatively short-lived but self-seeds easily. Origin: Southern Spain, North Africa. Hardiness: −10 to −12 °C. Drought resistance code: 5. Planting density: 9 per square metre. Other snapdragons are also easy to integrate in a groundcover garden: the large upright spikes of *Antirrhinum barrelieri*, for example, emerge elegantly from among groundcover plants in a gravel garden. *Antirrhinum majus* (with mauveish pink flowers) and *Antirrhinum latifolium* (with yellow flowers) colonize stony soils, stone steps and old walls, along with the wallflower (*Erysimum* × *cheiri*).

• ***Arenaria balearica*** forms a striking miniature carpet. In April-May its delicate pure white flowers open above the dark green background. The plant thrives in poor, stony or sandy soil (the name *Arenaria* derives from the Latin *arena*, "sand"). It is suitable for planting in the cracks between paving stones on a terrace or between stepping stones in semi-shade. When it grows in cracks between paving its roots benefit from the moisture that collects below the paving stones: it gives the best results in these

The delicate corollas of *Anemone coronaria* decorate wild lawns at the end of winter.

Arenaria balearica forms a miniature carpet that spreads between stones.

conditions. *Arenaria balearica* requires a light, perfectly drained soil. Origin: Corsica, Balearic Islands. Hardiness: −15 °C and below. Drought resistance code: 2. Planting density: 9 per square metre.

Artemisia alba (Asteraceae)

Origin: mountains of Southern Europe; **Height**: 50 to 60 cm; **Spread**: 80 cm or more; **Position**: sun; **Hardiness**: −15 °C and below; **Drought resistance code**: 3.5

This woody perennial makes a remarkable groundcover and possesses a discreet charm. Its semi-evergreen finely-cut leaves give off a strong smell of camphor. Its thick vegetation prevents the germination of weeds thanks to its allelopathic properties: the litter of fallen leaves that accumulates beneath the plant diffuses chemical substances that inhibit the germination of competitors. For the gardener, this type of plant represents a considerable amount of time saved in the maintenance of a groundcover garden: the plant weeds its own patch of soil by itself. *Artemisia alba* can be planted together with other species that have similar allelopathic properties to create large beds that require

The finely-cut leaves of *Artemisia alba* release chemical substances that inhibit the germination of competing species: this artemisia makes an excellent groundcover in large beds that need to be low maintenance.

minimal weeding: prostrate rosemaries, cistuses with a spreading habit, *Phlomis* species or sages. Its greyish yellow flowers, produced in summer, are of little visual interest: clipping the plant at the end of summer makes it rapidly regain the regular cushion shape that is this plant's main feature. *Artemisia alba* is unfussy as regards soil type. Planting density: 2 or 3 per square metre.
Propagation by softwood cuttings in spring.

Artemisia pedemontana
Synonym: *Artemisia lanata*

Origin: mountains of Southern Europe; **Height of foliage**: 1 to 5 cm depending on cultivation conditions; **Height when in flower**: 15 to 20 cm; **Spread**: 30 to 40 cm; **Position**: sun; **Hardiness**: −15 °C and below; **Drought resistance code**: 3.

It was quite by chance, when we were botanizing in the Sierra Ministra north-west of Madrid, that we first saw this plant growing in its natural habitat: it is always a real pleasure to see in the wild a plant that one has long known in the garden. *Artemisia pedemontana* grows in grazed steppes on very stony soil, which explains why it is so happy in the flowering steppe areas of our garden. Its silver foliage, covered in silky hairs, makes a soft little carpet. The silvery flowers are borne on supple spikes in May-June. In summer the foliage becomes sparser as the plant enters dormancy in order to withstand drought. *Artemisia pedemontana* can be planted with *Achillea tomentosa*, *Tanacetum*

The silver foliage of *Artemisia pedemontana* forms a low and soft-looking carpet. The plant is happy only in light soil, stony or sandy, with perfect drainage.

Artemisia 'Canescens' is a small groundcover plant which is happy in gravel gardens. Silver in summer, the foliage takes on violet hues in winter.

Artemisia arborescens 'Carcassonne' is a remarkable structural plant for large groundcover beds.

densum, Achillea umbellata and *Cerastium candidissimum* to form a striking carpet of different shades of grey and silver. *Artemisia pedemontana* requires a light sandy or stony soil with perfect drainage. It does not tolerate irrigation during hot periods: it thus needs to be grown in parts of the garden that receive no summer water. Planting density: 9 per square metre.
Propagation by division in autumn, or by soft-wood cuttings in spring.

• *Artemisia arborescens* 'Carcassonne' forms a large ball of silver leaves. We use it, together with *Artemisia thuscula,* synonym *Artemisia canariensis,* whose habit is very similar, as a structural plant in our gravel garden. These two species can also be used in large groundcover beds, where they require little maintenance thanks to their allelopathic properties. These plants are less attractive when their foliage becomes sparser after flowering: in our garden we clip them as soon as they start to flower in order to keep them more compact. Origin: Mediterranean Basin. Hardiness: −8 to −10 °C. Drought resistance code: 4. Planting density: 1 per square metre.

• *Artemisia* 'Canescens' forms a tough groundcover which is happy in flowering steppes or gravel gardens. In winter its silvery foliage takes on a striking grey-mauve hue. Origin uncertain. Hardiness: −15 °C and below. Drought resistance code: 3. Planting density: 4 per square metre.

• *Artemisia ludoviciana* 'Silver Queen' is a perennial that spreads rapidly thanks to its very powerful rhizomes. In spring it forms a fine silvery carpet, crowned with spikes of grey flowers in summer. In our garden we grow it together with *Euphorbia cyparissias,* another perennial with invasive rhizomes. Their foliage is complementary and they form great waves of vegetation across wild parts of the garden. To this mixture can be added *Achillea nobilis* which covers the ground in winter when the other two species lose their leaves. *Artemisia ludoviciana* can also be used to combat erosion on slopes where soil has been added.

Origin: North America. Hardiness: −15 °C and below. Drought resistance code: 3. Planting density: 2 per square metre.

Asphodelus fistulosus (Asphodelaceae)

Origin: Mediterranean Basin; **Height**: 50 cm; **Spread**: 30 cm; **Position**: sun; **Hardiness**: −12 to −15 °C; **Drought resistance code**: 5.

A perennial forming a clump of evergreen, upright cylindrical leaves. The pretty white flowers are highlighted by the star-shaped

Asphodelus fistulosus self-seeds prolifically in uncultivated parts of the garden, particularly if the soil has recently been disturbed. Here it colonizes a wild part of the garden together with *Euphorbia cyparissias.*

pattern of the fine dark veins. The plant is very early flowering and maintains a continuous cheering display from February through to June. Flowers are followed by capsules that release a large quantity of small black seeds. The plant self-seeds and easily colonizes uncultivated parts of the garden. It can be planted together with other pioneer plants that flower early, such as *Lavandula dentata*, *Euphorbia rigida* and *Euphorbia characias* subsp. *wulfenii*, to create great flowering scenes at the end of winter. *Asphodelus fistulosus* self-seeds abundantly in light stony or sandy soil with perfect drainage. Planting density: 4 per square metre. *Propagation by division or by lifting young plants at the end of winter.*

• **Asphodelus microcarpus** is a perennial whose rosette of leaves grows from a powerful rootstock of tuberous roots that serve as reserves for the plant to draw on during its summer dormancy. The handsome white flowers are borne on tall, branching inflorescences from April to June. In the wild, *Asphodelus microcarpus* can cover large areas when forest fires or over-grazing favour this species' colonizing potential. In our garden we use this asphodel as a vertical accent

Asphodelus microcarpus is an exceptionally tough plant. Here it has succeeded in growing through the surface of a small country road in the Mani peninsula of southern Greece.

In the wild *Ballota hirsuta* lives in poor and stony soil. Here it is growing between two rocks in the Sierra de Cazorla in southern Spain.

The tall silhouette of *Asphodelus microcarpus* lightens this large groundcover bed. In the foreground are *Santolina × lindavica*, *Santolina benthamiana*, *Stachys cretica*, *Ballota acetabulosa*, *Dorycnium pentaphyllum*, *Tanacetum densum*, *Centaurea bella* and *Euphorbia rigida*.

among cushion- or ball-shaped plants. It is a robust species, capable of surviving in the toughest soil conditions. It is long-lived. Origin: Mediterranean Basin. Hardiness: −12 to −15 °C. Drought resistance code: 5. Planting density: 4 per square metre.

Ballota hirsuta (Lamiaceae)

Origin: Spain, Portugal; **Height:** 60 cm; **Spread:** 60 cm; **Position:** sun; **Hardiness:** −10 to −12 °C; **Drought resistance code:** 5.

A woody perennial whose evergreen leaves are covered with fine silky hairs. The density of these hairs and the colour of the foliage change over the course of the seasons: the leaves are grey-green during the damp period and become silver-grey in the dry period. The discreet pinkish-white flowers appear in June-July. The plant forms ample spreading balls, whose dense vegetation prevents the germination of competing species. We use it as a structural plant in our gravel garden, where it may be associated with *Helianthemum caput-felis*, *Hypericum balearicum* or *Scabiosa minoana*. A light going-over with secateurs after it has finished flowering encourages the foliage to refurbish rapidly in early autumn. *Ballota hirsuta* prefers a well-drained stony or sandy soil. It cannot tolerate summer watering and should thus be planted in the unirrigated part of the garden. Planting density: 2 or 3 per square metre. *Propagation by seed in autumn or by softwood cuttings in spring.*

Ballota acetabulosa forms a magnificent cushion with silver leaves. A light clipping after flowering allows the plant to maintain a regular shape throughout the year.

• ***Ballota acetabulosa*** and ***Ballota pseudodictamnus*** both form broad silver-grey cushions. They can be associated with *Phlomis* species, cistuses with a spreading habit, lavenders and rosemaries to create large groundcover beds in parts of the garden that are not irrigated. Origin: Greece, Turkey. Hardiness: –10 to –12 °C. Drought resistance code: 5. Planting density: 2 or 3 per square metre.

• ***Bellis perennis***, the common lawn daisy, is one of the most ornamental perennials in wild lawns. Its plentiful white flowers open from February to May, with a peak around Easter. Many beneficial insects, including hoverflies and ladybirds, feed on

Brachypodium retusum is a very common grass in the garrigues of the South of France. If planted in gardens, it forms a humpy and wild-looking lawn.

the pollen that its flowers supply. Gourmet gardeners gather daisy leaves to make delicious wild salads. Origin: Europe, Western Asia. Hardiness: –15 °C and below. Drought resistance code: 3. Planting density: 9 per square metre to create small patches of daisies which will then self-seed over the entire wild lawn.

Brachypodium retusum (Poaceae)

Origin: Mediterranean Basin; **Height of foliage**: 20 cm; **Height when in flower**: 30 to 40 cm; **Spread**: 30 to 40 cm; **Position**: sun or semi-shade; **Hardiness**: –12 to –15 °C; **Drought resistance code**: 4.

A grass with narrow leaves that remain green year-round. The plant spreads slowly by means of its branching rhizomes. It gradually forms a wild-looking lawn that may be humpy to some extent. In the garrigue, it is a species that grows by the side of paths and in open spaces, often together with *Thymus vulgaris, Carex halleriana, Teucrium chamaedrys* and *Iris lutescens*. This plant association is easy to copy in parts of the garden that are not watered, preferably on poor and stony soil, to create a small area of "garrigue lawn", suitable for a moderate amount of foot traffic. The inflorescences, first green and then golden, appear in May and remain on the plant until the end of summer. *Brachypodium* can be mown to achieve a more even carpet. *Brachypodium retusum* is unfussy about soil type. It can cope with competition from the roots of pine trees and

can be planted in open spaces beneath trees. Planting density: 9 per square metre. *Propagation by seed sown in pots in spring. Sowing directly in the ground generally gives poor results (slowness in becoming established and competition from weeds).*

• ***Brachypodium phoenicoides*** is an invasive rhizomatous grass, useful for protecting slopes against erosion. Tough and adaptable, it is able to grow in the most difficult conditions. Origin: Mediterranean Basin. Hardiness: –15 °C and below. Drought resistance code: 5. Planting density: 2 or 3 per square metre.

• ***Bupleurum fruticosum***, or shrubby hare's ear, is a pioneer plant which self-seeds profusely in wild areas of the garden. This shrub, particularly resistant to drought and tough soil conditions, allows itself the luxury of flowering in full summer, when most Mediterranean species are dormant. Numerous insects visit it to make the most of the abundant source of nectar provided by its greenish-yellow flowers. To create the structure of a wild garden, one can use this bupleurum in conjunction with other pioneer plants such as *Dorycnium hirsutum, Coronilla valentina* subsp. *glauca, Teucrium flavum, Euphorbia characias* and *Viburnum tinus*. Origin: Mediterranean Basin. Hardiness: –12 to –15 °C. Drought resistance code: 5. Planting density: 1 per square metre.

• ***Bupleurum spinosum*** is happy in gravel gardens. It is eye-catching in summer and autumn, when its yellow flowers are gradually transformed into a curious tight mass of acid-green pedicels. Its growth is slow during the first years: this small miracle of a plant is not for impatient gardeners! Origin: the mountains of Spain and Morocco. Hardiness: –15 °C and below. Drought resistance code: 5. Planting density: 6 per square metre if one wants to create a uniform bed – but the spiny bupleurum shows its perfect ball shape to its best advantage when planted as a single specimen.

• ***Calamintha nepeta***, synonym *Clinopodium nepeta* subsp. *glandulosum,* is a perennial whose foliage gives off a strong fresh and minty scent when crushed. Anyone who walks in the garrigue is familiar with this scent: this *Calamintha* self-seeds happily

in the stones beside paths and when one treads on its compact vegetation it releases a great whiff of its scent. To re-create this sensation, we have planted a few specimens of *Calamintha nepeta* in our patch of flowering steppe, where it self-seeds freely in the gravel. The delicate inflorescences, of a pretty light blue, are produced in summer and at the beginning of autumn. Origin: Southern Europe, North Africa. Hardiness: −12 to −15 °C. Drought resistance code: 4. Planting density: 6 per square metre.

• *Carex halleriana* is a suckering perennial with narrow evergreen leaves that remain green year-round. Its spreading vegetation can be used in cracks between the paving stones of a terrace or between stepping stones. The plant can also be used to make a striking wild lawn in conjunction with *Brachypodium retusum* and various other carpeting garrigue plants which withstand moderate foot traffic. It likes dry and stony soil in sun or semi-shade. Origin: Central and Southern Europe, Western Asia, North Africa, Central America. Hardiness: −15 °C and below. Dryness code: 3. Planting density: 9 per square metre.

Centaurea bella (Asteraceae)
Synonym: *Psephellus bellus*

Origin: The Caucasus; **Height of foliage**: 10 to 15 cm; **Height when in flower**: 20 to 30 cm; **Spread**: 30 cm or more; **Position**: sun; **Hardiness**: −15 °C and below; **Drought resistance code**: 4.

This perennial might seem modest but it has many qualities: it is one of the best plants to use for small groundcover carpets in parts of the garden that receive no foot traffic. Its evergreen or semi-evergreen leaves, divided into irregular lobes, have silvery undersides and grey-green surfaces. The plant becomes dormant in very dry periods and may lose some of its leaves at the end of summer. The pretty mauve-pink flowers, rich in nectar, are produced in succession from March to the end of May. They attract numerous butterflies and beneficial insects like ladybirds. The plant forms a thick carpet which spreads gradually by layering and by suckers. Once it has become established, it requires practically no hand-weeding: the chemical substances exuded into the soil by its roots inhibit the germination of weeds (allelopathy). In our garden we like to grow it in association with *Tanacetum densum* and *Thymus ciliatus,* two other species whose remarkable allelopathic properties reduce the need for weeding. These three species all have grey-green or silvery grey foliage and complement one another perfectly. *Centaurea bella* prefers light, well-drained soil. It is a tough and easily grown plant, and long-lived. Planting density: 9 per square metre.
Propagation by division in autumn or by softwood cuttings in spring.

• *Centranthus ruber*, or valerian, is a pioneer plant which self-seeds prolifically on slopes and in wild parts of the garden. It produces its abundant red, pink, white or mauve flowers from May to July, and sometimes again in September-October. They attract numerous butterflies which use their long probosces to explore the store of nectar hidden in the flowers' spurs. Origin: Europe, North Africa, Asia Minor. Hardiness: −15 °C and below. Drought resistance code: 4. Planting density: 4 per square metre.

Centaurea bella makes a thick carpet which spreads slowly by layering and suckering.

The silver carpet of *Cerastium candidissimum* spreads over a stony slope. After its spring flowering the foliage partially dries out during the plant's summer dormancy before greening up again with the first autumn rains.

If one gives it regular water in summer, *Chamaemelum nobile* can be used as a carpet for small areas that receive moderate foot traffic.

• **Cerastium candidissimum** forms a thick and soft-looking carpet, with silver-white evergreen leaves. The foliage dries out partially when the plant becomes dormant during the summer drought, but is rapidly refurbished as soon as the first autumn rains arrive. The plant is covered in brilliant white flowers in May. Like many silver-leaved plants, *Cerastium candidissimum* likes poor stony or sandy soil with perfect drainage. Origin: the mountains of Greece. Hardiness: –12 to –15 °C. Drought resistance code: 3. Planting density: 9 per square metre.

• **Ceratostigma plumbaginoides** is irreplaceable in the garden: its deep ultramarine blue flowers appear at the end of summer and the beginning of autumn when most groundcover plants are dormant. Although the plant can resist drought, the flowering is markedly more abundant if an occasional watering is given during the summer: this little groundcover finds its place in one of the garden's intermediate watering zones. Its leaves, which it loses in winter, turn a lovely red in autumn. Origin: Western China. Hardiness: –15 °C and below. Drought resistance code: 3.5. Planting density: 9 per square metre.

• **Chamaemelum nobile** is covered with little white daisy flowers in June. The light green foliage makes a flat carpet, able to withstand moderate foot traffic. The leaves remain green throughout the winter but are lost during periods of great drought. It is possible to use *Chamaemelum* as a uniform carpeting plant if it is watered regularly in summer. In our garden we prefer to allow it to follow its natural cycle: we have planted it in our flowering steppe, where we enjoy its deliciously aromatic foliage during the wet season. At the end of summer there is nothing left but a carpet of gravel where the plant was. Origin: Europe, North Africa. Hardiness: –15 °C and below. Drought resistance code: 2. Planting density: 6 per square metre.

Cistus × florentinus 'Tramontane'
(Cistaceae)

Height: 30 cm; **Spread**: 60 to 80 cm; **Position**: sun or semi-shade; **Hardiness**: –12 to –15 °C; **Drought resistance code**: 4.

A hybrid of *Cistus monspeliensis* and *Cistus salviifolius* 'Prostratus', *Cistus × florentinus* 'Tramontane' is a sub-shrub with narrow dark green evergreen leaves. Its spreading vegetation forms a dense and even groundcover, which is covered in small white flowers in April-May. It can be used in the foreground of groundcover beds consisting of taller plants. Once established, a bed of cistuses needs no weeding. The foliage is partially lost when the plant enters into dormancy in periods of great drought: the fallen leaves then form a litter on the ground beneath the cistus and, as they decompose, release chemical substances which inhibit the germination of competing species (allelopathy). All cistuses are vulnerable to *Phytophthora*, a disease that develops if the soil is kept damp during hot weather. They should thus be planted only in zones of the garden that receive no irrigation. They appreciate poor soil, stony or sandy, with perfect drainage. Cistuses live for from

Cistus × florentinus 'Tramontane' has a spreading habit: it can be used as a low-growing groundcover in beds of perennials and shrubs. Here it is planted with *Erodium trifolium*, *Asphodelus microcarpus* and various euphorbias.

The pastel pink flowers of *Cistus* × *pauranthus* 'Natacha' begin to open in the morning light. The other cushion-forming plants which give structure to this bed include *Santolina viridis* 'Primrose Gem' and *Scabiosa cretica*.

Cistus × *pulverulentus* has very vigorous spreading vegetation. It is an excellent groundcover for slopes.

ten to fifteen years: the poorer the soil, the longer they live. Planting density: 2 or 3 per square metre.
Propagation by semi-ripe cuttings in autumn.

• **Cistus × ledon** produces a mass of small white flowers in May-June. However, it is above all its foliage that is worthy of note. The narrow sticky leaves, very aromatic in hot weather, are a dark green which looks

almost black in the burning light of high summer. We like to use it to create a strong contrast in beds of silver-leaved plants. Origin: a natural hybrid of *Cistus monspeliensis* and *Cistus laurifolius*, collected near the village of Saint-Chinian, in the Hérault region of France. Hardiness: −12 to −15 °C. Drought resistance code: 5. Planting density: 1 per square metre.

• **Cistus × pauranthus** 'Natacha' forms a perfectly regular cushion: it is one of the best groundcover cistuses in our garden. It can be used as a structural plant in gravel gardens or as part of the mixture in large groundcover beds. The small flowers, of a delicate ivory colour tinged with pink, open in April-May. Origin: a natural hybrid of *Cistus salviifolius* and *Cistus parviflorus*, collected on the Vaï peninsula in Crete. Hardiness: −6 to −8 °C. Drought resistance code: 5. Planting density: 2 or 3 per square metre.

• **Cistus × pulverulentus** is a vigorous ground-cover: in a few years it can attain a spread of 1 to 2 m. It can be mixed with the prostrate varieties of rosemary to give a dense cover on slopes. It blooms later than most cistuses, its dark pink flowers opening from May to the beginning of July. Origin: *Cistus × pulverulentus* is a natural hybrid of *Cistus albidus* and *Cistus crispus*. One can see fine specimens of it near the Abbey of Fontfroide in the Aude region of France. Hardiness: −10 to −12 °C. Drought resistance code: 4. Planting density: 1 per square metre.

• **Cistus creticus** 'Calcosalto' is a curiosity: the result of adaptation to wind and salt on the cliffs of Bonifacio where it originated (Calcosalto is the old name for Bonifacio), it forms a flat groundcover only a few centimetres high. The large pink flowers seem almost out of proportion on this miniature carpet. It is a striking groundcover to create a drift of low vegetation in a gravel garden. Hardiness: −8 to −10 °C. Drought resistance code: 5. Planting density: 6 per square metre.

Cistus creticus 'Cacosalto' is the smallest cistus in our collection: its ground-hugging vegetation is no more than a few centimetres in height.

• **Cistus × tardiflorens** is one of the most beautiful cistuses in our collection. Unlike most cistuses, which lose some of their leaves when they become dormant in summer, *Cistus × tardiflorens* becomes even more attractive in summer: with drought, its grey foliage, resembling that of an *Atriplex*, becomes silver and more and more luminous. Its flowering is also a surprise: the bright yellow flowers, marked with small black blotches, open over a long period, from May to July. We like to plant *Cistus × tardiflorens* with *Perovskia* 'Blue Spire' to create a blue and yellow picture which continues until late in the summer. *Cistus × tardiflorens* is the result of a cross, made by Jean-Pierre Demoly, between *Cistus atriplicifolius* and *Cistus halimifolius* (formerly called *Halimium*). Hardiness: −10 to −12 °C. Drought resistance code: 5. Planting density: 2 per square metre.

Among the cistuses that form large balls, ideal when one wants to create large groundcover beds to fill sizeable areas, we recommend *Cistus × skanbergii* (grey leaves and tender pink flowers), *Cistus × purpureus* (aromatic dark green leaves and large mauve-pink flowers with dark blotches), *Cistus × ultraviolaceus*, little known but interesting for its long flowering season (a spreading habit and very luminous mauve flowers) and *Cistus × verguinii* 'Paul Pècherat' (dark leaves and beautiful white flowers with dark red blotches). Finally, there are other cistuses that self-seed abundantly in poor stony soils, which can be used as pioneer plants to colonize slopes or wild areas of the garden, for example *Cistus albidus, Cistus monspeliensis* and *Cistus creticus*. I have deliberately limited this selection of cistuses in order to present here only those species and varieties that have a good tolerance of alkaline soils.

Clematis flammula (Ranunculaceae)
Virgin's Bower

Origin: Mediterranean Basin; **Height**: 50 cm or more (if growing without any support); **Spread**: 3 m and more; **Position**: sun; **Hardiness**: −12 to −15 °C; **Drought resistance code**: 4.

A sub-shrub with deciduous foliage. The twining petioles enable the plant to attach itself wherever it finds a support. If it does not find anything to climb on, it forms a spreading mass over the soil, which makes it a good groundcover, for example to cover slopes where the soil is poor. The plant is smothered in deliciously scented small pure white flowers from July to September. The dried inflorescences are decorative since each seed is equipped with a long feathery tail which allows it to be carried off by the wind. The plant self-seeds easily and can act as a pioneer plant to colonize wild areas of the garden. In groundcover beds it can be planted with *Leucophyllum langmaniae*, thus

creating an amazing flowering scene at the driest moment of summer. *Clematis flammula* is unfussy about soil type. Planting density: 1 per square metre.
Propagation by seed in autumn.

• **Clematis cirrhosa** likes growing on old walls and stony ground. Its handsome foliage remains green in winter but disappears completely in summer. Its creamy white flowers appear in winter. *Clematis cirrhosa* and *Clematis flammula* can be planted together to colonize stony slopes, their inverse growth cycles making them perfectly complementary. Origin: Mediterranean Basin. Hardiness: −12 to −15 °C. Drought resistance code: 5. Planting density: 1 per square metre.

Convolvulus sabatius (Convolvulaceae)
Origin: North Africa; **Height**: 20 cm; **Spread**: 30 to 40 cm; **Position**: sun; **Hardiness**: −10 to −12 °C (the plant is deciduous when temperatures reach −6 to −8 °C, but the rootstock is able to sprout again in spring); **Drought resistance code**: 3.

A perennial with evergreen downy light green leaves. The suckering clump forms a dense carpet. The very ornamental blue-mauve flowers are abundant from May to July. The plant can be set between stepping stones or can colonize flights of stone steps. It is capable of scrambling up a neighbouring plant. In our garden we like to combine it with *Lavandula dentata*, so that the very similarly coloured flowers of the two plants intermingle. *Convolvulus sabatius* likes light,

Convolvulus sabatius is a small groundcover that is useful for decorating the edges of paths, stepping stones or steps.

The silver foliage of *Convolvulus cneorum* disappears almost entirely beneath a mass of white flowers.

well-drained soils Planting density: 4 per square metre.
Propagation by division in autumn or softwood cuttings in spring.

• **Convolvulus cneorum** forms a handsome cushion of silky silvery leaves. It is covered in bright white flowers from April to June. The plant cannot tolerate watering during the hot time of year: it should thus be planted in a zone of the garden that receives no irrigation. It likes poor stony or sandy soils with perfect drainage. Origin: Croatia, Albania. Hardiness: −10 to −12 °C. Drought resistance code: 4 Planting density: 2 or 3 per square metre.

Coronilla minima (Fabaceae)

Origin: Southern Europe; **Height**: 15 to 20 cm, sometimes more; **Spread**: 30 to 40 cm; **Position**: sun; **Hardiness**: −15 °C and below; **Drought resistance code**: 5.

Sub-shrub with glaucous evergreen leaves. The plant forms a spreading cushion, which disappears beneath the bright yellow flowers in May-June. The roots are equipped with nodules that fix nitrogen from the air, enabling the plant to live in very poor stony soil. We like to grow it with *Salvia lavandulifolia* subsp. *blancoana* in order to have patches of brightly coloured flowers in our gravel garden in late spring. *Coronilla minima* requires a light soil, stony or sandy, with perfect drainage. The plant cannot tolerate irrigation in hot weather: it must thus be kept for the unirrigated zone of the garden. Planting density: 6 per square metre.
Propagation by seed which has first had boiling water poured over it, in autumn, or by softwood cuttings in spring.

• **Cotula lineariloba** forms a flat carpet of downy, finely-cut leaves, light green with a silvery sheen. The rounded heads of lemon yellow flowers open from April to June. In mild climates it is a very ornamental groundcover that can be included in mixed flowering carpets. Origin: Southern Africa. Hardiness: −4 to −6 °C. Drought resistance code: 3. Planting density: 4 per square metre.

• **Crocus goulimyi** is a bulbous plant whose pretty mauve flowers are much appreciated

in autumn when the dry garden is struggling to emerge from its summer lethargy. It can be planted more or less everywhere in a gravel garden or a flowering steppe, together with other early-flowering bulbs like *Crocus sativus* (saffron), *Sternbergia lutea* or *Colchicum lusitanum*. Origin: Greece. Hardiness: −15 °C and below. Drought resistance code: 5. Planting density: 16 per square metre.

• **Cyclamen hederifolium** naturalizes in shady parts of the garden, below shrubs or in the cracks between paving stones on a path or terrace. It is equally happy in stony

Cotula lineariloba is a small and very ornamental groundcover that can be grown in gardens with a mild climate. Its bright yellow flower heads mingle here with the luminous flowers of *Cistus* × *ultraviolaceus*.

soil and in moist soil. Its pretty pink flowers open in September-October and its marbled leaves spread to form a small carpet in winter and spring, before disappearing when the hot weather arrives. Origin: Southern Europe, Turkey. Hardiness: −15 °C and below. Drought resistance code: 5. Planting density: 9 per square metre.

• **Cymbalaria muralis**, or ivy-leaved toadflax, slips its long stems between stones, on

Cymbalaria muralis, or ivy-leaved toadflax, decorates steps and north-facing stone walls for many months of the year.

When it is watered regularly in summer, Cynodon 'Santa Ana' makes a robust lawn, perfectly suited to the heat of mediterranean summers.

Like all warm-season grasses, Cynodon 'Santa Ana' goes through a dormant period which is expressed as a complete yellowing of the leaves in winter. It is not until April that the first green shoots appear within the yellow carpet.

shady walls or between steps. Its delicate pale lilac-coloured flowers are produced in succession from July to October. Origin: South-East Europe (the plant has become naturalized in many regions around the Mediterranean). Hardiness: −15 °C and below. Drought resistance code: 4. Planting density: 9 per square metre.

Cynodon 'Santa Ana' (Poaceae)
Bermuda grass hybrid

Height of foliage: 2 to 15 cm depending on cultivation conditions and intensity of foot traffic; **Height when in flower:** 20 to 25 cm; **Spread:** 60 cm or more; **Position:** sun; **Hardiness:** −10 to −12 °C for established plantings (but only about −8 °C when newly-planted since the rhizomes have not yet gone deep); **Drought resistance code:** 2.

Cynodon 'Santa Ana' is one of the best warm-season grasses to replace a lawn in the mediterranean climate. It is not suitable for gardens in regions with harsh winters for when newly planted it is fairly sensitive to the cold. It is a hybrid of Cynodon dactylon, native to the Mediterranean Basin, and Cynodon transvaalensis, native to Southern Africa. Like all warm-season grasses, Cynodon has a dormant period in winter, which, in mediterranean gardens, means that from December to April its foliage turns completely yellow. Cynodon 'Santa Ana' is a sterile hybrid: its spikelets produce no seed and it can thus not be sown. It is planted in the form of small pot-grown plants raised from cuttings. It is easy to prepare these young plants in advance when one wants to plant a Cynodon lawn in successive sections in order to reduce the area that will need to be weeded by hand during the first year. In the hot season, which is this grass's growing season, the long rhizomes spread rapidly to colonize all the available space (the name Cynodon derives from the Greek kůon, "dog", and odous, "tooth", referring to the pointed white tips of the rhizomes which resemble dog teeth, hence its other name of dog's tooth grass).

Cynodon 'Santa Ana' forms a tough lawn that withstands foot traffic and is adapted to the heat of mediterranean summers. With regular irrigation, about once every ten days in summer, it is possible to achieve a very dense lawn whose appearance resembles that of a conventional lawn. An occasional mowing is needed to keep it short. It is also possible to water Cynodon less often, for example every three or four weeks in summer. Thanks to its rhizomes which can reach a depth of almost 2 m, it resists drought relatively well once it has been established for a few years. Under this regime it may enter partial dormancy at the end of summer, showing a progressive yellowing, before becoming green again with the first autumn rains. In parts of the garden that receive little irrigation, Cynodon 'Santa Ana' can also be mixed with other fast-growing groundcover plants, such as Achillea crithmifolia, Phyla canescens and Trifolium fragiferum, to form a wild-looking groundcover that withstands foot traffic and requires little maintenance.

In moist soil, Cynodon 'Santa Ana' can become invasive: it needs to be contained by an underground barrier, or by a close planting of evergreen shrubs that check the spread of its rhizomes. In mediterranean gardens, the problem of lateral invasiveness doesn't usually arise: the spread of this grass is significant only in parts of the garden that are irrigated. Scarification may be necessary every two or three years to remove the thick felty layer that gradually accumulates beneath its vegetation. Cynodon 'Santa Ana' is unfussy as regards soil type. It withstands salt spray by the sea. Planting density: 4 per square metre.
Propagation by division at the end of winter or by rhizome cuttings in June.

Dichondra repens (Convolvulaceae)
Synonym: Dichondra micrantha

Origin: Texas, New Mexico, North-West India, South Japan, China; **Height of foliage:** 1 to 10 cm depending on the conditions; **Spread:** 50 cm or more; **Position:** sun or shade; **Hardiness:** the foliage is burnt by the cold at −6 to −8 °C, but the stock resprouts after lower temperatures, of about −10 to −12 °C; **Drought resistance code:** 1.

A perennial with small evergreen leaves of a pretty fresh green. The plant spreads both by its underground rhizomes and by its lateral stems which root wherever they are in contact with the soil. It forms a low-growing and very ornamental carpet, useful when one wants to create small areas of a carpeting plant that can be walked on. The appearance of this carpet is variable, since the size of the leaves and the height of the vegetation depend on the position and on the frequency of irrigation. If the area is in full sun, frequent watering (about twice a week in summer) is necessary to obtain a dense carpet of small leaves that hug the soil. In shade watering can be less frequent and the leaves are often markedly larger. Too much watering is inadvisable for it can give rise to a rust disease which causes large circular spots on the leaves, making them wither. In prolonged periods of drought Dichondra loses its leaves. The plant then comes into leaf again with the first rains of autumn, the rhizomes serving as storage organs during the summer dormancy.

Dichondra can be planted as pot-grown

The ground-hugging foliage of *Dichondra repens* allows it to form a very even carpet

plants or by seed. Raising this plant from seed, however, has its problems: germination is slow and the sown area is invaded by rapidly germinating weeds which are hard to control. *Dichondra* can be planted in a mixture with carpeting perennials that thrive in shade, such as *Glechoma hederacea*, *Prunella vulgaris*, *Ajuga reptans* and *Viola hederacea*. This creates an attractive wild-looking lawn for a shady area. *Dichondra repens* prefers a friable soil that is fairly deep and well drained. Planting density: 4 per square metre.
Propagation by seed sown in pots, subsequently planted in the ground.

• *Dichondra argentea* forms an amazing silvery, silky carpet in gardens that are well protected from frost. It resists drought better than *Dichondra repens*. It can also be grown on the top of dry-stone walls or between steps, from which it cascades down. Origin: South-East United States. Hardiness: –2 to –4 °C (the leaves fall with the first frosts). Drought resistance code: 2. Planting density: 6 per square metre.

In gardens protected from frost, *Dichondra argentea* makes an amazing silver carpet.

• *Dimorphotheca caulescens*, whose flowering in pastel pink is spectacular, is of mountain origin: it resists cold better than its relation *Osteospermum fruticosum* but unfortunately tolerates drought less well. Origin: South Africa. Hardiness: –10 to –12 °C. Drought resistance code: 2. Planting density: 6 per square metre.

• *Dorycnium pentaphyllum* is covered in small white flowers, rich in nectar, which attract a multitude of beneficial insects. Sometimes a subtly flavoured honey is made from this plant. It self-seeds prolifically in poor soil, which it enriches thanks to the nitrogen-fixing nodules on its roots. It is a pioneer plant, useful for colonizing steep slopes or the wild parts of the garden, together with *Coronilla valentina* subsp. *glauca*, *Centranthus ruber* and *Euphorbia characias*. In very stony soil, *Dorycnium pentaphyllum* can be replaced by *Dorycnium hirsutum*, with handsome downy grey foliage. Origin: Mediterranean Basin. Hardiness: –12 to –15 °C. Drought resistance code: 5. Planting density: 2 per square metre.

• *Drosanthemum hispidum* is a fast-growing groundcover whose small succulent leaves act as water reserves, enabling the plant to survive in tough conditions. It can be planted to cascade from walls or used on rocky slopes, where its bright pink flowers are spectacular in April-May. Mixed with other plants of the Aizoaceae family, such as *Delosperma cooperi*, *Malephora lutea* and *Malephora crocea*, *Drosanthemum* provides

Dorycnium hirsutum is a pioneer plant which self-seeds abundantly in stony parts of the garden. Here it is growing with *Achillea coarctata*, *Geranium sanguineum* and *Achillea nobilis*.

Drosanthemum hispidum is a carpeting groundcover capable of living in very tough conditions, for example on green roofs in mediterranean regions.

an addition to the traditional range of *Sedum* species for planting on green roofs. With a substrate 20 cm thick (composed of equal parts of topsoil and pozzolano), it can get through the whole summer without watering. However, an occasional watering is necessary if the substrate is less thick. Origin: South Africa. Hardiness: –8 to –10 °C. Drought resistance code: 6. Planting density on slopes: 4 per square metre. Planting density on green roofs: 9 per square metre.

Dymondia margaretae (Asteraceae)
Synonym: ***Dymondia repens***

Origin: South Africa; **Height of foliage**: 1 to 5 cm, depending on cultivation conditions and foot traffic; **Spread**: 30 to 40 cm; **Position**: sun; **Hardiness**: –4 to –6 °C; **Drought resistance code**: 4.

An evergreen perennial forming a beautiful

The very dense foliage of *Dymondia margaretae* colonizes the cracks between paving on a path. In a mild climate it can also be used to create small and striking-looking carpets.

dense and very low-growing carpet that withstands a moderate degree of foot traffic. The narrow leaves, grey with silver borders, have an unusual texture, hard to the touch. The plant spreads slowly, by means of its stems which root wherever they are in contact with the soil. Its twisting roots, thick and deep, act as stores of water and nutrients for the plant. Drought-resistant, needing no mowing and leaving little space for competing weeds, *Dymondia* requires minimal maintenance once it is established. In gardens in mild climates it can be used to create an unusual-looking silvery carpet. It can also be used to fill the cracks between paving stones on terraces or between stepping stones. Small yellow flowers, barely visible in the midst of the foliage, open in June-July. Since its natural habitat is sandy, *Dymondia margaretae* requires a friable and light soil with perfect drainage. In clay soils

the addition of a large amount of sand benefits the plant. If the soil has been properly decompacted, the twisting roots will penetrate deep, thus guaranteeing the plant good resistance to drought. Planting density: 9 per square metre.

Propagation by division in autumn or by cuttings in spring.

Erica manipuliflora (Ericaceae)

Origin: South-East Europe, Turkey, Syria; **Height**: 60 to 80 cm; **Spread**: 60 to 80 cm; **Position**: sun or semi-shade; **Hardiness**: –12 to –15 °C; **Drought resistance code**: 5.

An evergreen shrub with fine dark green leaves. This beautiful heather, which tolerates alkaline conditions, is common in the Eastern Mediterranean Basin. It is seen both in coastal zones, as in the Mani peninsula of the southern Peloponnese, and in mountains, as for example at the foot of cedars in the western Taurus. Tolerating dryness, semi-shade and root competition, it often forms great ground-covering masses at the foot of trees. The flowers, a source of honey, are tightly packed along the stems and may be light pink or dark pink depending on the variety. They are produced for a long period, from September to November. The plant grows relatively slowly during the first years but the gardener's patience is amply rewarded by the beauty of the colourful spectacle it presents when bringing the garden to life in autumn. *Erica manipuliflora* is vulnerable to *Phytophthora*, a disease that develops if the soil is kept damp in the hot

season. It must thus be planted only in zones of the garden that receive no irrigation. It likes poor soil, stony or sandy, with perfect drainage. Planting density: 3 per square metre.

Propagation by cuttings taken from young non-flowering shoots, in autumn.

• *Erigeron karvinskianus* has small leaves which are evergreen or semi-evergreen depending on the winter cold. The supple mass of its foliage is covered in pinkish-white flowers from April to June, then again from September to November; flowering is often more abundant in autumn than in spring. Rich in pollen, the flowers attract numerous beneficial insects, including hoverflies, especially in late autumn when there are fewer flowers in the garden. *Erigeron karvinskianus* self-seeds into old stone walls, into cracks between paving stones on terraces and into stone steps. Origin: Mexico. Hardiness: –10 to –12 °C. Drought resistance code: 3. Planting density: 6 per square metre.

• *Erodium trifolium* is a small perennial that self-seeds easily among stones. The pretty white flowers, blotched with red, appear from the end of winter and continue successively until the heat arrives. The leaves disappear completely in summer: the plant becomes dormant and lives on the reserves accumulated in its fleshy roots. The rosettes of downy leaves reappear with the first rains of autumn. *Erodium trifolium* can be

Erica manipuliflora in the mountains of northern Syria, near the Turkish border. This particularly robust heather tolerates alkaline soils and competition from tree roots.

Erigeron karvinskianus self-seeds generously in a flight of old stone steps (Jardin des Sambucs.)

Erodium trifolium flowers at the end of winter. This very ornamental species self-seeds easily in stony parts of the garden.

associated with other plants that self-seed generously, such a *Erigeron karvinskianus*, *Geranium sanguineum*, *Nepeta racemosa* or *Euphorbia myrsinites*, to create little flowering scenes in the stony parts of the garden, whose composition changes from year to year. Origin: Asia Minor. Hardiness: −12 to −15 °C. Drought resistance code: 4. Planting density: 9 per square metre.

• *Eschscholzia californica*, California poppy, produces a multitude of brightly coloured flowers. They are rich in nectar and attract to the garden many beneficial insects such as hoverflies. It is a short-lived perennial which self-seeds easily when the soil is free from vegetation: scratch the soil beneath the plant to encourage re-seeding in autumn. It can be used in annual flowering meadows, where its long flowering period is a delight. It is sometimes held to be invasive, although it disappears as soon as it meets competition from a herbaceous carpet. It can sometimes self-seed for a few years on disturbed land, for example after construction work, but there have been no reports of a negative impact in South-West Europe. Origin: South-West United States. Hardiness: −12 to −15 °C. Drought resistance code: 5. Planting density: 4 per square metre if pot-grown plants are used, but direct sowing is the most common means of propagation.

Euphorbia rigida (Euphorbiaceae)

Origin: Mediterranean Basin, Asia Minor; **Height**: 50 cm; **Spread**: 60 cm; **Position**: sun; **Hardiness**: −15 °C and below; **Drought resistance code**: 5.

This perennial with thick evergreen leaves arranged in regular spirals along the stems, is one of the most beautiful plants in our garden. In winter its grey-blue foliage takes on amazing pinkish-mauve hues, especially in years of extreme cold. The bright yellow flowers appear at the end of January, when most plants in the garden are still dormant. In late spring the bracts gradually turn deep red: this is the moment when the plant is at its most spectacular. In summer the luminous foliage remains magnificent, even in periods of intense drought. We like to grow this plant with other species whose foliage is particularly attractive in summer, such as *Phlomis chrysophylla*, *Hypericum balearicum*, *Coleonema album* and *Leucophyllum*

Euphorbia rigida in its natural habitat in the mountains of Sicily.

langmaniae. It self-seeds profusely in the garden. As with all euphorbias, the white latex that oozes out if you cut off a bit of the plant irritates the skin, mucous membranes and eyes: it is better to wear gloves if you need to pull out euphorbias that have self-seeded too freely. *Euphorbia rigida* likes poor stony or sandy soils with perfect drainage. Planting density: 3 or 4 per square metre.
Propagation by seed in autumn.

• *Euphorbia ceratocarpa* is a vigorous plant which also attracts a host of beneficial insects, a real sight for the amateur entomologist. Its generous production of yellow-green flowers continues from April to July, lightening large groundcover beds. It is a tough plant that is easy to grow. Origin: Sicily. Hardiness: –10 to –12 °C. Drought resistance code: 4. Planting density: 1 per square metre.

• *Euphorbia* 'Copton Ash' forms a cushion of very fine blue-green leaves. The plant is covered in acid yellow-green flowers from May to July. These flowers, shiny with nectar, attract a whole corps de ballet of insects, including countless hoverflies and ladybirds. *Euphorbia* 'Copton Ash' is a hybrid of two species native to the South of France, *Euphorbia nicaeensis* and *Euphorbia seguieriana*. Hardiness: –12 to –15 °C. Drought resistance code: 4. Planting density: 4 per square metre.

• *Euphorbia characias* is a pioneer plant which self-seeds easily in the wild parts of the garden or on degraded slopes. It is also happy in gravel gardens, where it colonizes

Euphorbia ceratocarpa is rich in nectar and its generous flowering attracts a remarkable range of insects. We see here the elegant long hoverfly, *Sphaerophoria scripta* (1), the seven-spotted ladybird, *Coccinella septempunctata* (2), a metallic-coloured cuckoo wasp, *Chrysis ignita* (3), whose larvae are cuckoo-like parasites in wasps' nests, a large, fat bluebottle, *Caliphora vicina* (4), and the amazing assassin bug, *Rhynocoris iracundus* (5) which does not feed on nectar itself but lies in wait for the many other insects visiting the euphorbia to hunt them with its sharp, bayonet-like rostrum.

1

2

3

4

5

In the depths of winter, when the garden is still dormant and flowers are rare, the luminous colour of euphorbias brings a cheerful note to groundcover beds. Here we see *Euphorbia characias* subsp. *wulfenii* (left foreground), which flowers almost as early as *Euphorbia rigida* (on the right).

Euphorbia dendroides has a remarkable silhouette that gives structure to the landscape (here on the island of Amorgos in the Cyclades). Perfectly resistant to drought, it has a growth cycle which is the inverse of many temperate-climate plants: its foliage is light green in winter, then takes on yellow, red or orange tints in spring and drops completely in early summer.

the spaces between lower-growing plants. The subspecies originating in the Eastern Mediterranean, *Euphorbia characias* subsp. *wulfenii*, has the most spectacular flowering. It begins to flower almost as early as *Euphorbia rigida*. In our garden we grow these two euphorbias together in a small winter-flowering bed of yellows and blues, with *Iris unguicularis*, *Helianthemum alypoides*, *Lavandula dentata*, *Teucrium fruticans* 'Ouarzazate' and *Rosmarinus officinalis* 'Sappho'. Origin: Mediterranean Basin. Hardiness: −12 to −15 °C. Drought resistance code: 5. Planting density: 2 per square metre.

• *Euphorbia cyparissias* is a rhizomatous species which invades uncultivated areas of the garden. It can be grown in association with other pioneer plants like *Achillea coarctata* or *Asphodelus fistulosus* to create the first line of plants in a wild garden. Origin: Europe. Hardiness: −15 °C and below. Drought resistance code: 3. Planting density: 2 per square metre.

• *Euphorbia dendroides* is a plant whose striking silhouette gives structure to large groundcover beds in gardens situated in mild climates. Its leaves fall at the end of spring to reveal the perfect regularity of its branching architecture. Origin: Mediterranean Basin. Hardiness: −6 to −8 °C (the plant resists cold better in very dry soil). Drought resistance code: 5. Planting density: 1 per square metre.

The vegetation of *Frankenia laevis* forms an even carpet. Dark green in summer, it takes on lovely red or mauve tints during the winter cold.

• *Euphorbia myrsinites* has thick blue-grey leaves arranged in a spiral along the prostrate stems. The plant self-seeds abundantly in poor and stony soil. We like to grow it in association with *Erodium trifolium*, *Glaucium flavum*, *Goniolimon speciosum* and *Pallenis maritima* to create pictures that change from year to year in the rocky areas of our garden. Origin: Southern Europe, North Africa, Central Asia. Hardiness: −15 °C and below. Drought resistance code: 5. Planting density: 6 per square metre.

• *Euphorbia spinosa* is a compact plant whose rock-hugging cushions cling to limestone cliffs. One can see good colonies of it in the hinterland of Menton, near the pretty villages of Sainte-Agnès or Gorbio. In the garden the plant grows slowly but is very long-lived. It naturally takes the shape of a perfectly regular dome, as if it were pruned regularly. Origin: Mediterranean Basin.

Hardiness: −12 to −15 °C. Drought resistance code: 4. Planting density: 3 or 4 per square metre.

Frankenia laevis (Frankeniaceae)
Origin: coasts of South-West Europe; **Height**: 1 to 4 cm depending on cultivation conditions and degree of foot traffic; **Spread**: 50 cm and more; **Position**: sun; **Hardiness**: −12 to −15 °C; **Drought resistance code**: 2.

A remarkable low-growing carpet with small dark green evergreen leaves. The plant spreads by means of its lateral stems which root wherever they are in contact with the soil and the dense vegetation forms a very even carpet that withstands a moderate amount of foot traffic. In winter, the foliage becomes marbled with a red or purplish colour, both striking and very ornamental. The small pink flowers open in May-June. In summer *Frankenia* needs to be watered about once every ten days if its foliage is to maintain a good appearance in the dry season. If it receives no water, the plant becomes dormant and loses some of its leaves, then the foliage is refurbished as soon as the first autumn rains arrive. *Frankenia laevis* is generally used as a carpeting plant for small areas of a few dozen square metres only, for it requires regular hand-weeding. In late spring it may be subject to attack from aphids, which are quickly controlled by the arrival of lacewings, hoverflies and ladybirds. If you want to cover larger areas,

Frankenia can be planted together with other carpeting plants such as *Thymus hirsutus*, *Thymus herba-barona* and *Thymus ciliatus* to form mixed flowering carpets that require a lot less maintenance than single-species carpets. In the wild *Frankenia laevis* grows among rocks beside the sea, on small ledges where there is a little sandy soil. In the garden it has a longer life if one plants it in light, perfectly drained soil. It tolerates salt spray by the sea and saline soil. Planting density: 4 per square metre.
Propagation by cuttings in spring.

Geranium macrorrhizum
(Geraniaceae)
Origin: Central and Southern Europe; **Height:** 30 cm; **Spread:** 40 cm or more; **Position:** shade or semi-shade; **Hardiness:** −15 °C and below; **Drought resistance code:** 3.

A rhizomatous perennial with evergreen or semi-evergreen green leaves. Some of the leaves take on a lovely red hue in autumn and winter. The plant spreads slowly by means of its rhizomes and in time forms a dense groundcover. If you look at the leaf surface with a magnifying glass, two distinct kinds of hairs are apparent: long silky hairs, which give a slightly grey tinge to the leaves, and shorter hairs bearing a minute shining droplet, which is a small essential oil gland. When you crush the leaves, these glandular hairs break and the plant gives off a powerful and delicious scent, at once woody and fruity, which remains on the fingers for a long time. The essential oil of this plant is famed as a popular medicine in Central Europe, and particularly for its aphrodisiac virtues: *Geranium macrorrhizum* is traditionally cultivated for distillation in Bulgaria, where it is called *zdravets* (from *zdrave*, which means "health" in Bulgarian). It is a good groundcover for shade and semi-shade, and is able to withstand root competition beneath trees. In our garden it grows in a shady area beneath old cypress trees, where few plants thrive. Its pretty mauve-pink flowers, with a long bunch of protruding stamens, appear from April to June. In prolonged periods of drought the plant becomes dormant and loses some of its leaves, drawing on the reserves contained in its thick roots. If you wish the plant to maintain its handsome foliage throughout the year, you can give it an occasional watering in summer because it tolerates irrigation well and can be planted in either the irrigated or the unirrigated zones of the garden. *Geranium macrorrhizum* prefers friable and fairly deep soils that are well drained. Planting density: 6 per square metre.
Propagation by rhizome cuttings in early winter.

• *Geranium* '**Rambling Robin**' is a remarkable fast-growing groundcover, which likes shade or semi-shade in a mild climate. Its finely-cut evergreen foliage is covered in pale blue-mauve flowers from April to June. It is a hybrid of two species native to South Africa, *Geranium incanum*, from which it has inherited its attractive cut foliage, and *Geranium robustum*, which has given it its rapid growth. Hardiness: −6 to −8 °C. Drought resistance code: 2. Planting density: 3 or 4 per square metre.

• *Geranium sanguineum* is an easily grown robust perennial that is equally happy in sun or shade. Its magenta flowers are produced in succession over a long period, from April to June and then again in autumn. Origin: Europe, Turkey. Hardiness: −15 °C and below. Drought resistance code: 4. Planting density: 6 to 9 per square metre.

• *Geranium* × *cantabrigiense* '**Biokovo**' has bright green aromatic semi-evergreen leaves. It spreads slowly by suckering and can easily colonize the cracks betwen paving stones on a terrace or stone steps, in either shade or semi-shade. Its pinkish-white flowers open in May-June. The cultivar 'Karmina' has bright pink flowers. *Geranium* × *cantabrigiense* varieties are hybrids of *Geranium macrorrhizum* and *Geranium dalmaticum*. Hardiness: −15 °C or below. Drought resistance code: 3. Planting density: 9 per square metre.

• *Glaucium flavum*, or horned poppy, is a short-lived perennial whose rosettes of wavy leaves, silvery and downy, are very ornamental. The large bright yellow flowers appear in summer. They are followed by narrow seedpods which open suddenly to project a shower of small black seeds thus enabling the plant to migrate year by year throughout the

Geranium 'Rambling Robin' is a fast-growing groundcover that likes shade or semi-shade. The flowers are delicately veined to guide the insects which come to feed from the nectar glands at the bottom of the corolla.

Geranium sanguineum is a tough groundcover that can adapt to different situations, in shade as well as in full sun.

Glaucium flavum is a pioneer species that self-seeds in disturbed ground, as here beside the road round the Bay of Alcúdia in Mallorca.

garden. The horned poppy, which probably originated in the Middle East, naturalized all round the Mediterranean several thousand years ago by spreading along paths and in the poor and uncultivated soils that it favours. Hardiness: −12 to −15 °C. Drought resistance code: 5. Planting density: 6 per square metre.

Glechoma hederacea (Lamiaceae)
Ground-ivy

Origin: Europe; **Height**: from 5 to 15 cm depending on conditions; **Spread**: 50 cm or more; **Position**: shade or semi-shade; **Hardiness**: −15 °C and below; **Drought resistance code**: 2.

A perennial with dark green evergreen leaves. It forms a dense groundcover thanks to its fast-growing stems which spread in all directions and root wherever they are in contact with the soil. The blue-mauve flowers, a source of honey, appear in May-June. Ground-ivy is happy on the edge of woodland, at the foot of hedges, or in the shadow of north-facing façades. In the unirrigated zones of the garden it loses some of its leaves in summer, then is refurbished with the first autumn rains. It can be used as a carpet from which emerge perennials that appreciate semi-shade, such as *Salvia spathacea*, *Helleborus argutifolius* or *Lobelia laxiflora* var. *angustifolia*. It can also be planted in the shade in association with *Dichondra repens*, *Prunella vulgaris* and *Viola hederacea* to create small patches of lawn that can be walked on and need only occasional watering. And finally it can be used to create large groundcover scenes, in shade or semi-shade, planted together with *Malvastrum lateritium*, *Ajuga reptans* and *Geranium sanguineum*. *Glechoma hederacea* is unfussy about soil type. It is an easily grown and long-lived plant. It grows faster in friable, fairly deep, well-drained soil. Planting density: 4 per square metre.
Propagation by division or by softwood cuttings in early spring.

• **Globularia alypum** is a compact shrub which is happy in stony ground. Its grey-blue foliage remains attractive in summer, even in periods of great drought. The bright blue flowers open in winter, from the end of January. It can be grown in association with other early-flowering species that like poor and stony soils, such as *Euphorbia rigida* or *Lavandula dentata*. Origin: Mediterranean Basin. Hardiness: −12 to −15 °C. Drought resistance code: 6. Planting density: 6 per square metre.

• **Goniolimon speciosum** is a small perennial whose graceful and prolonged summer flowering is much appreciated in dry gardens. The plant self-seeds willingly among stones or along gravel paths. In our garden we like to grow it in association with *Origanum laevigatum*, which also flowers over a long period in summer. Origin: steppes of Mongolia and Siberia. Hardiness: −15 °C and below. Drought resistance code: 5. Planting density: 9 per square metre.

• **Halimione portulacoides,** synonym *Atriplex portulacoides*, or sea purslane, is a vigorous groundcover with small silvery-grey evergreen leaves. It thrives in zones where periods of dryness are interspersed with temporary flooding, such as at the bottom of retention ponds or on canal banks. It is happy in saline soils near the sea, and its edible leaves have a pronounced salty taste (the name *Halimione* derives from the Greek *halos*, "salt"). Birds like its leaves and peck at the young shoots. It is also browsed by sheep in coastal salt meadows, where it can form huge spreading expanses. In gardens beside the sea it can be mown regularly to give an amazing grey lawn that withstands moderate foot traffic. Origin: coasts of the Mediterranean, the Atlantic, the Black Sea

Glechoma hederacea, or ground-ivy, is an easily grown ornamental groundcover for shady areas of the garden.

In the Jardin des Plantes at Montpellier ivy replaces lawn below centuries-old trees.

maintain good foliage during the dry season. It can also be used in the cracks between paving stones on a terrace, where it self-seeds cheerfully. In this case its roots spread out beneath the paving, where they find a little moisture. *Herniaria glabra* likes light sandy or stony soils with perfect drainage. Origin: Europe, Asia Minor, North Africa. Hardiness: –15 °C and below. Drought resistance code: 2. Planting density: 9 per square metre.

• ***Hertia cheirifolia*** has thick blueish-grey evergreen leaves. The plant forms a large prostrate groundcover, very ornamental when it flows over the top of a stone wall. The sparse yellow flowers appear at the end of winter. Origin: North Africa. Hardiness: –12 to –15 °C. Drought resistance code: 4. Planting density: 4 per square metre.

• ***Hyparrhenia hirta*** is a grass that is common in all the hot regions of the Mediterranean Basin: it is a pioneer species which self-seeds at roadsides and on abandoned land, sometimes forming a large-scale groundcover mass that turns golden in summer. The plant cannot tolerate too much humidity: it likes poor stony or sandy soil with perfect drainage. Origin: Mediterranean Basin. Hardiness: –8 to –10 °C (the plant resists cold better in very dry soil). Drought resistance code: 5. Planting density: 4 per square metre.

• ***Hypericum balearicum*** is a sub-shrub which grows in the rocks of the Sierra de Tramuntana in Mallorca. The dark green mass of its thick vegetation contrasts with the pale colour of the limestone rock. The plant spreads slowly to form a regular ball shape. In our garden it is one of the plants whose foliage remains attractive in summer, even during periods of great drought. The small leathery leaves, with wavy margins, give off a pleasant smell when crushed. The bright yellow flowers open from May to July. Origin: Balearic Islands. Hardiness: –12 to –15 °C. Drought resistance code: 5. Planting density: 3 or 4 per square metre.

and the North Sea. Hardiness: –15 °C and below. Drought resistance code: 5. Planting density: 3 or 4 per square metre.

• ***Hedera helix***, ivy, forms large groundcover carpets beneath trees. In the Jardin des Plantes at Montpellier, for example, it covers huge areas beneath trees that are hundreds of years old, punctuated by clumps of acanthus. Its creeping stems root on contact with the soil and its thick foliage tends to strangle any competing vegetation. An unusual option is to mow ivy regularly in order to obtain a very low-growing carpet which can withstand a moderate amount of foot traffic. It is one of the best solutions for replacing a lawn in the most inhospitable parts of the garden where shade and root competition are so great that other lawn alternatives are not feasible. Check annually that the ivy does not invade tree trunks for it likes to climb skywards as much as it likes to crawl over the ground. But allow ivy to climb on an old wall or a dead tree in one spot in the garden so you can enjoy its deliciously scented autumn flowering. The flowers are an exceptional source of nectar and pollen which benefit bees, hoverflies, ladybirds and other beneficial insects. They are followed by a generous crop of berries, which garden birds love in winter. There are many ivy species and cultivars, of differing leaf size and colour. In our garden the one that gives the best result is the common small-leaved ivy. Origin: Europe, Asia,

North Africa. Hardiness: –15 °C and below. Drought resistance code: 4. Planting density: 1 plant per 2 square metres.

• ***Helichrysum orientale*** is happy in gravel gardens, in poor, perfectly drained soil, where it forms a magnificent cushion of silver leaves. The golden yellow flowers, borne on supple stems, open in June. This species is vulnerable to *Phytophthora*: it should be reserved for unirrigated parts of the garden. We like to use its beautiful yellow flowers in beds where blue is the dominant colour, composed for example of *Lavandula* × *ginginsii* 'Goodwin Creek Grey', *Salvia interrupta* and *Perovskia* 'Blue Spire'. Origin: islands of the Mediterranean Basin. Hardiness: –10 to –12 °C. Drought resistance code: 4. Planting density: 2 or 3 per square metre.

• ***Herniaria glabra*** forms a low-growing carpet of tiny light green evergreen leaves. The plant spreads by means of its lateral stems which root wherever they are in contact with the soil. It can be used as a carpet for small surfaces subject to a moderate degree of foot traffic. It may be planted in association with the dark foliage of *Thymus praecox* and *Thymus serpyllum* 'Elfin' to create small mossy-looking carpets that mingle different shades of green. In parts of the garden which are not irrigated, the plant loses some of its leaves in summer; however, an occasional watering will enable it to

Hypericum olympicum 'Citrinum' makes a handsome groundcover with compact vegetation. Its pale yellow flowers completely cover the foliage in June.

Ipheion uniflorum 'Rolf Fiedler' self-seeds into the cracks in a paved path. (Garden of Joëlle and Lauw de Jager, nursery Bulb'Argence.)

• ***Hypericum olympicum* 'Citrinum'** forms a flattened cushion, very dense and regular. In May-June the small blueish-green leaves are covered in pretty lemon yellow flowers, topped by a tangled bunch of protruding stamens. This plant can be used, for example, between stepping stones, together with other plants that form low cushions such as *Rhodanthemum catananche*, *Veronica polifolia* or *Thymus camphoratus*. Origin: Greece, the Balkans, Turkey. Hardiness: −15 °C and below. Drought resistance code: 3. Planting density: 9 per square metre.

• ***Ipheion uniflorum* 'Rolf Fiedler'**, synonym *Tristagma peregrinans* 'Rolf Fiedler', naturalizes freely at the foot of stone walls, between paving stones on a terrace or in the midst of carpeting groundcover plants. Its generous flowering is very ornamental. In our garden we have planted it in the middle of a carpet of *Potentilla neumanniana*: in April the bright blue flowers of the *Ipheion* cultivar emerge from the brilliant yellow carpet of the potentilla. *Ipheion uniflorum*, the species, has beautiful white flowers, sometimes lightly tinged with blue. Origin: Argentina, Uruguay. Hardiness: −12 to −15 °C. Drought resistance code: 4. Planting density: 16 per square metre.

Iris lutescens (Iridaceae)

Origin: Southern Europe; **Height**: 15 cm; **Spread**: 20 to 30 cm; **Position**: sun; **Hardiness**: −15 °C and below; **Drought resistance code**: 5.

The dwarf iris of the garrigue is an excellent small groundcover which tolerates tough conditions. In the wild, it is found growing among stones along the edges of paths. Wild boars help it to spread by cutting up its rhizomes as they root about in the top layers of the soil. From March its large yellow, blue, mauve or white flowers, which seem out of proportion to the small leaves, transform the stony expanses of the garrigue into a delightful and colourful scene that heralds the end of winter. Thanks to its thick rhizomes which act as storage organs, it resists drought perfectly. It may lose its leaves at the end of summer when it becomes dormant, but new leaves are rapidly produced in autumn. In the garden it can be planted together with other garrigue plants like *Brachypodium retusum*, *Teucrium chamaedrys*, *Carex halleriana* or *Potentilla neumanniana* to create small areas of wild lawn on dry and stony soil, suitable for a moderate degree of foot traffic. It can also be used as a complement to sedums in order to add variety to green roof planting in mediterranean regions. In this case one can plant it in association with the *Sedum* species most resistant to drought, such as *Sedum gypsicola*, *Sedum sediforme*, *Sedum ochroleucum* and *Sedum album*, as well as with plants that self-seed abundantly in substrates containing a large proportion of pozzolano, such as *Asphodelus fistulosus* or *Salvia verbenaca*. The planting density varies according to the way the plant is used and the desired effect: 9 per square metre in a mixed planting, 16 per square metre in a single-species planting.

Propagation by fresh seed sown in summer: germination occurs at the beginning of autumn. If the seed is sown in autumn, the seeds will not germinate until the following year.

• ***Iris × germanica*** is an unbeatable groundcover for the stabilizing of poor, dry slopes: the network of rhizomes retains the soil and combats erosion effectively. By contrast, in good garden soil, large plantings of this iris are easily invaded by competing weeds and require regular weeding. To reduce the amount of maintenance needed, these irises can be planted in a gravel garden, where their elegant flowers emerge each year from among the lower-growing plants. Origin uncertain, *Iris × germanica* probably being a hybrid of several European species.

The rhizomes of *Iris × germanica* have insinuated themselves into the cracks in a dry-stone wall. A particularly frugal plant, the bearded iris is happy in the poorest soils

The Algerian iris (*Iris unguicularis*) has a remarkable quality: its delicate flowers open in mid-winter

Hardiness: −15 °C and below. Drought resistance code: 5. Planting density: 9 per square metre.

• *Iris unguicularis*, the Algerian iris, has narrow, graceful evergreen foliage. It forms dense clumps, less vulnerable to competition from weeds than *Iris × germanica*. The flowers are white, light blue or mauve-blue depending on the variety and appear in mid-winter, with flowering continuing from December to March. The seed is dispersed by ants and the Algerian iris naturalizes easily. In our garden it self-seeds in the mixture of soil and gravel that marks the transition between the gravel paths and the groundcover beds. Grown in association with *Euphorbia rigida*, it gives a winter-flowering picture that changes from year

This garrigue lawn comprises *Iris lutescens* and *Brachypodium retusum*. It will support some foot traffic and is adapted to poor, dry, stony ground.

to year as both plants self-seed liberally in the gravel. Origin: North Africa, Eastern Mediterranean Basin. Hardiness: −12 to −15 °C. Drought resistance code: 5. Planting density: 6 per square metre.

• *Jasminum nudiflorum*, winter jasmine, has long supple branches which root on contact with the soil. The abundant bright yellow flowers appear from December to February. Although it is often grown as a climbing plant, winter jasmine also makes a very good groundcover: tough, adaptable to many situations and long-lived. It is as happy in sun as it is in shade. It can be used equally well as a large groundcover on slopes or cascading over a wall. Although the foliage is deciduous in winter, the thick mass of interweaving stems is enough to cover the ground throughout the year, even when the plant has lost its leaves. The main disadvantage of winter jasmine is that it grows very slowly during the first years. It can be associated with other, faster-growing, twining plants, such as *Clematis cirrhosa*, which also flowers in winter, or *Lonicera splendida*, a beautiful honeysuckle with a vigorous carpeting habit. Origin: China. Hardiness: −15 °C and below. Drought resistance code: 3. Planting density: 1 per square metre.

• *Juniperus horizontalis* 'Blue Chips' forms an excellent carpeting groundcover after a few years. Its blueish grey foliage, dense and even, is effective in preventing

the germination of weeds thanks to the allelopathic properties of the essential oil given off by its leaves. Its growth is relatively slow: it is possible to fill the space around the *Juniperus* temporarily by sowing annuals or short-lived perennials, for example a mixture of love-in-a-mist and *Eschscholzia californica*. These plants will self-seed there until the *Juniperus* has completely covered the soil. Origin: North America. Hardiness: −15 °C and below. Drought resistance code: 4. Planting density: 1 per square metre.

• *Lantana montevidensis* has spreading branches which cascade down if it has been planted at the top of a wall. In gardens protected from frost it is a handsome evergreen groundcover, but elsewhere, for example in the Montpellier region of southern France, it is usually deciduous. In harsh winters the stems may partially die back from the cold, but the plant comes back vigorously from the rootstock in spring. In favourable conditions, the mauve flowers may be produced continually from May to October. Flowering in summer is more abundant if the plant receives occasional water. *Lantana montevidensis* is a plant that is happy in close proximity to the house, where it benefits both from the heat it absorbs from south-facing walls and from the water given to pot plants on the terrace or in the patio. The flowers are rich in nectar and attract numerous butterflies, while in winter the berries offer food much valued by birds. Origin: South America. Hardiness: the foliage is deciduous at −4 °C, but the plant can resprout after temperatures of −8 to −10 °C. Drought resistance code: 3. Planting density: 2 or 3 per square metre.

Lavandula × chaytorae (Lamiaceae)
Height of foliage: 20 to 30 cm; **Height when in flower**: 40 to 50 cm; **Spread**: 40 cm; **Position**: sun; **Hardiness**: −12 to −15 °C; **Drought resistance code**: 4.

Lavandula × chaytorae is a hybrid of two lavenders that are native to mountains: *Lavandula angustifolia*, which grows in the Alpes of Haute Provence, and *Lavandula lanata,* which grows in the mountains of southern Spain. This hybrid combines the qualities of its two parents: its drought resistance and silver foliage come from *Lavandula lanata*, while its tolerance of cold and its compact habit come from *Lavandula*

angustifolia. The flowers, a rich and deep mauve, appear from June to the end of July, sometimes even to the beginning of August. Among all the lavenders in our collection, *Lavandula × chaytorae* is the one that lives longest. In our gravel garden we like to grow it beside other silver-leaved plants, such as *Teucrium cossonii*, *Achillea umbellata* or *Salvia lavandulifolia* subsp. *oxyodon*, which make a very attractive sight throughout the year, even when they are not in flower. There are several cultivars of *Lavandula × chaytorae*, including 'Richard Gray', which forms a beautiful regular cushion, 'Silver Frost', which has the most luminously silver foliage, and 'Sawyers', whose spreading vegetation remains very low. All these cultivars have identical requirements: they cannot tolerate irrigation in summer and need poor stony or sandy soil with perfect drainage. Planting density: 6 per square metre.
Propagation by ripe wood cuttings in autumn.

• *Lavandula dentata* is a pioneer plant that colonizes the edges of paths and degraded garrigue in southern Spain and Morocco. It self-seeds abundantly in poor and stony soils. In gardens situated in mild climates its outstanding flowering continues for more than eight months, lasting from autumn to spring. The plant then becomes dormant with the advent of the hot season, just

when most other lavenders are starting to flower. In our garden the cold prevents it from flowering in early winter, but by way of compensation it seems even more abundant when the plant bursts into flower in March. The leaf colour varies according to the variety. The species type found in Spain has light green leaves, the variety found in the Atlas Mountains has grey foliage, and the variety that grows on the coast between Essaouira and Agadir, near Cape Rirh, has velvety silver foliage which turns almost white in summer. The flowers may be pale

The early flowering of *Lavandula dentata* stands out in a large bed containing a mixture of lavenders, achilleas, *Phlomis*, *Anthyllis* and salvias.

Lavandula dentata 'Adrar M'Korn' is a cultivar with dark flowers.

Lavandula × chaytorae forms a fine regular cushion. Of all our lavenders, this is the one best suited to small groundcover beds in combination with other cushion-shaped plants. Here it is growing with *Santolina × lindavica*.

Among the many cultivars of *Lavandula* × *intermedia*, 'Alba' is distinguished by the remarkable abundance of its pure white flowers.

mauve, violet-blue or pink according to the cultivar. We particularly like two cultivars, named after their places of origin in Morocco: 'Adrar M'Korn', with dark flowers, and 'Imi n'Ifri', with pale pink flowers. Origin: Iberian peninsula, Morocco. Hardiness: –6 to –8 °C (it resists cold better in very dry soil). Drought resistance code: 6. Planting density: 2 or 3 per square metre.

• *Lavandula* × *ginginsii* 'Goodwin Creek Grey' is an excellent groundcover plant for mild climates. It forms a large spreading cushion whose toothed leaves recall its parent *Lavandula dentata*. Its dark violet-coloured flowers, borne on long branching spikes, continue from spring to the beginning of the summer. It is happy in the driest parts of the garden, in poor, stony soil with perfect drainage. In our garden we like to grow it in association with other plants with blue-mauve flowers which appreciate the same growing conditions, such as *Salvia interrupta*, *Salvia candelabrum* and *Salvia*

clevelandii. Origin: a hybrid of *Lavandula dentata* and *Lavandula lanata*. Hardiness: –6 to –8 °C (it resists cold better in very dry soil). Drought resistance code: 5. Planting density: 2 or 3 per square metre.

• *Lavandula* × *intermedia* is vulnerable to die-back caused by the diseases that develop if one keeps the soil moist during hot weather; this lavender should be planted only in the zone of the garden that receives no irrigation. To ensure that the plant has a good lifespan, it is better to avoid planting it in uniform masses, which promote the rapid spread of diseases. If you wish to create a large lavender bed, it is preferable to plant many species and cultivars together: the staggered flowering seasons, the diversity of flower colours which range from white to pale blue to mauve or violet-blue, and the grey, green or silvery foliage are all worth making the most of in a large groundcover garden. In our own garden we like to complete these mixed beds with plants whose

flowering serves as a visual counterpoint, such as *Santolina* × *lindavica*, *Anthyllis cytisoides*, *Hypericum empetrifolium* or *Cistus* × *tardiflorens*. The spent flowering stems of *Lavandula* × *intermedia* can be clipped off in mid-summer: the foliage is then rapidly refurbished in autumn and one can enjoy the compact ball shapes which give structure to the garden all winter long. Covering the soil with a mineral mulch enables one to plant lavenders far enough apart to emphasize their natural growth habits, while at the same time reducing the amount of weeding needed. Here are some cultivars of *Lavandula* × *intermedia* which do well in our gravel garden: 'Super', whose sky-blue flowers are particularly abundant, 'Grosso', with violet-blue flowers, 'Alba', with magnificent white flowers, and 'Nizza', whose lovely silvery-grey foliage forms a vigorous mass. *Lavandula* × *intermedia* is a hybrid of *Lavandula angustifolia* and *Lavandula latifolia*, which both grow in stony soils: both it and its cultivars prefer poor soils, stony or sandy, with perfect drainage. Hardiness: −15 °C and below. Drought resistance code: 4.

• *Lavandula × losae* is a little-known plant, with magnificent foliage: in our collection, it is without doubt the lavender with the most beautiful leaves, silvery and woolly. It is only happy in poor and stony soils: if you garden on clay soil it is not worth bothering with – it will remain feeble and straggly, then little by little will die. It is a hybrid of *Lavandula lanata* and *Lavandula latifolia* and, although most lavender hybrids are sterile (as for example *Lavandula × intermedia* and its cultivars), this particular one is fertile: the dried flower spikes bear numerous small shiny black seeds, which self-sow willingly among stones. It is thus a good idea to wait until the seeds have fallen to the ground before clipping off the faded spikes. This lavender can be planted to seed itself on top of a dry-stone wall or between stone steps. Its branching spikes form an airy mass of very dark violet-blue flowers, which contrast with the very pale silvery foliage. We like to grow *Lavandula × losae* with other woolly-leaved plants that self-seed among stones, such as *Sideritis cypria* or *Stachys cretica*. Hardiness: −10 to −12 ° (it resists cold best in very dry soil). Drought resistance code: 4. Planting density: 4 per square metre.

Leucophyllum langmaniae
(Scrophulariaceae)

Origin: Mexico; **Height**: 80 cm to 1 m; **Spread**: 1 m; **Position**: sun; **Hardiness**: −10 to −12 °C; **Drought resistance code**: 6.

A shrub with grey-green, slightly velvety evergreen leaves. The very dense foliage forms a regular rounded mass. The bright pink flowers appear in successive waves from late August to October. The density of the flowers varies: at the beginning of flowering they are often not very abundant and blend into the foliage prettily. Then come further waves of flowers, sometimes so profuse that the foliage is completely hidden and for a few weeks the plant is the main point of interest in the garden, at a time of year when few plants are flowering. To break the austerity of the dry garden at the end of

summer, *Leucophyllum langmaniae* can be planted with a selection of the plants whose flowering brightens groundcover beds at the same season, such as *Salvia chamaedryoides*, *Epilobium canum* 'Catalina', *Stipa calamagrostis*, *Colchicum lusitanum* and *Sternbergia lutea*. Native to the shallow soils of the Chihuahua desert, *Leucophyllum langmaniae* likes poor soil with perfect drainage. Planting density: 1 per square metre.
Propagation by semi-ripe cuttings in autumn.

Limoniastrum monopetalum 'Carnaval' (Plumbaginaceae)

Origin: Mediterranean littoral; **Height**: 25 cm; **Spread**: 1 m; **Position**: sun; **Hardiness**: −10 to −12 °C; **Drought resistance code**: 5.

A sub-shrub with silver-grey evergreen leaves. The plant forms an excellent, dense groundcover, effective in limiting competition from weeds. It spreads laterally thanks to its prostrate branches which root on contact with the soil. It grows naturally at the edge of coastal mudflats and is thus well able to survive both temporary flooding and periods of intense drought. It withstands salt spray perfectly well. The thick and leathery leaves have a curious granular texture due to the salt crystals that are exuded by their cells which accumulate on the leaf surfaces. In the garden it is easy to grow: it grows faster in a friable well-drained soil but is able to adapt to many different conditions. It makes a very handsome groundcover on a slope or

in a gravel garden. The cultivar 'Carnaval' has a particularly carpeting habit, with striking flowers. The supple inflorescences, more or less lying on the foliage, look bicoloured: the small flowers are violet-pink when they open, then turn pale pink before they fade. *Limoniastrum monopetalum* is a protected species in France. Although the cultivar 'Carnaval' can be planted in gardens, large-scale planting to rehabilitate coastal environments requires the propagation of genetic stock that is local, as well as permission from the relevant authorities. In other countries of South-West Europe, the plant's status is very different: for example, in spite of the fact that it is native to the Iberian peninsula, *Limoniastrum monopetalum* is considered to be a potentially invasive plant in the Balearic Islands. *Limoniastrum* thus demonstrates the diversity of possible points of view as regards the conservation of plants. Planting density: 1 per square metre.
Propagation by cuttings from young shoots in autumn or spring, or by seed in autumn.

• *Limonium pruinosum* is a small perennial pioneer plant which self-seeds easily in tough conditions. It tolerates both poor, stony soils and clay soils that are sometimes waterlogged – something relatively rare

Limoniastrum monopetalum 'Carnaval' makes a powerful groundcover whose dense vegetation limits competition from weeds effectively.

in mediterranean plants. It can resist episodes of the most intense drought. The first time we saw this plant was beside a track in the Negev Desert, one of the driest places around the Mediterranean. It is partially deciduous in summer, which reduces water loss from the leaves, but the light mass of small mauve flowers remains ornamental throughout the summer. In autumn the spent inflorescences can be cut back. The rosettes of thick leaves then make pretty cushions that last all winter. Origin: North Africa, Middle East. Hardiness: –10 to –12 °C. Drought resistance code: 6. Planting density: 9 per square metre.

Lonicera splendida has twining stems that form a dense groundcover. The flowers appear in spring, perfuming the air with their sweet scent.

• ***Lonicera splendida*** is a honeysuckle with semi-evergreen leaves whose pretty yellow and white flowers, abundant and sweetly scented, are pollinated by butterflies. The plant makes a vigorous groundcover thanks to its twining branches which root wherever they are in contact with the soil. Its supple vegetation is easily integrated into large groundcover beds, among cistuses, rosemaries and *Phlomis species*. Origin: mountains of Southern Spain. Hardiness: –12 to –15 °C. Drought resistance code: 4. Planting density: 1 per square metre.

• ***Lotus corniculatus***, bird's-foot trefoil, is a small groundcover that naturalizes easily in wild lawns or flowering steppes, where it can withstand regular foot traffic. Its bright yellow flowers appear in abundance from May to July and are rich in nectar. They attract many beneficial insects to the garden, such as hoverflies and lacewings. *Lotus corniculatus* forms a small flattened cushion, very ornamental when entirely covered in flowers. If it is mown, it produces new flower buds shortly afterwards.

In wild lawns it can be grown with *Prunella vulgaris, Bellis perennis, Potentilla neumanniana* and *Plantago coronopus*. In flowering steppes it can be planted on a bed of gravel with *Thymus praecox, Teucrium aureum* and *Achillea odorata* to create ornamental scenes that resemble the natural steppes seen on the Larzac plateau. In poor soils it aids the growth of surrounding plants thanks to the nitrogen-fixing nodules on its roots. It can be planted together with the strawberry clover to fertilize Bermuda grass lawns naturally. This plant is easy to grow. It is unfussy about soil type, doing equally well in heavy soil and in stony soil. Origin: Europe, Asia, North Africa. Hardiness: –15 °C and below. Drought resistance code: 3. Planting density: 9 per square metre.

Matricaria tchihatchewii (Asteraceae)

Origin: Asia Minor; **Height of foliage**: 2 to 5 cm depending on cultivation conditions and amount of foot traffic; **Height when in flower**: 15 to 20 cm; **Spread**: 50 cm and more; **Position**: sun or semi-shade; **Hardiness**: –15 °C and below; **Drought resistance code**: 1.5.

A carpeting perennial with finely-cut evergreen leaves of a pretty light green. The stems root on contact with the soil and form an even carpet capable of withstanding a moderate degree of foot traffic. This *Matricaria* has long been famed as an alternative to lawn: it was already described as one of the best groundcovers suitable for foot traffic in the French encyclopaedic

almanac *Le Bon Jardinier* [The Good Gardener] in the 19th century. The arrival of lawns composed entirely of grass caused it to be forgotten, in the same way that the achilleas and clovers, formerly considered as useful groundcovers, came to be thought of as weeds to do battle with.

There is an interesting mutually beneficial interaction between matricaria and the marmalade hoverfly *(Episyrphus balteatus)*. In late spring the matricaria is covered in small white daisies, rich in pollen, which attract the hoverflies. Just at that moment the turgescent tissues of the matricaria are subject to attack by aphids, barely visible since they hide in the leaf axils yet numerous enough to weaken the plant for a short while. Luckily, the hoverflies attracted by the flowers may lay numerous tiny white eggs that hatch to release an army of little transparent larvae which feed exclusively on aphids. Most of the time the gardener is blissfully unaware that all this is taking place: we have been growing *Matricaria tchihatchewii* in our garden for more than twenty years, yet it was only recently that we took the time to notice the silent battle unfolding beneath our feet each year. The outcome of this battle is in any case not a foregone conclusion since it depends on the overall practices adopted by the gardener. In a garden where chemical treatments are used to combat

Matricaria tchihatchewii makes a carpet covered in small white daisy flowers in late spring.

The blue flowers of *Muscari neglectum* mingle with the yellow flowers of hawk's beard in this wild lawn consisting of clover, daisies, plantains and black medick.

pests, hoverflies, which are particularly sensitive to the chemical constituents of garden insecticides, rapidly disappear, to the great joy of the greenfly. On the contrary, in a garden designed to encourage the presence of beneficial insects (see page 151), the aphid populations on *Matricaria* are only a transitory problem.

Athough its vegetation is low, *Matricaria* can be mown once a year, after flowering, to remove the faded flower heads. In summer it needs to be watered about once a week to remain green during the dry season. If it receives no water the plant becomes dormant and loses some of its leaves until it is refurbished by the first autumn rains. It is generally used as a carpet to cover smaller areas of a few dozen square metres, since it requires hand-weeding. If larger areas are to be covered, it can be mixed with other carpeting plants such as *Thymus hirsutus*, *Achillea crithmifolia* and *Trifolium fragiferum* to create large flowering groundcovers that need less maintenance than single-species carpets. *Matricaria tchihatchewii* is unfussy about soil type. However, it grows faster during the first year in friable, deeply decompacted and well-drained soils. Planting density: 4 per square metre. *Propagation by softwood cuttings in autumn.*

• **Medicago arborea**, the tree medick, is a pioneer plant which self-seeds easily on degraded slopes or in the wild parts of the garden. The orange-yellow flowers appear in winter and early spring. Rich in nectar, they attract numerous beneficial insects at a season when other flowers are still few. It can be planted in large groundcover beds together with other early-flowering species such as *Teucrium fruticans*, *Coronilla valentina* subsp. *glauca* and *Rosmarinus officinalis* 'Spice Islands', a vigorous rosemary with bright blue flowers. Origin: Eastern Mediterranean Basin, naturalized in Italy, France and Spain. Hardiness: −10 to −12 °C. Drought resistance code: 4. Planting density: 1 per square metre.

• **Medicago sativa**, lucerne, has roots which can reach a depth of more than 2 m, giving the plant an exceptional resistance to drought. We have noticed in the Middle East, from where the plant originates, that lucerne is one of the last plants to survive on roadsides as one approaches desert areas. In spite of the heat and drought, it is able to flower uninterruptedly from June to November in gardens in the South of France. It can be planted with other perennials that flower all summer long in dry ground, like mallow, fennel and wild chicory, to colonize the wild parts of the garden. These four species all have strong twisting roots which help decompact the soil. All are sources of honey and attract into the garden a large number of beneficial insects such as hoverflies, lacewings and ladybirds. Lucerne has become naturalized on all continents and is sometimes considered to be an invasive plant, in spite of the fact that no negative impact from it has been cited. Hardiness: −15 °C and below. Drought resistance code: 6. Planting density: 4 per square metre if pot-grown plants are used, but this species is more often sown directly *in situ* since it germinates easily in the open ground.

• **Muscari neglectum**, the common grape hyacinth, decorates thin lawns in spring, where its tight clusters of dark blue-mauve, almost black, flowers mingle with the yellow flowers of dandelions, black medick (*Medicago lupulina*) and hawk's beard (*Crepis sancta*). The small flowers are bell-shaped, their narrow openings fringed with a toothed white crown that serves as a visual guide to pollinators. The flowers contain abundant nectar, very desirable to bees and hoverflies. They are pleasantly scented (the name *Muscari* derives from the Latin *muscus*, "musk"). *Muscari neglectum* self-seeds easily in wild lawns, and also spreads by means of its numerous bulbils. Other *Muscari* and related species are equally easy to grow, such as *Leopoldia comosa*, the tasselled grape hyacinth, and *Muscari armeniacum*, with particularly ornamental flower spikes. They can be planted together with many other bulbous species which combine to transform a neglected lawn into a striking and refined sight: *Ornithogalum umbellatum* or Star-of-Bethlehem, *Narcissus tazetta*, *Anemone coronaria*, *Ipheion uniflorum*, *Crocus speciosus* or *Crocus tommasinianus*. Origin: Southern Europe, North Africa, Asia Minor. Hardiness: −15 °C and below. Drought resistance code: 4. Planting density: 16 per square metre.

• **Myoporum parvifolium** is a vigorous carpeting groundcover plant suitable for gardens in mild climates. Its spreading or fountaining stems hug the ground. Its small thick leaves form a dense mat, reputed to delay fire in regions where there is an increased risk of forest fires. The plant is covered in small honey-bearing flowers from May to July. Origin: Australia. Hardiness: −4 to −6 °C. Drought resistance code: 4. Planting density: 2 or 3 per square metre.

• **Narcissus tazetta** grows wild in the dry grasslands around the Mediterranean,

and continue successively throughout the winter. It can be associated with different varieties of *Iris unguicularis* to create pretty flowering scenes at Christmas.

• **Nepeta racemosa** seeds itself freely between stepping stones or stone steps. In late spring its pretty pale blue flowers make a light mass above the grey leaves. It can be combined with *Erigeron karvinskianus*, *Geranium sanguineum* and *Lotus corniculatus* to add flowers for a long period to low walls and old steps. Origin: the Caucasus, Turkey, Iran. Hardiness: −15 °C and below. Drought resistance code: 4. Planting density: 9 per square metre.

• **Ononis speciosa** has sticky, dark green, very aromatic foliage. In April the plant is covered in lemon-yellow flowers arranged in very ornamental narrow clusters. The

Ononis speciosa is a tough species which can be included in large groundcover beds.

A few months after being planted, *Narcissus* 'Paper White' is already in full flower. Between the narcissi one can just make out the young carpeting plants which will in the future form our garden's "flowering steppe".

often in hollows in damp valleys, but also in dry meadows and on rocky hillsides. Magnificent colonies of this narcissus can be seen in olive groves on Greek islands, growing with anemones and *Muscari*. Its white flowers, with an orange corolla, appear from February to April. They are very decorative and sweetly scented. In the garden, *Narcissus tazetta* naturalizes easily in mixed lawns consisting of daisies, clover and self-heal. It is necessary to wait until the narcissus leaves have turned yellow in late spring before giving the first mowing. It can also be planted between ball- or cushion-shaped plants in a gravel garden, along with other elegant species such as *Narcissus jonquilla* or *Narcissus*

bulbocodium. Origin: Mediterranean Basin. Hardiness: −12 to −15 °C. Drought resistance code: 3. Planting density: 16 per square metre.

Many other narcissi can also be used in groundcover gardens. The hybrid 'Tête à Tête', for example, is a dwarf narcissus which can be planted directly into the middle of carpets of *Frankenia laevis*, *Thymus ciliatus* or *Cerastium candidissimum*. *Narcissus × odorus* is a more vigorous hybrid that can colonize large areas of wild lawns, making a spectacular effect at the beginning of spring every year. *Narcissus* 'Paper White', also called 'Totus Albus', has white, heavily-scented flowers that open in early December

Narcissus 'Tête-à-Tête' is a dwarf narcissus, useful as an addition to groundcover carpets and gravel gardens. Here we have planted it in the middle of a cushion of *Cerastium candidissimum*. In the foreground the powerful flowering spike of an *Asphodelus microcarpus* is developing.

foliage is partially deciduous in summer, thus allowing the plant to resist long periods of drought. We have observed that it copes well with competition from the roots of old trees like pines or cypresses. This tough species deserves to be better known. It can be used in large beds of perennials and shrubs, together with cistuses, euphorbias, scabious and *Phlomis*. Origin: Southern Spain. Hardiness: –10 to –12 °C. Drought resistance code: 5. Planting density: 2 per square metre.

Ophiopogon japonicus (Liliaceae)
Lily turf

Origin: Japan, Korea; **Height**: 5 to 20 cm depending on cultivation conditions and degree of foot traffic; **Spread**: 20 cm or more; **Position**: sun or shade; **Hardiness**: –12 to –15 °C; **Drought resistance code**: 2.

A perennial with narrow dark green evergreen leaves that forms a very dense carpet. The plant spreads slowly by means of its creeping rhizomes. In summer short racemes of white flowers appear, often partially concealed by the tough foliage. The flowers are followed by ornamental berries of an amazing china blue colour. Although *Ophiopogon* tolerates sun, it is more often used in shady sites where the range of suitable groundcovers is markedly more restricted. In the Botanical Garden of Lisbon, for example, this plant covers the soil at the foot of centuries-old trees. It may be mown if one wants a very low-growing carpet that can withstand moderate foot traffic. It tolerates drought but gives better results if regularly watered, about once a week during the hot season. It forms a very ornamental carpet but its slow rate of growth limits its use to small areas because of the amount of weeding needed during its first years. To cover larger areas, one could plant section by section, *Ophiopogon* being easy to propagate from plants that are already established. In parts of the garden that are regularly irrigated, it is possible to plant *Ophiopogon* together with faster-growing groundcovers such as *Soleirolia soleirolii*, *Dichondra repens* or *Glechoma hederacea*, which temporarily occupy the free space then progressively cede their place to the *Ophiopogon*. *Ophiopogon japonicus* prefers friable, well-drained soil. Planting density: 25 per square metre.
Propagation by seed in autumn or by division in autumn or spring.

Origanum vulgare (Lamiaceae)
Oregano

Origin: Europe, Asia; **Height of foliage**: 5 to 10 cm; **Height when in flower**: 40 to 50 cm; **Spread**: 50 cm and more; **Position**: sun; **Hardiness**: –15 °C and below; **Drought resistance code**: 3.

A perennial with light green, downy semi-evergreen leaves. The plant spreads by means of its rhizomes. Glands on the lamina are pierced whenever one brushes against the plant, releasing the essential oil which possesses aromatic and allelopathic qualities. In the garden, oregano makes an excellent groundcover requiring minimal maintenance: once it is well established, no weeding is necessary. The subspecies *hirtum*, whose carpeting vegetation is particularly vigorous, has white flowers, while the subspecies *vulgare*, whose groundcover potential is more modest, has pink flowers. The flowers open in June-July and stay ornamental for a long time thanks to the bracts which remain on the inflorescences. At the end of summer the faded inflorescences can be cut down, to allow the new shoots to form a dense carpet quickly. In our garden we like to plant oregano with other perennials that possess allelopathic properties, for example *Achillea coarctata*, *Centaurea bella* and *Thymus ciliatus*, in order to create large groundcover beds that require a reduced amount of maintenance. Oregano likes light, well-drained soils. Planting density: 4 per square metre.
Propagation by seed or division in autumn, or by softwood cuttings in spring.

• ***Origanum laevigatum*** is distinguished by its light mass of small violet-pink flowers which are produced in succession all summer long, in spite of drought and heat. The foliage is dark green in winter but takes on a blueish tinge when the plant is preparing to flower. The rhizomatous stock develops into a small, dense groundcover, with the same allelopathic properties as *Origanum vulgare*. The different oregano species cross-breed easily, so that in gardens one may find interesting hybrids between *Origanum laevigatum* and *Origanum vulgare*, for example the variety named 'Hopley's', whose flowering is particularly generous. Origin: Turkey, Cyprus. Hardiness: –12 to –15 °C. Drought resistance code: 4. Planting density: 6 per square metre.

Many other oreganos have a place in the groundcover garden. *Origanum microphyllum* forms a small cushion of grey leaves, covered in a mist of mauve flowers in early summer. *Origanum dictamnus*, or dittany, has beautiful drooping inflorescences whose curious green bracts turn a mauveish pink as flowering continues. Its leaves, covered in silver hairs, give off a particularly powerful scent when crushed, at once powerful, sharp and spicy. It is happy in gravel gardens with perfect drainage. *Origanum scabrum* subsp. *pulchrum* produces a spectacular show of mauveish pink flowers in the middle of the summer, at a time when most of the plants in the garden are dormant. *Origanum* 'Kent Beauty', a hybrid of *Origanum scabrum* and *Origanum rotundifolium*, forms a small, spreading groundcover, whose leaves are deciduous in winter. Its drooping inflorescences have very decorative bracts, pink mixed with green. *Origanum majorana* var. *tenuifolium*, which for a long time we grew under the mistaken name of *Origanum dubium*, forms a regular ball of velvety grey evergreen leaves whose sweet and powdery

In spite of drought and heat, the pinkish-mauve flowers of *Origanum laevigatum* appear in succession throughout the summer. Here it is mixed with the mauve flowers of *Goniolimon speciosum*, another perennial remarkable for its long summer flowering.

The drooping inflorescences of *Origanum* 'Kent Beauty' have green bracts which change colour as flowering progresses: they start off pale green, then turn pale pink and finally purple.

scent is extraordinary – it is one of the most aromatic plants in our garden.

• ***Osteospermum caulescens*** has spectacular pale pink flowers and is of mountain origin. Resists cold better than *Osteospermum fruticosum* but tolerates drought less well. Origin: South Africa. Hardiness: –10 to –12 °C. Drought resistance: 2. Planting density: 6 per square metre.

• ***Osteospermum fruticosum*** is a groundcover appreciated for its rapid growth and abundant flowering in gardens that are situated in mild climates. It spreads over the soil or cascades down if one plants it at the top of a wall. The mauve flowers open at the end of January and continue in succession until May. The cultivar 'Album' has beautiful white flowers with a mauve tinge on the backs of their petals. Origin: South Africa. Hardiness: about –5 to –7 °C. Drought resistance code: 4. Planting density: 2 or 3 per square metre.

In gardens situated in a mild climate, the mauve flowers of *Osteospermum fruticosum* open in January.

Pallenis maritima (Asteraceae)

Synonym: *Asteriscus maritimus*

Origin: Western Mediterranean Basin; **Height**: 15 to 20 cm; **Spread**: 40 cm; **Position**: sun; **Hardiness**: –6 to –8 °C; **Drought resistance code**: 4.5.

A perennial with thick, dark green, evergreen leaves that forms a small spreading cushion. The daisy-like bright yellow flowers open from April to June. The extensive root system allows the plant to anchor itself in crevices in sea cliffs, where it grows almost without competition thanks to its ability to withstand direct contact with salt spray. The plant self-seeds easily in poor and stony soil. It is one of the best groundcover plants for rocks by the sea, where it can be grown together with *Crithmum maritimum*,

or samphire, and *Lotus cytisoides*. These native plants are useful when one is trying to replace Hottentot Figs (*Carpobrotus* sp.), which are invasive on coasts. In a mild climate, *Pallenis maritima* is equally happy in gardens situated far from the sea: it can be used in the cracks between paving stones on a terrace or between stepping stones. It requires a light stony or sandy soil with perfect drainage. Planting density: 6 per square metre.

Propagation by seed in autumn or by softwood cuttings in autumn or spring.

Phillyrea angustifolia (Oleaceae)

Origin: Mediterranean Basin; **Height**: up to 2 to 3 m, but tolerates being kept lower by regular pruning; **Spread**: 2 m; **Position**: sun or shade; **Hardiness**: –12 to –15 °C; **Drought resistance code**: 5.

A shrub with narrow, leathery, dark green evergreen leaves. *Phillyrea* holds a preeminent position as a groundcover beside the sea. It is salt-tolerant and can be used as a front-line plant right on the coast. Wind, sand and salt spray will then sculpt its vegetation into a large, low-growing cushion that is very striking. In regions where goats put a lot of pressure on garrigue vegetation, as in the Greek islands for example, one may also see phillyreas hugging the rocks, forming curious woody-based carpets. In the garden, inspired by these natural scenes, one can create large groundcover beds using

Pallenis maritima self-seeds easily in stony soil. Here it forms a pretty, irregular groundcover beneath *Helichrysum orientale*.

When battered by wind and salt spray, phillyrea grows into a strong, ground-hugging cushion, as here at Cape Creus in Spanish Catalonia. In the garden one can easily sculpt the vegetation of phillyrea into a broad, spreading ball.

phillyrea along with other evergreen shrubs such as lentisk, wild olive and bupleurum. These shrubs should be pruned once a year to keep them at the desired height. They are usually planted at a low density, for in time their lateral spread is significant. A mineral mulch will limit the germination of weeds during the first years until the thick vegetation of the shrub covers the whole bed. Alternatively, fast-growing pioneer plants can be used in this type of planting, such as for example *Achillea nobilis*, *Achillea crithmifolia* and *Achillea coarctata*, whose herbaceous vegetation will temporarily fill the spaces between the structural plants. The small flowers of the phillyrea appear in spring – not very visible but a rich source of honey. In winter the berries are an important food for birds at a time when other sources of food, such as insects, are less available. *Phillyrea* is unfussy about soil type. Planting density: from 1 per square metre to 1 per 2 square metres, depending on the rapidity of coverage desired.
Propagation by fresh seed in autumn or by softwood cuttings in spring.

Phlomis × *cytherea* (Lamiaceae)

Origin: natural hybrid in Crete and other Aegean islands (the name *cytherea* derives

This groundcover bed requires little maintenance as the dense vegetation of the spreading cushion-shaped plants limits competition from weeds. This planting consists of *Euphorbia spinosa* (in the foreground), *Artemisia alba* (in the middle) and *Phlomis* 'Edward Bowles' (in the background). The silver foliage in the right foreground is that of *Artemisia arborescens* 'Carcassonne'.

Phlomis × *cytherea* naturally maintains a compact ball shape.

from Cythera, an island off the south of the Peloponnese); **Height**: 60 to 80 cm; **Spread**: 80 cm; **Position**: sun; **Hardiness**: –10 to –12 °C; **Drought resistance code**: 5.

A shrub with evergreen leaves that are grey-green on the surface and cottony white on the underside. The leaves are slightly rolled in at the edges, creating an elegant silver margin. The bright yellow flowers appear in April-May. The plant forms a spreading ball, whose attractive regular shape contributes to the structure of a gravel garden. As the leaves are renewed each year, little by little a thick litter of old leaves accumulates round the base of the *Phlomis* which inhibits the germination of weeds though the chemical substances it releases as the leaves decompose (allelopathy). In our garden we like to plant *Phlomis* × *cytherea* together with other ball-shaped plants such as *Ballota hirsuta*, *Santolina* × *lindavica* and *Cistus* × *pauranthus* 'Natacha', all of which are plants that require little maintenance apart from an annual pruning. Pruning *Phlomis* is not a pleasant task for the minute hairs that cover the leaves detach easily and can irritate one's throat. To avoid this problem, we prefer to prune *Phlomis* in damp weather, for example just after the first autumn rain, since

the hairs don't fly about when the leaves are wet. The dry inflorescences arranged in tiers remain ornamental throughout the summer, which is another reason to delay pruning until autumn. *Phlomis* × *cytherea* requires well-drained soil. Planting density: 2 per square metre.
Propagation by semi-ripe cuttings in autumn.

• ***Phlomis chrysophylla*** has grey-green leaves which in summer are covered in a thick down of yellow hairs. It is a relatively slow-growing shrub that requires little maintenance: it keeps its compact shape without pruning. Its golden summer foliage can be used to create interesting contrasts in large groundcover beds. It can be planted with other plants whose foliage is particularly attractive in summer, such as *Cistus* × *tardiflorens*, with silver foliage, *Phlomis purpurea* subsp. *almeriensis*, with luminous, almost white foliage, *Hypericum balearicum*, with light green foliage, or *Cistus* × *ledon*, with very dark foliage that looks almost black in the summer light. Origin: Lebanon, Syria, Jordan. Hardiness: –10 to –12 °C. Drought resistance code: 6. Planting density: 2 per square metre.

• ***Phlomis* 'Edward Bowles'** is probably a hybrid of a herbaceous *Phlomis* with a suckering habit (*Phlomis russeliana*) and a shrubby *Phlomis* (*Phlomis fruticosa*). Combining the characteristics of both its parents, it forms a vigorous spreading groundcover whose large leaves are evergreen or semi-evergreen (they sometimes fall in extremely cold weather). The pale yellow flowers are arranged in whorls along the long stems that emerge from the foliage. This *Phlomis*, a hybrid acquired by the

A soft combination of *Phlomis purpurea* and *Artemisia thuscula* in a large groundcover bed.

In our garden *Phyla canescens* loses all its leaves in winter. We have to wait until April before the new vegetation pushes up through the network of bare stems that covers the ground in winter.

Hillier nursery in England, is adaptable to different growing conditions. It is often used in England in mixed borders where it is valued for its generous flowering. One can see it, for example, in a long border at the Cambridge Botanic Gardens, where is is planted with *Stipa gigantea* and *Verbena bonariensis*, to make a very ornamental display in late spring. Hardiness: –12 to –15 °C. Drought resistance code: 3. Planting density: 1 or 2 per square metre.

• *Phlomis lychnitis* is a small carpeting groundcover with pretty grey leaves. It is happy in poor and stony soils. Its yellow flowers, borne on short inflorescences, are very abundant in May. In our gravel garden we like to plant it with other grey-leaved carpeting plants that flower at the same time, such as *Salvia lavandulifolia* subsp. *oxyodon*, *Cerastium candidissimum* or *Teucrium cossonii*. It can also be planted in areas of garrigue lawn, together with *Brachypodium retusum*, *Carex halleriana*, *Iris lutescens*, *Salvia verbenaca* and *Thymus vulgaris*. Origin: South of France, Spain, Portugal. Hardiness: –12 to –15 °C. Drought resistance code: 5. Planting density: 6 per square metre.

• *Phlomis purpurea* is easy to grow and is happy in poor and stony soils. It is of unfailing value in large groundcover beds, where it can be planted with other shrubs like *Scabiosa cretica*, *Cistus × skanbergii* and *Artemisia thuscula*. The species has delicate pink flowers which blend into the downy grey foliage. The cultivar *Phlomis purpurea* 'Alba' has lovely white flowers, while the leaves of *Phlomis purpurea* subsp. *almeriensis* become a very luminous silver colour in periods of extreme drought. Origin: Spain, Portugal. Hardiness: –10 to –12 °C (the plant

is less hardy in wet soil). Drought resistance code: 5. Planting density: 1 per square metre.

Phyla canescens (Verbenaceae) Lippia

Synonyms: *Lippia canescens*, *Lippia repens*.
Origin: South America, naturalized in many parts of the world; **Height**: 1 to about 5 cm, depending on cultivation conditions and degree of foot traffic; **Spread**: 1 m or more; **Position**: sun or semi-shade; **Hardiness**: –10 to –12 °C; **Drought resistance code**: 3.

A perennial with small green leaves, deciduous in winter. The pinkish white flowers, which are scented and a good source of honey, are produced in succession throughout the summer. The plant spreads rapidly by means of its lateral stems that root on contact with the soil. *Phyla* makes an excellent groundcover, robust and easy to grow. Its water requirements are low, it withstands intense foot traffic and it is not prone to diseases. It requires neither fertilizing nor mowing. With a deep watering once or twice a month in the hot season it will give a beautiful, even carpet, but it is also possible not to water *Phyla* at all once it is established; in this case its vegetation becomes partially dormant in late summer. It has received a favourable vote from many gardeners and represents one of the best alternatives to lawn in mediterranean gardens, allowing the gardener to save on water consumption, fertilizers and pesticides. Nevertheless, in our experience there is no "miracle groundcover plant": *Phyla* also has a few drawbacks. In the South of France, for example, it loses all

its leaves in winter, with the result that the groundcover carpet no longer looks ornamental. With the first frosts the vegetation takes on a curious dark appearance which is not attractive, since the dead leaves remain on the plant for some time. In late winter, when the leaves have fallen, the bare skeleton of stems shows, close to the ground. The *Phyla* carpet is now temporarily vulnerable to competition from weeds. Thus at this time of year one or two hand-weeding sessions are needed, until the *Phyla* comes back into leaf during April. Hence single-species plantings of *Phyla* are suitable only for modest areas of a few dozen square metres, so that the weeding required does not become

Phyla canescens is one of the groundcover plants that can be walked on and requires less maintenance than a conventional lawn. It can be grown in association with many other carpeting groundcovers such as achilleas, clovers and creeping thymes.

too much of a constraint. When larger areas are to be planted one can opt instead for mixed plantings so as to benefit from the remarkable qualities of *Phyla* while at the same time limiting its disadvantages.

In our experience, *Phyla* goes well with species that have a complementary growth cycle, such as *Trifolium fragiferum, Achillea crithmifolia, Thymus ciliatus* or *Thymus hirsutus*. In this way one obtains a carpet suitable for foot traffic which requires a limited amount of weeding since the soil has better coverage throughout the year. The diversity of foliage colours also serves to mask the possible presence of young weeds. Weeding can be replaced by occasional mowing, which prevents the weeds from growing tall. Some gardeners also choose to mow *Phyla* in order to cut off its flowers in summer, to avoid the presence of bees. Bees may indeed be perceived as a nuisance, either for psychological reasons (they are often confused with wasps), or because the area planted with *Phyla* is in a part of the garden where one often goes barefoot (bees are not aggressive but can sting if they feel directly threatened, for example if crushed when you step on them). A small manual lawn mower with a spiral blade is perfectly suitable for mowing *Phyla*: a quick going over with the mower is enough to cut off all the flowers.

Phyla is unfussy about soil type tolerating both light soils and clay soils that are sometimes waterlogged. It withstands salt spray as well as high concentrations of salt in the soil. It can even withstand temporary flooding. In its natural habitat (the flooding pampas of South America), its seeds are dispersed by the flow of water during floods, and the plant seeds easily in salty mud. In some specific environments (salt pastures in areas prone to flooding), where the combined action of grazing, salt and floods almost totally prevents the regeneration of the native flora, *Phyla* can become the dominant species. It can then invade vast areas and have a negative impact on the profitability of pasture land, since livestock will rarely eat it. This is what has happened in, for example, the salt pastures of the lower valley of the River Aude, in Southern France. To avoid spreading *Phyla* into this type of environment, we call on those responsible for landscapes not to plant *Phyla* in zones subject to flooding (marshes, river banks, salt flood meadows). In the mediterranean garden, however, *Phyla*

is valuable for its many qualities, both ornamental and practical: it consumes little water and requires no fertilizers or pesticides, and it is one of the groundcover plants suitable for foot traffic that requires the least maintenance compared to a conventional lawn.

Pilosella officinarum
Synonym: *Hieracium pilosella*
(Asteraceae) Mouse-ear hawkweed

Origin: Europe, Asia Minor, North Africa; **Height of foliage**: 2 to 10 cm depending on cultivation conditions and degree of foot traffic; **Height when in flower**: 20 cm; **Spread**: 40 cm or more; **Position**: sun or semi-shade; **Hardiness**: –15 °C and below; **Drought resistance code**: 3.

A perennial with evergreen leaves arranged in ground-hugging rosettes. The grey-green leaves have long hairs on their surfaces, while the undersides are covered with a fine silver down. The plant spreads by means of stolons which root on contact with the soil, producing new rosettes around the mother plant each year. In time the mouse-ear hawkweed forms an even carpet of closely packed grey leaves. The yellow flowers, borne on short upright peduncles, appear in May-June. The plant is known for its allelopathic properties: its roots exude chemical substances which inhibit the germination of competing species. It is sometimes used in organic farming as a "herbicidal plant", for example to cover the ground between rows in orchards or vineyards. In the garden it can be used to make a natural-looking

carpet that withstands moderate foot traffic. It can also be used in mixed flowering carpets, requiring little maintenance once established: it is possible to eliminate almost entirely the need for weeding if one plants mouse-ear hawkweed together with other carpeting species with allelopathic properties, for example *Achillea crithmifolia, Centaurea bella, Origanum vulgare, Tanacetum densum* or *Thymus ciliatus*. In parts of the garden that are not irrigated, mouse-ear hawkweed may lose some of its leaves during prolonged droughts. The foliage is rapidly refurbished as soon as the first autumn rains arrive. An occasional watering allows the plant to retain good dense foliage in summer. Unfussy about soil type, mouse-ear hawkweed establishes faster in a light, well-drained soil. It is a tough and adaptable plant, and long-lived. Planting density: 6 per square metre.

Propagation by division in autumn, or by seed in spring, sown in pots. Sowing in the open ground gives rather haphazard results as the germination rate is uneven.

• *Pistacia lentiscus*, the lentisk or mastic, sometimes forms amazing ground-hugging carpets in the wild, for example by the sea when it is sculpted by the wind and the salt spray. Like phillyrea, it can be used to create

The lawn on a badly maintained sports ground is gradually invaded by mouse-ear hawkweed (*Pilosella officinarum*), which spreads into a wild-looking groundcover. The herbicidal properties of mouse-ear hawkweed limit competition from taller plants.

The lentisk is a shrub which has a carpeting habit when it grows near the sea. Adaptable to many different conditions, it is one of the easiest Mediterranean shrubs to prune to form the backbone of large groundcover beds.

Potentilla neumanniana withstands foot traffic and makes a beautiful flowering carpet in spring. Without irrigation, the foliage is partially deciduous in summer.

the backbone for large groundcover beds, occasionally sculpted by the gardener. Both tough and adaptable, it thrives where few other plants manage to grow, for example under oaks or pines. In difficult sites one can combine it with other evergreen shrubs that are equally happy in sun or in dense shade, such as myrtle, phillyrea or laurustinus. It can also be planted in association with *Ampelodesmos mauritanicus*, a powerful grass that does well in the shade of pine trees in spite of competition from the trees' roots. Origin: Mediterranean Basin. Hardiness: –12 to –15 °C. Planting density: from 1 per square metre to 1 per 4 square metres, depending on how quickly one wants the space covered. Drought resistance code: 6.

• *Plantago coronopus*, the buck's-horn plantain, develops its thick leaves in ground-hugging rosettes. It is often seen beside paths, where it is walked on regularly. It can be planted together with the strawberry clover to make a tough groundcover which requires little maintenance. On the coast one may also find the buck's-horn plantain growing with *Frankenia laevis*: this mixture is easy to reproduce successfully in the garden in poor and stony soil. In richer soils, the buck's-horn plantain has a tendency to grow taller and form a fat clump. In this case you can gather the edible leaves, which have a delicate taste, and use them as a basis for

The buck's-horn plantain is often seen growing at the edges of paths, where it is regularly walked on. Here it grows with *Frankenia laevis* along the Sentier des Douaniers at Cap Corse, Corsica.

wild salads. The inflorescences of the buck's-horn plantain attract a small black ladybird, *Scymnus frontalis*, whose cottony larvae are greedy devourers of aphids. Among the other plantains common in wild lawns, we may mention *Plantago lanceolata*, which is happy in dry soil, and *Plantago major*, which prefers damper soil or irrigated lawns. Origin: Europe, Central and Western Asia, North Africa. Hardiness: –15 °C and below. Drought resistance code: 4. Planting density: 9 per square metre.

• *Potentilla neumanniana,* synonym *Potentilla verna*, spring cinquefoil, forms a remarkable carpet of yellow flowers in spring. Its pretty cut foliage, evergreen in winter, is summer-deciduous in unwatered areas of the garden. This potentilla can withstand moderate foot traffic. It can be planted together with other carpeting plants to create beautiful mixed flowering carpets, for example

The leaves of *Potentilla neumanniana* are evergreen in winter. Covered in a light down of silky hairs, they are picked out in hoar frost on winter mornings.

Thymus praecox, Matricaria tchihatchewii, Lotus corniculatus or *Achillea tomentosa*. Origin: Southern Europe. Hardiness: –15 °C and below. Planting density: 6 per square metre. Drought resistance code: 3.

• *Prunella hyssopifolia* increases laterally by means of its spreading stems which root on contact with the soil. Its narrow leaves are evergreen in winter and partially deciduous in summer, when the plant becomes dormant in order to reduce water losses during the dry period. The very ornamental violet-blue flowers apear in June-July. They

Self-heal is a lawn "weed". It can be planted with clover, achilleas, cinquefoil and plantains to form the basis of a wild lawn that is easy to maintain.

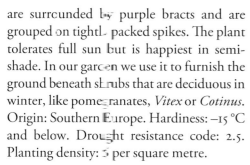

Rhodanthemum catananche is slow-growing. After a few years it makes a very attractive small groundcover.

Putoria calabrica is a small groundcover with a spreading or cascading habit. Its bright pink flowers, rich in nectar, open in May-June to the delight of all the butterflies.

are surrounded by purple bracts and are grouped on tightly packed spikes. The plant tolerates full sun but is happiest in semishade. In our garden we use it to furnish the ground beneath shrubs that are deciduous in winter, like pomegranates, *Vitex* or *Cotinus*. Origin: Southern Europe. Hardiness: −15 °C and below. Drought resistance code: 2.5. Planting density: 5 per square metre.

• *Prunella vulgaris*, or self-heal, grows with clovers, plantains daisies and dandelions in wild lawns that receive occasional irrigation in summer. Its violet-blue flowers, grouped in short clusters that just top the leaves, are rich in nectar and attract many beneficial insects such as hoverflies. Origin: Europe, North Africa, Asia Minor. Hardiness: −15 °C and below. Drought resistance code: 2. Planting density: 6 per square metre.

• *Putoria calabrica* has small bright green evergreen leaves that give off a pleasant scent when crushed. It is a prostrate subshrub whose woody stems, spreading or falling, cling to the surfaces of rocks. The small bright pink flowers appear in May-June. They attract a host of butterflies which plunge their probosces into the tubular corollas to extract the abundant nectar. The flowers are followed by small black berries

which attract birds in autumn and early winter. It is a striking plant that deserves to be better known as it is ornamental throughout the year. It can be planted at the foot of a wall or between steps with a south-facing orientation, where it benefits from the heat given off from the stones, for it is a plant that doesn't much like the cold. Origin: Southern Mediterranean Basin. Hardiness: −6 to −8 °C. Drought resistance code: 4. Planting density: 4 per square metre.

• *Rhodanthemum catananche* is slowgrowing. It forms a low carpet of finely-cut leaves that slip easily between stepping stones or stone steps. Its delicate flowers, borne on short flowering stems, mingle ivory, pastel pink and soft orange tones and are very ornamental. Origin: Morocco. Hardiness: −10 to −12 °C. Drought resistance code: 3. Planting density: 9 per square metre.

• *Rhodanthemum hosmariense* forms a magnificent cushion of grey and silky leaves. It is happy in stony parts of the garden, in very well-drained soil. In our gravel garden we have planted it with *Tanacetum densum*, *Artemisia pedemontana* and *Achillea umbellata* to create a low river of silver foliage in the midst of taller plants. From February onwards, the daisy flowers of the

Rhodanthemum hosmariense flowers from February onwards. Here it serves as the foreground for a groundcover bed of grey-leaved plants consisting of *Phlomis lychnitis*, *Artemisia pedemontana*, *Euphorbia myrsinites*, *Centaurea bella* and *Scabiosa minoana*.

Rhodanthemum light up this pretty carpet. Origin: Morocco. Hardiness: –10 to –12 °C. Drought resistance code: 4. Planting density: 6 per square metre.

Rosmarinus (Lamiaceae) Rosemary
Rosemaries are unbeatable plants in ground-cover gardens. The cultivars with a spreading or falling habit, such as for example 'Bonifacio' or 'Punta di Canelle', are exceptional plants for covering large slopes or for cascading down high walls. The carpeting cultivars with more compact vegetation, such as 'Barcelone' or 'Montagnette', are suitable for decorating the edges of flights of steps or the tops of low walls. The cultivars that develop into huge balls, such as 'Ulysse' or 'Santa Barbara Blue', find their place in large groundcover beds. Finally, some little-known hybrids, such as *Rosmarinus × mendizabalii* or *Rosmarinus × noeanus* can show to good advantage in gravel gardens or rock gardens. The amazing diversity of the rosemaries can also be seen in their flower colour, which can be white ('Blanc des Calanques'), pink ('Sierra de Cazorla'), pale mauve ('Boule'), bright blue ('Sappho') or violet ('Cap Pertusato'). It is expressed too in the subtle variations in the size and colour of their leaves. The leaves can, for example, be broad and bright green ('Spice Islands'), dark green and needle-like ('Sappho'), golden ('Joyce de Baggio') or grey and silky *(Rosmarinus × mendizabalii)*.

The evergreen foliage of rosemaries covers the ground extremely well, leaving little room for competition from weeds. The leaves are equipped with essential oil glands which release chemical substances that effectively inhibit the germination of competing species. Thus beds of rosemaries require only a limited amount of maintenance since they don't need any hand-weeding once they are well established. The main work consists of lightly clipping the tips of the stems once a year in order for the rosemaries to retain a good, dense habit in the long term. But this can hardly be called a chore: the rosemaries smell so good that clipping them is a pleasure. In our garden we prefer to clip them at the end of spring, when all cultivars have ceased flowering. The rosemary clippings can be used beneath other plants as a mulch with anti-germination properties.

All rosemaries need soil with perfect drainage. In the wild they grow in poor and

The remarkable diversity of rosemaries may be seen in the colour of their flowers, which can be white, pink, mauve or bright blue, as in this plant growing on a cliff at Cap Corse in Corsica.

stony soils: thus when planting them in the garden one must never try to give them a little help by adding potting compost or fertilizer. When filling in the planting hole it is better to offer them some spadefuls of sand and pebbles, to perfect the drainage at the level of the plant's crown. Like many shrubs originating from Mediterranean garrigues, rosemaries are prone to be killed by cryptogamic diseases like *Phytophthora*, which develop in hot and humid conditions. Hence they should be planted only in parts of the garden that receive no irrigation. To avoid spreading diseases, mixed beds composed of several varieties are preferable to large uniform plantings.

Rosemaries resist drought well (drought resistance code: 4). However, in exceptionally dry years one should not be taken aback

A rosemary in its natural habitat, on top of cliffs at Bonifacio, Corsica. All rosemaries like poor, stony soil with perfect drainage. Too rich a soil shortens their life span markedly.

An exceptional drought on Cap Corse in autumn 2007. During long periods of drought rosemaries reduce their photosynthesis and become dormant. They take on an extraordinary golden colour as they await the first rains that will turn them green once more.

A rosemary cascading down limestone rocks in the mountains of Mallorca. This type of rosemary is particularly useful for covering large spaces that require low maintenance

by the surprising appearance they may have at the end of summer. In order to limit water losses, the edges of the leaves roll inwards, forming a narrow gutter which protects the stomata through which the plant transpires. Simultaneously the plant limits its photosynthesis, so that growth almost completely stops during periods of intense drought. The leaves become narrower and narrower and progressively turn yellow, with the result that by the end of summer the foliage can take on an amazing golden colour. Only the narrow rolled-in leaf margins remain green, protected by the cottony hairs that cover the undersides of the leaves. The slowing down of photosynthesis enables the plant to survive periods of exceptional drought. The leaves become green again with the first autumn rains and the rosemary starts to grow again, shortly before showing its first flower buds. This is the time when the plant is easiest to propagate, by short cuttings of the new autumn shoots.

Of all the plant collections that Clara and I have built up in our garden, the collection of rosemaries is one of our favourites. The aroma of the foliage, the succession of flowerings in autumn and winter, the host of insects that hasten to make the most of the generous source of nectar: all these are

things of which we never tire. In our garden we study their flowering, their scent, their habit, their resistance to cold and their long-term behaviour – some cultivars about which we were enthusiastic at first proved to be disappointing because of their short life, while others on the contrary are remarkably long-lived.

I present here a selection of the best rosemary cultivars for groundcover, classifying them by use. The flowering dates given are only indicative, for the flowering time of rosemaries may vary greatly from year to year. It depends a lot on the climate conditions, for example the intensity of drought at the end of the year, how wet the autumn is, and the occurrence of very cold periods which can limit winter flowering. The dimensions I indicate refer to adult plants, ten years old, which have benefited from a light pinching off of their tips each year.

Rosemaries with a spreading or cascading habit

This group includes cultivars with very vigorous vegetation, especially useful when one wants to cover large slopes with as little maintenance as possible. The prostrate stems root on contact with the soil, allowing the plant to continue spreading laterally even when very old. The planting density can vary from 1 plant per square metre to 1 plant per 4 square metres, depending on how quickly you want the space to be filled. Rosemaries with a spreading habit can be combined with other vigorous groundcover

plants such as, for example, *Cistus × pulverulentus*, *Sarcopoterium spinosum* or *Limoniastrum monopetalum* 'Carnaval', to create the permanent structure of large groundcover beds on large slopes. Pioneer species can be planted between the structural plants to complete this type of planting, for example species that self-seed prolifically on slopes such as *Dorycnium hirsutum*, *Euphorbia characias* and *Salvia sclarea*, or species that sucker rapidly such as *Achillea nobilis*, *Achillea crithmifolia* and *Achillea coarctata*.

• *Rosmarinus officinalis* 'Baie de Douarnenez'
Grey-green leaves and fast-growing vegetation. The sinuous stems, whose tips may turn upwards or downwards, form a hairy-looking tangled mass. Large dark blue flowers, flowering spectacular in winter. Height: 40 to 60 cm. Spread: 2 to 3 m. Hardiness: −10 to −12 °C.

• *Rosmarinus officinalis* 'Bonifacio'
A selection with bright blue flowers from one of the magnificent rosemaries that grow on top of the cliffs at Bonifacio, Corsica. Rapid growth and handsome, dark green, regular vegetation. Flowering in late winter and early spring. Height: 30 to 40 cm. Spread: 2 to 3 m. Hardiness: −8 to −10 °C (the plant is hardier in very dry stony soil).

Like many rosemaries with a spreading habit, the plant often called *Rosmarinus officinalis* (Prostratus Group) can either spread over the soil or cascade vertically from the top of a wall.

Rosmarinus officinalis 'Boule' is a cultivar with extremely vigorous vegetation: it is the strongest growing rosemary of them all. It has pale mauve flowers arranged along the creeping stems which layer as they spread over the soil.

• *Rosmarinus officinalis* 'Boule'

A cultivar with extremely powerful vegetation: it is the most vigorous of all rosemaries. The oldest specimen in our garden is about 60 cm high and 4 m wide, and its long lateral vegetation is still growing. No doubt it is the plant's ability to layer very easily that gives it such vigour. Large pale blue-mauve flowers, packed along the stems. Flowering in late winter and early spring. If this rosemary is planted above a wall or on a steep slope it makes a spectacular cascade. Hardiness: –12 to –15 °C.

• *Rosmarinus officinalis* 'Cap Pertusato'

A selection with very dark flowers of one of the prostrate rosemaries growing on the limestone plateau of Cape Pertusato, the southernmost point of Corsica. When they first open the flowers are a beautiful dark violet, then their colour becomes progressively lighter until it is a luminous blue before the flowers die. Height: 60 to 80 cm. Spread: 1.50 m. Hardiness: –8 to –10 °C (the plant is hardier in very dry stony soil).

• *Rosmarinus officinalis* 'Punta di Canelle'

Narrow pale green leaves and small dark blue flowers. The vegetation falls naturally in a cascade, making it an excellent choice for planting at the top of a low wall. Flowering in late winter. Height: 60 to 80 cm. Spread: 3 m. Hardiness: –8 to –10 °C. This cultivar is happy only in stony soil. It is short-lived if the soil does not have adequate drainage.

• *Rosmarinus officinalis* 'Rose de Corse'

Small grey-green leaves packed along the stems. Abundant pale pink flowers in late winter give this fine rosemary a striking appearance. It is a cultivar of one of the many prostrate rosemaries that colonize slopes and cliffs on the west coast of the Corsican cape. Height: 50 cm. Spread: 1.50 to 2 m. Hardiness: –8 to –10 °C.

• *Rosmarinus officinalis* (Prostratus Group)

I am referring here to the plant often called *R. officinalis* var. *repens*. Pale blue flowers in late winter, rapid growth and low vegetation. If it is planted above a wall, the vegetation will hang down in a beautiful even sheet that is very ornamental. Height: 30 to 40 cm. Spread: 2 to 3 m. Hardiness: –10 to –12 °C.

Rosemaries with a ball-shaped habit

This group includes cultivars that form large balls, often as wide as they are tall. They are robust plants suitable for lage groundcover beds where they can be planted together with other Mediterranean shrubs such as *Cistus* × *verguinii*, *Phlomis purpurea*, *Artemisia thuscula*, *Euphorbia ceratocarpa* or *Teucrium fruticans*. The planting density is usually 1 per square metre.

• *Rosmarinus officinalis* 'Blanc des Calanques'

Long dark green leaves, contrasting with pretty pure white flowers. Flowering in late winter and early spring. Height: 60 to 80 cm. Spread: 80 cm to 1 m. Hardiness: –10 to –12 °C.

Rosmarinus officinalis 'Spice Islands' grows fast. It forms a massive ball, useful for giving structure to large groundcover beds.

• *Rosmarinus officinalis* 'Corsican Blue'

An old cultivar that has rightly become a garden classic because of its beautiful dark flowers. The plant forms a massive ball, more or less spreading. Its habit is uneven, with some stems being upright and others drooping. Flowering in winter and spring. Height: 80 cm to 1 m. Spread: 1.50 m or more. Hardiness: –8 to –10 °C.

• *Rosmarinus officinalis* 'Joyce de Baggio'

A cultivar with a compact habit, striking for the colour of its foliage. The very fine leaves have a golden hue in autumn, winter and spring, then turn light green during the summer drought. The very sticky young shoots are particularly aromatic. The pale blue flowers are not produced in abundance. Height: 60 cm. Spread: 80 cm. Hardiness: –10 to –12 °C.

• *Rosmarinus officinalis* 'Santa Barbara Blue'

Dark green leaves and a handsome very regular ball shape, thick and compact. Bright blue flowers in late winter. Height: 80 cm to 1 m. Spread: 1 m. Hardiness: –10 to –12 °C.

• *Rosmarinus officinalis* 'Sappho'

Very fine needle-like leaves. Flowers of a remarkable bright blue, reminiscent of the blue of some ceanothuses such as *Ceanothus* 'Concha'. The flowers grow progressively paler before withering. The plant

is magnificent when in full flower in late winter. It can be used in large groundcover beds in association with *Coronilla valentina* subsp. *glauca* 'Citrina', whose pale yellow sets off the intense colour of the rosemary. The sticky young shoots are highly aromatic. Height: 80 cm to 1 m. Spread: 1 m. Hardiness: −10 to −12 °C. This cultivar is happy in sandy or stony soil with perfect drainage. It is short-lived in heavy soil.

• *Rosmarinus officinalis* 'Sierra de Cazorla'
Green leaves and large pale pink flowers veined with dark pink. Abundant flowering in autumn and early winter, sometimes repeated in spring. Height: 1 m. Spread: 1 m. Hardiness: −10 to −12 °C. This cultivar is happy only in sandy or stony soil with perfect drainage. It is short-lived in heavy soil.

• *Rosmarinus officinalis* 'Spice Islands'
A cultivar remarkable for its rapid growth. It is distinguished by its fine bright green foliage, broad and spatulate. Large bright blue flowers, a particularly good source of honey, in mid-winter. Height: 1.25 m. Spread: 1.25 m. Hardiness: −10 to −12 °C. Of all the different rosemaries in our collection, this robust cultivar seems to be the least fussy about type of soil: it thrives in stony soil but is equally tolerant of heavier soils.

• *Rosmarinus officinalis* 'Vicomte de Noailles'
A compact cultivar with narrow grey-green leaves. Abundant pale pink flowers, streaked with mauve. Flowers in the depths of winter. Height: 60 cm. Spread: 80 cm. Hardiness: −8 to −10 °C.

• *Rosmarinus × mendizabalii*
The fine foliage of this hybrid with its musical name is a reminder of its two parents: *Rosmarinus officinalis*, with green leaves, and *Rosmarinus tomentosus*, a little-known species with silver leaves. The elegant grey and slightly silky leaves of the hybrid are remarkably aromatic (a strong smell of camphor). Luminous blue flowers in winter and spring. A native of the sea cliffs of Southern Andalucia. *Rosmarinus × mendizabalii* requires poor stony soil that is perfectly drained. Height: 60 to 80 cm. Spread: 80 cm to 1 m. Hardiness: −8 to −10 °C (the plant is hardier in very dry soil). Drought resistance code: 5.

Small rosemaries

The cultivars 'Barcelone' and 'Montagnette' are distinguished by their ground-hugging vegetation and their limited lateral spread. They can be place above low walls over which they will make a small and ornamental cascade. Another small rosemary, *Rosmarinus × noeanus,* has, on the contrary, an upright habit. It is interesting for its long flowering season and can be used in gravel gardens together with other winter-flowering plants such as *Iris unguicularis* or *Lavandula dentata*. Planting density: 2 or 3 per square metre.

• *Rosmarinus officinalis* 'Barcelone'
Grey-green leaves and pale mauve flowers in late winter. Height: 10 to 15 cm. Spread: 60 to 80 cm. Hardiness: −6 to −8 °C.

• *Rosmarinus officinalis* 'Montagnette'
Dark green leaves set off pretty pure white flowers. Winter- and spring-flowering. Height: 10 to 15 cm. Spread: 80 cm. Hardiness: −10 to −12 °C.

• *Rosmarinus × noeanus*
A hybrid of *Rosmarinus officinalis* and another little-known species, *Rosmarinus eriocalyx*, which is native to Southern Spain and North Africa. The flowers, which are a pretty, luminous mauve and particularly abundant, are grouped on small lateral branches. In our garden *Rosmarinus × noeanus* is the only rosemary to flower uninterruptedly in autumn, winter and spring, to

Rosmarinus officinalis 'Montagnette' has a ground-hugging habit. Its lovely pure white flowers contrast well with the dark foliage

the very great pleasure of bees and numerous other beneficial insects which come to feed on this generous source of nectar. The plant is happy in areas of the garden where the soil is poor, stony and perfectly drained. Height: 60 cm. Spread: 60 cm. Hardiness: −8 to −10 °C.

Salvia 'Bee's Bliss' (Lamiaceae)

Origin: probable hybrid of *Salvia leucophylla* and *Salvia sonomensis*, both native to California. **Height of foliage**: 20 to 30 cm; **Height when in flower**: 40 cm; **Spread**: 80 cm or more; **Position**: sun; **Hardiness**: −6 to −8 °C (the plant is hardier in very dry soil); **Drought resistance code**: 5.

A sub-shrub with vigorous carpeting vegetation which makes an excellent groundcover in mild climates. The plant spreads by means of its long lateral stems which root on contact with the soil. It can also cascade from the top of a low wall. The pretty pale

Salvia 'Bee's Bliss' is a groundcover that is easy to grow in gardens with a mild climate.

Salvia fruticosa does well in our gravel garden in perfectly drained soil.

Salvia interrupta is planted in a raised border which ensures good drainage. (Jardin des Plantes, Montpellier.)

The carpeting vegetation of *Salvia multicaulis* spreads by means of its short rhizomes. These rhizomes act as storage organs when the plant becomes dormant in summer, temporarily losing almost all its leaves.

mauve flowers, which appear in April-May, attract a host of butterflies. The downy grey evergreen leaves release a strong scent when crushed. If you look at the undersides of the leaves with a magnifying glass, you will be able to make out tiny waxy pearls nestling under the dense mass of silver hairs which are the glands that produce the essential oil. As with all aromatic-leaved salvias, the essential oil contains chemical substances that inhibit the germination of competing species (allelopathy). Depending on the species, these chemical substances can be leached by the rain, diffused by the decomposition of fallen leaves or, as is the case with *Salvia* 'Bee's Bliss', deposited on the soil beneath the foliage like a fine dew. Despite the thinness of its carpeting vegetation, this makes *Salvia* 'Bee's Bliss' less vulnerable to competition from weeds. This salvia requires a poor stony or sandy soil with perfect drainage. Planting density: 2 or 3 per square metre.
Propagation by semi-ripe cuttings in autumn.

• **Salvia fruticosa** forms a beautiful rounded mass of very aromatic leaves. It is covered in pinkish mauve flowers in spring. In our gravel garden we like to grow it with the plants that accompany it in the wild: *Ballota pseudodictamnus*, with silvery foliage, *Salvia pomifera*, with lovely blue-mauve flowers, *Satureja thymbra*, a vigorous savory with pink flowers, and *Thymbra capitata*, the Cretan thyme that flowers in early summer. Origin: Mediterranean Basin. Hardiness: –8 to –10 °C (it resists cold better in very dry soil). Drought resistance code: 4. Planting density: 2 per square metre.

• **Salvia interrupta** bears beautiful spikes of blue-mauve flowers in May-June. The plant forms a large spreading clump. In light, perfectly drained soil it makes a remarkable groundcover and is long-lived. By contrast, in heavy soil the plant rapidly dies. Origin: Morocco. Hardiness: –10 to –12 °C. Drought resistance code: 4. Planting density: 2 or 3 per square metre.

There are many hybrids between *Salvia fruticosa*, *Salvia officinalis*, *Salvia interrupta* and *Salvia candelabrum* that often flower spectacularly in spring. All these hybrids like perfectly drained soils and make good groundcovers for a gravel garden.

• **Salvia lavandulifolia subsp. *blancoana*** forms a carpeting groundcover, very ornamental in spring when it is covered in bright blue flowers. It is a tough plant and long-lived provided that one takes care to plant it in poor stony soil with perfect drainage. In our gravel garden we have combined it with *Achillea coarctata* and *Tanacetum densum*, two other groundcover plants that can serve as a foreground for taller plantings. Origin: Southern Spain, North Africa. Hardiness: –12 to –15 °C. Drought resistance code: 4. Planting density: 6 per square metre.

Salvia multicaulis

Origin: Asia Minor; **Height of foliage**: 2 to 5 cm; **Height when in flower**: 25 cm; **Spread**: 40 cm; **Position**: sun; **Hardiness**: –12 to –15 °C; **Drought resistance code**: 4.

A perennial with grey-green leaves that remain on the plant in winter and are dropped in the summer after flowering. The plant spreads slowly by means of its rhizomes and forms a small and very low-growing groundcover. Native to the grazed steppes of Turkey, Syria and Iraq, it thrives in stony soils. It is one of the few salvias in our collection whose foliage can withstand a moderate amount of foot traffic when the plant is not in flower. In our garden we like to plant it in patches of flowering steppe, where the lack of leaves in summer is amply compensated for by its marvellous flowering. The pale mauve flowers are borne on short flowering stems, closely packed together (the name *multicaulis* derives from the Latin *multus*, "many", and *caulis*, "stem"). They open in April, surrounded by dark calyces. Little by little these calyces fatten until they form large parchment-textured balls squeezed up against each other. They remain on the plant after flowering is over and take on a bright purple colour, so that this modest steppe plant turns into one of the most spectacular plants in our garden for a few weeks. Planting density: 6 per square metre.
Propagation by seed in autumn or by division in autumn or winter.

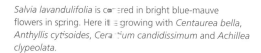

Salvia lavandulifolia is covered in bright blue-mauve flowers in spring. Here it is growing with *Centaurea bella*, *Anthyllis cytisoides*, *Cerastium candidissimum* and *Achillea clypeolata*.

Salvia spathacea likes shade or semi-shade, for example at the edge of undergrowth.

• **Salvia spathacea** spreads slowly by means of its rhizomes and forms a robust groundcover. Its highly aromatic dark green leaves are evergreen. The glandulous inflorescences, also very aromatic, form upright spikes from April to June. The delicate dark pink flowers are held in curious reddish-brown bracts. The plant tolerates sun but does even better in shade. It is happy in open undergrowth beneath holm oaks. In our garden we like to plant it with other shade-loving groundcovers such as *Vinca minor*, *Glechoma hederacea* or *Geranium macrorrhizum*. Origin California. Hardiness: –10 to –12 °C. Drought resistance code: 3. Planting density: 3 or 4 per square metre.

• **Salvia verbenaca** is a small perennial whose leaves are arranged in rosettes. The spikes of blue-mauve flowers are produced in succession over a long period, from March to June. The plant self-seeds prolifically in poor and stony soils. It can be planted together with other species that self-seed generously, such as *Scabiosa argentea*, *Goniolimon speciosum*, *Glaucium flavum* or *Asphodelus fistulosus*. These pioneer plants make it possible to create light and flowery scenes along paths in the spaces between stepping stones or in the stony and wild parts of the garden. This salvia can also be used to add to the range of carpeting plants

on green roofs: it will seed itself there freely, even after the driest summers. Origin: Southern Europe. Hardiness: –15 °C and below. Drought resistance code: 3. Planting density: 9 per square metre.

• **Sanguisorba minor**, salad burnet, is a perennial with cut leaves which thrives in wild lawns that receive little irrigation planted together with other species such as bird's-foot trefoil (*Lotus corniculatus*), strawberry clover (*Trifolium fragiferum*), spring

cinquefoil (*Potentilla neumanniana)* and black medick (*Medicago lupulina*). When one is sowing a mixed lawn *in situ*, the salad burnet has one great advantage: while most of the species that make up a mixed lawn germinate slowly, making the "ecological" lawn sometimes hard to get going, salad burnet by contrast germinates very rapidly.

Salvia verbenaca self-seeds abundantly in stony soil. Here the narrow inflorescences of the salvia mingle with the blue flower heads of *Orlaya grandiflora* in a lovely natural scene beside a path in the garrigue.

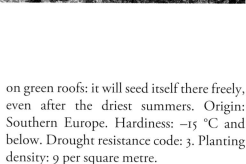

If sowing is carried out during September, the seeds will have sprouted by the end of October. The young leaves taste of cucumber and fresh walnuts and can be eaten in salads together with the tender new shoots of poppies and daisies. Origin: Europe, Asia Minor, North Africa. Hardiness: −15 °C and below. Drought resistance code: 3. Planting density: 9 per square metre.

Santolina magonica (Asteraceae)

Origin: Balearic Islands; **Height of foliage**: 25 to 30 cm; **Height when in flower**: 40 cm; **Spread**: 60 to 80 cm; **Position**: sun; **Hardiness**: −10 to −12 °C; **Drought resistance code**: 5.

A sub-shrub with evergreen silvery grey leaves. Magnificent colonies of *Santolina magonica* can be seen on the rocky coast of the Levant peninsula in Mallorca. This species is distinguished from the common santolina by its more carpeting habit: of all the different santolinas that we grow, this one makes the best groundcover. Its numerous lateral branches produce horizontal stems that root easily on contact with the soil. It is a fairly slow-growing plant but develops into a handsome flattened cushion. *Santolina magonica* is also distinguished from other santolinas by the scent of its foliage: a very pleasant fresh and invigorating aroma reminiscent of eucalyptus and mint. The very abundant orange-yellow flowers appear in May-June. Their pollen attracts a multitude of beneficial insects; one may, for example, see on the flowers minute black ladybirds belonging to the genus *Scymnus*, whose curious cottony larvae are particularly effective at devouring colonies of aphids. As with all santolinas, clipping after flowering will keep the plant more compact. *Santolina magonica* is prone to succumb to cryptogamic diseases, such as *Phytophthora*, that develop in hot and moist conditions. It should thus be planted in the zone of the garden that is not irrigated. It prefers poor soils, stony or sandy, with perfect drainage. In coastal gardens it withstands direct salt spray, making it one of the few plants that can be used in the first line, right beside the sea. Planting density: 2 or 3 per square metre.
Propagation by semi-ripe cuttings in autumn.

Many other santolinas are also very useful in groundcover gardens. We may mention the common santolina, or lavender cotton, *Santolina chamaecyparissus*, a robust and

Santolina magonica and *Helichrysum stoechas* make a plant barrier right by the sea on the Levant peninsula, Mallorca.

The massive cushions of *Sarcopoterium spinosum* lose almost all their leaves in periods of great drought, as here on a stony scree in the foothills of the Western Taurus in Turkey.

vigorous plant which is particularly long-lived provided that it is planted in soil that is very dry in summer – it hates summer irrigation; *Santolina viridis* 'Primrose Gem', a green-leaved santolina with pastel yellow flowers whose dark cushions make a good contrast amid grey-leaved plants; *Santolina benthamiana* which has creamy-yellow flowers; and *Santolina × lindavica*, one of my favourites for the extraordinary luminosity of it soft primrose-yellow flowers.

• *Sarcopoterium spinosum* has a very striking texture when it loses most of its leaves in summer to reveal the geometrical structure of its thorns. It makes a powerful groundcover that forms a huge cushion, which may reach a spread of more than 2 m when it finds conditions that suit it. In our garden the oldest specimen is more than 3 m wide. However, it is fairly fussy about growing conditions and requires light, perfectly drained soil. In heavy soils *Sarcopoterium* limps along then quietly dies since it cannot tolerate stagnant damp. Origin: Eastern Mediterranean Basin. Hardiness: −10 to −15 °C depending on the wetness of the soil. Drought resistance code: 6. Planting density: 1 per square metre.

• *Scabiosa argentea* is a small herbaceous plant with cut grey-green leaves. Its suckering stock spreads slowly to form a small, silky-looking cushion. The light inflorescences bear pretty creamy-white flowers produced in succession throughout the summer. They are rich in nectar and attract numerous pollinators and beneficial insects. The plant self-seeds easily in the garden. Origin: Mediterranean Basin. Hardiness: −15 °C and below. Drought resistance code: 4. Planting density: 9 per square metre.

The pale mauve flowers of *Scabiosa minoana* go well with its silvery-grey foliage.

In large groundcover beds *Scabiosa cretica* is a plant that attracts attention over many months: when its flowering is over, the dried inflorescences remain ornamental for a long time. Here it is growing with *Lavandula × intermedia* 'Grosso', *Phlomis lychnitis* and *Santolina rosmarinifolia*.

Securigera varia forms an invasive groundcover in wild parts of the garden. Here it is with *Centaurea scabiosa* colonizing a slope by the road on the Larzac plateau.

• **Scabiosa cretica** forms a vigorous spreading ball. The handsome grey-green foliage is evergreen in winter and partially deciduous at the end of summer in times of great drought. It is rapidly refurbished as soon as the first autumn rains arrive. The abundant lavender-blue flowers appear from March to July and are followed by very ornamental seedheads. In our garden we like to plant it with other plants that form spreading balls like *Cistus × pauranthus* 'Natacha', *Santolina viridis* 'Primrose Gem' or *Salvia fruticosa*. Origin: islands of the Mediterranean Basin. Hardiness: −10 to −12 °C. Drought resistance code: 4. Planting density: 2 per square metre.

• **Scabiosa minoana**, similar to *Scabiosa cretica*, can be distinguished by its magnificent silky silvery-grey foliage, which sets off well the pretty pale mauve flowers. It is a tough and fast-growing plant that requires a light soil with perfect drainage. Origin: Crete. Hardiness: −10 to −12 °C. Drought resistance code: 4. Planting density: 2 per square metre.

• **Securigera varia** is a perennial that tends to be invasive, with beautiful pink flowers in June. It suckers vigorously and self-seeds on slopes or in wild parts of the garden. Origin: Southern Europe, South-West Asia. Hardiness: −15 °C and below. Drought resistance code: 3. Planting density: 1 per square metre.

Sedum album (Crassulaceae)
White stonecrop

Origin: Europe, Asia Minor, North Africa; **Height of foliage**: 2 to 3 cm; **Height when in flower**: 10 to 15 cm; **Spread**: 30 cm or more; **Position**: sun; **Hardiness**: −15 °C and below; **Drought resistance code**: 4.

A perennial with small light green fleshy leaves, which turn pink or red in winter. *Sedum album* grows wild in shallow stony soils, often in fine gravel on the edges of paths, where it makes a pretty, low-growing carpet. It also grows in crannies between the stones of old walls, or sometimes on old roofs, where it makes the most of the slight accumulation of dust, moss and debris to put down shallow roots. Its ability to resist drought is excellent, thanks to its succulent leaves which store significant amounts of water. Its stems put out aerial roots that slip between stones until they find a little earth in which to anchor themselves. The leaves break off the stems easily and also root when they fall on to the ground, which enables the *Sedum* to regenerate after disturbances. The small white flowers appear in June-July, arranged in panicles borne on short upright stems. Planting density: 9 per square metre. *Propagation by cuttings taken from short stem sections or by leaf cuttings.*

• **Sedum album 'Coral Carpet'** has smaller leaves, tightly packed along the stems. It forms a fast-growing carpet with a very uniform appearance. Its leaves take on a magnificent dark red colour throughout the entire winter, then become green again with the new growth of spring. Its toughness, its rapid growth and the seasonal variation in its colour make it one of the best sedums for green roofs.

• **Sedum gypsicola**
The plant usually grown under the name *Sedum gypsicola* is probably a hybrid of *Sedum album* and *Sedum gypsicola*. Whatever its exact parentage may be, it is

Sedum species are traditionally used in Northern Europe to make thick carpets that allow green roofs to be planted on a shallow substrate, with a depth of about 6 to 8 cm. This substrate usually consists of a mixture of peat and pozzolano whose low density limits the weight on the load-bearing structure. In mediterranean regions, the climate conditions make this type of arrangement very much less successful. In our experience, however, there are various options for green roofs that are feasible in regions where there is a pronounced summer drought.

• The first option consists of accepting that in summer *Sedum* species have meagre vegetation and huddle in on themselves, surviving as best they can. In the mediterranean climate sedums can indeed survive without water in a shallow substrate, but do not provide an effective cover for the roof. They can be planted together with the dwarf iris, *Iris lutescens*, which is also able to survive in very tough conditions thanks to its thick rhizomes that act as reserves during the period of hydric deficit.

• A second option is to increase the depth of the substrate substantially (18 to 20 cm),

adding to the peat-pozzolano mixture from 40 to 50% of topsoil, in order to provide the roots with a medium that has better potential as a buffer. If the most drought-resistant *Sedum* species are then chosen, it is possible to achieve a relatively uniform coverage of the roof without summer watering. The range of sedums can be completed by other succulent plants that tolerate the same conditions, such as *Drosanthemum hispidum*, *Malephora crocea* or *Malephora lutea*. The depth of the substrate also allows summer-dormant bulbs to be used (*Sternbergia*, *Crocus*, *Narcissus*, *Allium*) and pioneer herbaceous plants whose abundant production of seeds ensures that they continue from year to year. Such pioneer plants might include, for example, *Salvia verbenaca*, *Scabiosa argentea*, *Goniolimon speciosum*, *Glaucium flavum*, *Asphodelus fistulosus*, *Stipa tenuissima*, *Nigella damascena* or *Eschscholzia californica*.

• A third option consists of integrating the concept of the green roof into a honeycomb-like complex, proposed by many professional roofing experts, which serves both as a drainage system and for water storage. An occasional watering of the roof (about twice a month in summer)

makes even more diversified planting possible, always provided that the substrate is deep enough. Sedums, irises, bulbous plants and pioneer plants can then be completed by the whole range of perennial plants that grow in flowering steppes, such as carpeting thymes, achilleas, *Phyla* or *Centaurea bella*. In spite of the watering, the consumption of mains water may be zero if a system for harvesting and storing rainwater is installed. If this is the case, the roof serves a double function as a green space and as a surface for harvesting the water used to meet its needs.

• Apart from the traditional benefits of a green roof (thermal insulation, air purification, regulation of water run-off), plantings that include a large range of species also become a refuge for insects and birds, contributing to the biodiversity of urban areas. From this point of view, *Sedum* species always remain an important element in the range of plants used, whatever technical option has been chosen. Their flowers constitute an important source of pollen that attracts numerous insects, for example the very elegant long hoverfly, *Sphaerophoria scripta*, whose larvae devour aphids avidly.

a very interesting *Sedum* for the mediterranean climate since it possesses remarkable qualities. Of all the carpeting sedums that we have tried out in our garden, it is not only the most vigorous but also the most drought-resistant. Its behaviour on green roofs with only a shallow substrate is excellent. Its small evergreen leaves, thick and spatulate, are a lovely bright green. They take on a tinge of red in winter. Flowering is spectacular: in June the panicles of white flowers cover the foliage completely. Origin uncertain. Hardiness: −10 to −12 °C. Drought resistance code: 5. Planting density: 9 per square metre.

• ***Sedum ochroleucum*** grows in the stony expanses of the garrigue, between rocks and

Sedum album takes on a pink or red colour in winter. Its succulent leaves store water, enabling the plant to survive in very harsh conditions.

Sedum gypsicola has some remarkable qualities: of all the sedums that we have been able to trial, it is not only the most vigorous but also the most drought-resistant. Its bright green foliage disappears beneath the white flowers in June.

Sedum ochroleucum and Thymus hirsutus on a green roof that gets occasional watering. If the substrate is deep enough, it is possible to expand the range of groundcover plants that can be used on green roofs in mediterranean regions.

on old walls. Its slender leaves, arranged in very regular spirals around the stems, are grey-green in summer and take on a lovely greyish-purple colour in winter. In early summer the plant is covered in pale yellow flowers, at the same time very soft and luminous (the name *ochroleucum* derives from the Greek *ochros*, "pale yellow", and *leucos*, "white", "bright"). It can be planted in old walls, together with houseleeks such as *Sempervivum tectorum*, *Sempervivum calcaratum* or *Sempervivum arachnoideum*. It also withstands the difficult conditions on green roofs very well. Origin: Southern Europe, Asia Minor. Hardiness: −15 °C. Drought resistance code: 4. Planting density: 16 per square metre.

• **Sedum sediforme**, or Mediterranean stonecrop, has slender grey-green succulent leaves tightly packed along its stems. In early summer its numerous pale yellow flowers light up walls and garrigue screes. Their abundant pollen attracts a multitude of pollinators. This is a tough and undemanding plant that can be used in the most difficult situations. In the mediterranean climate it is the best *Sedum* species to use with *Sedum gypsicola* on unirrigated green roofs where

Sedum sediforme is a tough species that can be used in the most difficult conditions.

A bee harvests pollen from an inflorescence of Sedum sediforme. The planting on green roofs can offer food and shelter to many beneficial insects.

the substrate must be of little depth because of the load-bearing limits of the structure. Origin: Mediterranean Basin. Hardiness: −15 °C and below. Drought resistance code: 5. Planting density: 9 per square metre.

• **Silene ucrainica** forms a large regular cushion of dark green leaves. In May the plant is covered in a light mass of supple inflorescences. The pink flowers are graceful, their fringed petals delicately curling inwards. *Silene ucrainica* is easy to grow and long-lived. In our garden we use it in large groundcover beds together with other cushion-forming plants such as *Helichrysum orientale*, *Lavandula × chaytorae*, *Thymbra capitata* and *Santolina magonica*. Origin: Ukraine. Hardiness: −15 °C and below. Drought resistance code: 3. Planting density: 2 or 3 per square metre.

Silene ucrainica spreads into a magnificent cushion, which is covered in pink flowers in May. Easy to grow, it makes a robust groundcover that deserves to be better known.

Soleirolia soleirolii (Urticaceae), Mind-Your-Own-Business

Origin: Corsica, Sardinia; **Height**: 2 to 10 cm depending on cultivation conditions; **Spread**: 40 cm or more; **Position**: shade or semi-shade;

Hardiness: the foliage blackens at the first touch of frost but the rootstock sprouts again in spring from –8 to –10 °C; **Drought resistance code**: 1.

A perennial with tiny light green leaves tightly packed together, forming a striking-looking mossy carpet. *Soleirolia* needs regular humidity. In the mediterranean climate it can be used to colonize the cracks between paving stones on a terrace, in the shade beneath a pergola, or on the north side of the house: its roots benefit from the moisture trapped below the paving stones and thus need less frequent watering. In parts of the garden that receive frequent irrigation it is possible to use *Soleirolia soleirolii* in a mixture of other shade-loving groundcovers with relatively high water requirements, such as *Dichondra repens* or *Ophiopogon japonicus*. Planting density: 9 per square metre.

Propagation by division in autumn or spring.

Stachys byzantina (Lamiaceae)

Origin: from the Caucasus to Iran; **Height of foliage**: 15 cm; **Height when in flower**: 50 cm or more; **Spread**: 40 to 50 cm; **Position**: sun; **Hardiness**: –15 °C and below; **Drought resistance code**: 3.

A perennial whose evergreen leaves are long, grey and downy, turning silver in summer. The plant is sometimes called "lamb's ears" because of the long silky hairs that seem carefully combed on both sides of each leaf. The suckering stock slowly spreads laterally and the plant forms a very ornamental spreading cushion. At the beginning of summer the woolly spikes bear small mauve-pink flowers, visited by numerous pollinating insects such as carpenter bees. The very abundant flowering tends to exhaust the plant. Clipping off the dried inflorescences after flowering allows the vegetation to be refurbished rapidly in early autumn. In our garden, we nevertheless like to leave a few of the inflorescences unclipped, in order for the plant to self-seed prolifically, especially in areas where the soil is covered by a mineral mulch. *Stachys byzantina* likes soil that is friable, deeply decompacted and perfectly drained. It is short-lived in places where the soil remains wet for a long time in winter. Planting density: 4 per square metre.

Propagation by seed in autumn or by cuttings from suckers in autumn or spring.

Stachys byzantina likes well-drained soil in a gravel garden, since its magnificent woolly silver foliage cannot tolerate stagnant damp. The plants growing with it here are *Anthyllis cytisoides*, *Lavandula* × *intermedia*, *Helichrysum orientale* and *Centaurea bella*.

Stenotaphrum secundatum (Poaceae)

Origin: hot regions of America and Africa; **Height**: 5 to 20 cm depending on cultivation conditions and degree of foot traffic; **Spread**: 60 to 80 cm or more; **Position**: sun; **Hardiness**: –6 to –8 ° C for short periods (new plantings are more sensitive to the cold); **Drought resistance code**: 1.

A large-leaved grass, which spreads rapidly by means of its interweaving network of subterranean rhizomes and by its long above-ground stolons. In mild climates the plant makes an amazing and very dense lawn, which feels like a flexible mattress underfoot. To confuse matters, *Stenotaphrum secundatum* is sometimes called Kikuyu grass. However, Kikuyu grass is in fact another warm-season grass, *Pennisetum clandestinum*, which looks fairly similar to *Stenotaphrum* but whose invasive potential represents a major disadvantage. *Stenotaphrum* requires regular watering, about once a week during the summer, in order for its foliage to remain good and uniform. Once well established, it can go for several weeks without water, for instance if one is going away on holiday. After being abandoned for a while, a few closely spaced waterings will rapidly make it look good again. Numerous spikelets appear above the foliage in summer, and the *Stenotaphrum* then needs to be mown several times if it is to remain a handsome lawn. These spikelets are sterile, with the result that there is no risk of the plant self-seeding beyond its designated area. Like all macrothermic grasses (see page 41), *Stenotaphrum* becomes dormant in winter when the soil gets cold: it ceases photosynthesis and survives thanks to its rhizomes, which act as storage organs. The foliage now becomes a not very ornamental yellow-brown. It greens up again relatively late in the spring, when the soil has warmed up thoroughly, generally at the end of April but sometimes not until the beginning of May. By contrast, in regions with a mild climate *Stenotaphrum* stays green almost throughout the whole winter: these are the regions where it is most widely used to replace lawns. *Stenotaphrum secundatum* is unfussy about soil type but grows faster in a friable soil that has been deeply decompacted. Planting density: 4 per square metre.

Propagation by cuttings in early summer.

Stipa calamagrostis (Poaceae)

Origin: Southern Europe; **Height of foliage**: 50 cm; **Height when in flower**: 70 cm; **Spread**: 80 cm; **Position**: sun; **Hardiness**: –15 °C and below; **Drought resistance code**: 4.

A grass with narrow leaves, which are green in summer and turn golden in winter. The stock suckers slowly and in time the plant forms a broad, supple mass with a fountaining habit. The inflorescences, first green then golden, appear in early summer. They remain for many months on the plant, which stays ornamental until the beginning of the winter. In our garden we like to grow it in association with other species that are particularly attractive in early autumn, such as *Salvia microphylla*, *Salvia greggii*, *Salvia chamaedryoides*, *Epilobium canum* or *Erica manipuliflora*. In the wild *Stipa calamagrostis* thrives in degraded garrigues, growing on rocky slopes together with cistuses and euphorbias. Fine colonies are to be seen in the hinterland of Menton, on the rocky peaks of the villages of Sainte-Agnès and Gorbio, which mark the transition between the coastal area and the foothills of the Maritime Alps. In the garden *Stipa calamagrostis* prefers a poor stony or sandy soil with perfect drainage. It is a tough and long-lived grass. Planting density: 2 per square metre. *Propagation by seed in autumn or by division in autumn or winter.*

The "angel's hair" of *Stipa barbata* stirs in the slightest breeze. The plant has seeded itself here in front of one of the best groundcover cistuses in our garden, *Cistus* × *pulverulentus*.

The golden inflorescences of *Stipa calamagrostis* last for many months, from July to December. Among the plants in this autumn scene are *Salvia chamaedryoides*, *Phlomis chrysophylla*, *Artemisia thuscula* and *Euphorbia characias* subsp. *wulfenii*. The *Stipa* is planted beneath a *Pistacia chinensis*.

• **Stipa barbata** has "angel's hair" inflorescences that float in the slightest breeze. The thin foliage is compensated for by the exceptional beauty of the plant when it flowers in June. This grass self-seeds easily on stony ground. It can be grown with other pioneer species such as *Centranthus ruber* or *Gaura lindheimeri* to create magnificent ornamental plantings whose composition slowly changes from year to year. Another grass species with "angel's hair" inflorescences is *Stipa pennata*, which makes an extraordinary

sight in the windswept landscapes of the Larzac plateau. Origin: Southern Europe, Asia Minor, North Africa. Hardiness: −12 to −15 °C. Drought resistance code: 5. Planting density: 6 per square metre.

• **Stipa juncea** is a grass with light foliage which colonizes the edges of stony paths in the garrigues of the South of France. The silver spikelets appear in late spring. This plant is happy in flowering steppes, where its fine silhouette emerges from among the

carpeting plants. It can be grown with other light-foliaged grasses, such as *Stipa pennata* or *Stipa barbata*. Origin: South-West Europe, North Africa. Hardiness: −15 °C and below. Drought resistance code: 4. Planting density: 4 per square metre.

• **Stipa tenuissima**, synonym *Nassella tenuissima*, forms a supple mass whose very narrow leaves are constantly swayed by the wind. Although it is fairly short-lived, it is a pioneer plant which self-seeds easily along paths or in areas of open ground where it meets no competition. Its ability to seed itself has led to questions about its potential invasiveness. In its natural environment the plant is spread by sheep – the seeds agglomerate in prickly balls which easily stick to their wool. These balls of seeds also roll along the ground, blown by the wind, and the plant seeds itself wherever they come to rest, for example at the foot of a wall, fence or hedgerow. However they are not carried great distances by the wind, unlike the seeds

The massive flowering of *Stipa pennata* creates a transient vision of movement which for a few weeks transforms the austere landscape of the Larzac plateau.

of *Stipa* species which are equipped with long feathery awns. *Stipa tenuissima* presents no risk of escaping from the garden and seeding itself far away. Nevertheless in some parts of the world it is reported to be invasive in specific environments such as over-grazed steppes, where it can have a real negative impact: it reduces the profitability of the pastures since it is not eaten by sheep. We thus recommend to landscape managers that they avoid using *Stipa tenuissima* in agricultural areas near pastures in steppes, for example along roads where it could be disseminated by passing sheep. In gardens, on the contrary, *Stipa tenuissima* is worth using for its many qualities, both ornamental and practical: it requires no water, no fertilizers and no pesticides and does not need any maintenance. Origin: Texas, Mexico. Hardiness: –12 to –15 °C. Drought resistance code: 5. Planting density: 4 per square metre.

Tanacetum densum (Asteraceae)

Origin: Anatolia; **Height**: 15 cm; **Spread**: 40 cm; **Position**: sun; **Hardiness**: –15 °C and below; **Drought resistance code**: 4.

A sub-shrub with spreading vegetation that forms a thick and soft-looking carpet. The plant spreads by means of its lateral stems which root on contact with the soil. The supple inflorescences bear numerous little yellow flowers from May to July. The small leaves are delicately cut like the feathers of a bird, each segment being itself cut into tiny regular teeth. Covered in a thick down of white hairs, the leaves resemble finely worked silver lace. When crushed between the fingers, they release an essential oil with a mild scent of camphor, olive oil and bay leaves, reminiscent of the soap factories in the souk of Aleppo. This essential oil contains chemical substances which limit the germination of competing species (allelopathy). *Tanacetum* thus makes a groundcover which requires little maintenance because once it is established it doesn't need any hand-weeding. In our garden we like to grow it with other plants that resist competition, such as *Centaurea bella* or *Teucrium marum*, in order to create large groundcover beds that require minimal maintenance. *Tanacetum densum* needs poor soil, stony or sandy. In our experience, provided that the soil is adequately drained this is a robust and particularly long-lived plant. Planting density: 9 per square metre.

Propagation by division in autumn or by softwood cuttings in spring.

• ***Teucrium flavum*** forms a pretty ball of dark green leaves. It is a pioneer plant that self-seeds abundantly in uncultivated parts of the garden. The pale yellow flowers appear from May to July. They are rich in nectar and attract numerous beneficial insects. Origin: Mediterranean Basin. Hardiness: –12 to –15 °C. Drought resistance code: 3.5. Planting density: 4 per square metre.

• ***Teucrium fruticans* 'Agadir'** is a cultivar of the shrubby germander which we have selected for its fine foliage that is silver in winter and becomes almost white in summer. The very bright blue flowers are well set off by the pale foliage. In our garden the mixture of *Teucrium fruticans* 'Agadir', *Rosmarinus officinalis* 'Sappho', *Euphorbia*

In our garden a specimen of *Stipa tenuissima* which has seeded itself into the gravel stands like a sentinel beside a path. Among the plants in this groundcover scene are *Achillea umbellata*, *Ballota acetabulosa*, *Euphorbia cyparissias*, *Euphorbia characias* subsp. *wulfenii* and *Salvia fruticosa*.

dendroides and *Euphorbia characias* subsp. *wulfenii* creates a magnificent yellow and blue picture in late winter. Origin: South-Western Mediterranean Basin. Hardiness: –10 to –12 °C. Drought resistance code: 4. Planting density: 1 per square metre.

• ***Teucrium marum*** has small silver leaves that are very aromatic with a piquant scent. The plant forms a handsome flattened cushion of very dense and regular vegetation. Although relatively slow-growing, it makes an excellent groundcover that is long-lived in our garden. The pinkish mauve flowers appear from June to early August, attracting

numerous bees which come for the abundant nectar at a time when there are not many plants flowering. At the end of summer some of the leaves may fall, revealing the decorative framework of silvery stems. *Teucrium marum* can be grown with other species that flower in early summer, such as *Origanum laevigatum* or *Goniolimon speciosum*. Origin: islands of the Western Mediterranean Basin. Hardiness: –10 to –12 °C. Drought resistance code: 5. Planting density: 6 per square metre.

Many other *Teucrium* species that form small groundcover cushions are useful for creating a wave-like structure in gravel gardens. We may mention, for example, *Teucrium aureum*, whose almost white foliage is covered

in acid yellow-green flowers, *Teucrium cossonii*, whose beautiful silver foliage serves as a screen that sets off its mauve flowers, *Teucrium divaricatum*, whose pinkish mauve flowers emerge from bright green foliage, or *Teucrium lusitanicum*, which forms a robust cushion of golden-grey foliage. In the steppe grazing lands of the Larzac plateau, the lovely *Teucrium montanum* is to be found, whose vegetation, flattened to the ground by wind, cold and passing sheep, is adorned with large creamy-yellow flowers. Native to the garrigues of the South of France, the wall germander *(Teucrium chamaedrys)* is a herbaceous plant which suckers among the stones at the

The mauve-pink flowers of *Teucrium marum* appear from June to August, at a time when there are few flowers in dry gardens.

Teucrium cossonii is one of the most beautiful groundcovers in our garden. It thrives in light soil, stony or sandy, with perfect drainage.

Teucrium chamaedrys is a discreet but particularly robust plant. It can be planted with *Brachypodium retusum* and *Iris lutescens* to create a wild lawn suitable for garrigue conditions.

Thymbra capitata has a fine late flowering. In our garden it starts to flower at the end of June.

Thymbra capitata and *Sarcopoterium spinosum* are the dominant plants in this mountain landscape in southern Crete.

cushions of *Sarcopoterium spinosum*. In some Aegean islands these two species dominate the entire landscape, where the tough living conditions associated with dryness, poor soil, salt spray and the everyday pressure of goats favour plants that grow in cushions. In spite of an absence of goats, in our garden *Thymbra capitata* preserves its stiff cushion shape, huddled in on itself. It has evolved several strategies to resist drought: the length of its root system, which enables it to explore an important water reserve, its small needle-like leaves whose thick cuticle limits water loss, and the partial falling of its foliage during prolonged drought. This loss of leaves reveals the decorative silvery branch structure, for the stems are covered in a dense felt consisting of minute white

side of paths. It is particularly drought-resistant and can be planted in garrigue grassland consisting of *Brachypodium retusum*, *Carex halleriana* and *Iris lutescens*. Finally *Teucrium × lucidrys* forms a vigorous cushion of bright green evergreen leaves and its abundant pink flowers in early summer attract numerous pollinators and beneficial insects.

Thymbra capitata
Synonym: *Thymus capitatus*

Origin: Mediterranean Basin; **Height**: 40 to 50 cm; **Spread**: 50 cm; **Position**: sun; **Hardiness**: –10 to –12 °C; **Drought resistance code**: 5.

Formerly classified as a *Thymus* species, *Thymbra capitata* is a plant that is very common in the Eastern Mediterranean Basin. It colonizes degraded garrigues, growing between the stones in the driest areas, often in the company of magnificent spiny

hairs. In spite of the seasonal changes in its vegetation, *Thymbra capitata* remains attractive all year long, even in times of great drought. The leaves of *Thymbra capitata* release a powerful scent when crushed, similar to that of savory. The pinkish mauve flowers appear in June-July, when thyme species have finished flowering. They are much appreciated by bees, which find in them an abundant source of nectar. In our garden we like to grow this plant with another cushion-shaped species, *Teucrium marum*, whose late flowering is also appreciated by bees. *Thymbra capitata* likes poor stony or sandy soil with perfect drainage. It is long-lived, especially if one takes care to trim its tips every year, one's secateurs filling the role of rapacious goats. Planting density: 4 per square metre.
Propagation by seed in autumn or by cuttings in spring.

Thymus (Lamiaceae)

The thymes are unbeatable plants for groundcover gardens. Known for their culinary and medicinal uses since antiquity, they are aromatic plants famed for the powerful scent of their foliage. The essential oil produced by the tiny glands hidden on the undersides of the leaves contains chemical substances that limit attacks by insect pests and inhibit the germination of competing species (allelopathy). The anti-germinating activity of the essential oil is complemented by the exudations directly released from the roots, whose herbicidal properties also contribute to the suppression of competitors. The thymes are excellent groundcover plants in gardens for they require little weeding. They can be divided into two large groups, according to the way they are used as groundcover: on the one hand carpeting thymes which form a very low-growing groundcover, and on the other hand those that have a cushion- or ball-shaped habit.

Thymes with a carpeting habit

This group includes thymes whose lateral stems root on contact with the soil, forming fine, even carpets. On small areas they can be remarkable as a uniform, single-species planting. A striking flowering carpet can be created by mixing different species at random. When planted on gravel, the carpeting thymes can also create a pedestrian surface suitable for foot traffic in flowering steppes.

Thymus ciliatus, a robust and adaptable plant, is easy to grow. It can be planted together with *Achillea crithmifolia* to create a groundcover that withstands a moderate amount of foot traffic.

Thymus ciliatus

Origin: North Africa; **Height**: 2 to 8 cm depending on cultivation conditions and degree of foot traffic; **Spread**: 50 cm or more; **Position**: sun; **Hardiness**: −12 to −15 °C; **Drought resistance code**: 2.5.

A sub-shrub with a vigorous carpeting habit, which withstands a moderate amount of foot traffic. The long white hairs on the leaves, visible to the naked eye, resemble eyelashes, hence the specific epithet *ciliatus*. When the leaves are crushed, they give off a scent which is initially like freshly cut hay then develops a hotter, spicy note. The pink flowers, a source of honey, appear in May. Grouped together in heads tightly packed together, they form a downy mass which completely hides the foliage. The evergreen leaves change colour over the course of the year: grey-mauve in winter they become grey-green in the spring growing season, then take on an amazing rusty-red hue in periods of prolonged drought. At the end of the summer the plant becomes dormant, losing some of its leaves. Irrigation approximately once a fortnight in summer will allow the plant to maintain handsome foliage throughout the year. In this way *Thymus ciliatus* can be used to create an even single-species planting in small areas. It is easy to grow and suitable for many different situations. For larger areas, it can be planted together with other vigorous carpeting plants such as *Thymus hirsutus, Phyla canescens* or *Achillea crithmifolia*, to make a flowering carpet that requires little maintenance. *Thymus ciliatus* is unfussy as regards soil type but grows faster in light, well-drained soil. Planting density: 4 per square metre.
Propagation by division in autumn or by softwood tip cuttings in autumn or spring.

Thymus herba-barona

Origin: Corsica, Sardinia, Balearic Islands; **Height**: 2 to 10 cm depending on cultivation conditions and degree of foot traffic; **Spread**: 40 cm or more; **Position**: sun; **Hardiness**: −12 to −15 °C; **Drought resistance code**: 2.

A sub-shrub with small dark green evergreen leaves that sometimes take on violet hues in winter. It makes a fine uniform carpet that withstands moderate foot traffic. When the leaves are crushed they release a pleasant scent: initially this is fresh and reminiscent of citrus peel but a few seconds later the scent develops a peppery note rather like cumin. *Thymus herba-barona* loses some of its leaves in prolonged droughts. Watering approximately once a fortnight in summer will allow the plant to maintain handsome foliage throughout the year. The bright pink flowers appear in May-June. *Thymus herba-barona* can serve as the basis for a striking flowering carpet consisting of a mixture of scented thymes such as *Thymus ciliatus, Thymus praecox* subsp. *polytrichus, Thymus praecox, Thymus pannonicus* and *Thymus serpyllum* 'Lemon Curd': simply walking on these thymes releases a delicious bouquet of scents. *Thymus herba-barona* likes being planted on a bed of gravel, which is effective in conserving moisture in the soil between waterings. Planting density: 6 per square metre.
Propagation by division in autumn or by softwood tip cuttings in autumn or in spring.

Thymus hirsutus

Origin (probable): Crimea, Balkans; **Height**: 3 to 5 cm; **Spread**: 50 cm and more; **Position**: sun; **Hardiness**: −15 °C and below. **Drought resistance code**: 2.

Thymus hirsutus has handsome neat foliage and flowers abundantly. It is one of the best plants for creating a uniform carpet in small areas.

The nomenclature of thymes is complex, and although we have our doubts about the validity of the name *Thymus hirsutus* to designate a carpeting thyme which we have been growing for many years it is the one we are using at the moment. This thyme is also known as *Thymus roegneri* and sometimes known as *Thymus glabrescens* subsp. *urumovii*. It is possible that it is one of the many cultivars of *Thymus serpyllum*. Whatever its name, it is a remarkable groundcover plant: in our experience, it is one of the best plants for small single-species carpets suitable for occasional foot traffic. It is a tough and adaptable species that is long-lived. Its fast-growing stems root easily on contact with the soil and the plant forms a handsome low-growing carpet, capable of withstanding moderate foot traffic. Its June flowering is spectacular: the tight mass of bright pink flowers, a very good source of honey, covers the dark green foliage completely. In our garden *Thymus hirsutus* loses some of its leaves in prolonged droughts. Irrigation every ten or fifteen days enables the plant to maintain good foliage throughout the year. Unfussy about soil type, it nevertheless grows faster in light well-drained soil. It can also be planted together with other carpeting plants that flower profusely, such *Matricaria tchihatchewii*, *Potentilla neumanniana* and *Phyla canescens*, to create large mixed carpets, very ornamental in late spring and early summer. Planting density: 4 per square metre.

Propagation by division in autumn or by softwood tip cuttings in autumn or spring.

• **Thymus praecox** subsp. *polytrichus* has dark green leaves that turn partially red in winter. It forms an even carpet that can withstand a moderate amount of foot traffic. The leaves release a pleasant scent of bergamot when crushed. The bright pink flowers appear in May. In unirrigated zones of the garden the plant loses some of its leaves when it becomes dormant in late summer. It can be watered about once a fortnight in summer in order for its foliage to remain in good condition throughout the year. The bright pink flowers appear in May. *Thymus praecox* subsp. *polytrichus* resists drought better when it is planted on gravel. Origin: mountains of Southern Europe. Hardiness: −15 °C and below. Drought resistance code: 2. Planting density: 6 per square metre.

• **Thymus serpyllum** 'Elfin' forms a miniature carpet of tiny leaves closely crammed together, giving the plant a very striking mossy look. It is often used in Japanese-inspired gardens. It is happy in the cracks between paving stones on a terrace or among stepping stones, where it benefits from the underlying moisture trapped beneath the stones. Origin: Europe. Hardiness: −15 °C and below. Drought resistance code: 2. Planting density: 16 per square metre.

Among the many other carpeting thymes which might form part of mixed carpets, we may mention *Thymus praecox*, which is happy in stony soils and whose aromatic foliage is covered in bright pink flowers, *Thymus pannonicus*, with toothed leaves and tender mauve flowers, *Thymus leucotrichus* subsp. *neiceffii*, with silver-grey leaves that form a very low-growing carpet, *Thymus serpyllum* 'Album', with light green leaves and pure white flowers, and *Thymus serpyllum* 'Lemon Curd', with thick vegetation and a delicious lemony scent. The planting density for these carpeting thymes is generally 6 per square metre.

Thymes with a cushion- or ball-shaped habit

This group contains thymes whose woody branching stems form compact balls that spread to a greater or lesser extent. While the carpeting thymes, native to mountain

Like many carpeting thymes, *Thymus praecox* grows wild in stony steppes, as here on the Larzac plateau.

Thymus mastichina in the Sierra de Huetor, north of Granada.

regions, appreciate occasional irrigation in summer, by contrast the cushion- or ball-shaped thymes mostly originate from the plains and coasts of the Mediterranean in an environment subject to prolonged summer drought; all the thymes in this group are thus resistant to drought. They cannot tolerate summer watering as they are prone to be killed by diseases like *Phytophthora* which spread in hot and damp conditions. They should thus be planted only in zones of the garden that receive no irrigation.

Thymus camphoratus

Origin: Southern Portugal; **Height:** 20 to 30 cm; **Spread:** 40 cm or more; **Position:** sun; **Hardiness:** −10 to −12 °C; **Drought resistance code:** 3.

A sub-shrub with evergreen dark green leaves. The plant forms a handsome and regular dense cushion. Its profuse pale pink flowers, a good source of honey, appear in May. When crushed, its foliage releases a powerful scent of camphor and turpentine which remains on one's fingers for a long time. *Thymus camphoratus* prefers poor soils, stony or sandy, that are perfectly drained. In a gravel garden it can be planted with other species that form compact cushions, such as *Rhodanthemum hosmariense*, *Teucrium lusitanicum* and *Veronica polifolia*. Planting density: 6 per square metre.
Propagation by cuttings in autumn or spring.

• *Thymus mastichina* forms an airy ball, covered in beautiful creamy-white, cottony-looking flowers in May-June. When crushed, the silver foliage gives off a powerful scent reminiscent of eucalyptus, liquorice and turpentine. It grows in poor and stony soil in the mountains of Southern Spain and Portugal. It is happy in gravel gardens, where it can be planted with other plants with very aromatic foliage such as *Salvia clevelandii*, *Origanum majorana* var. *tenuifolium* and *Artemisia herba-alba*. Origin: Iberian peninsula. Hardiness: −10 to −12 °C. Drought resistance: 5. Planting density: 9 per square metre.

• *Thymus vulgaris*, the common thyme of the garrigue, forms a spreading cushion, covered in small pink flowers in spring. Very variable in the wild, its foliage can be green, grey or silvery. The form we grow in our garden has grey leaves and a particularly strong scent. In periods of extreme drought it loses almost all its leaves, tiny buds packed into the old leaf axils maintaining a slower rate of photosynthesis. The plant rapidly puts out new leaves with the first autumn rains. It self-seeds prolifically in poor and stony soil and we leave it to its own devices in a small bed where many other plants self-seed freely, including *Stachys cretica*, *Euphorbia myrsinites* and *Asphodeline lutea*. Origin: Western Mediterranean Basin. Hardiness: −12 to −15 °C. Drought resistance code: 4. Planting density: 9 per square metre.

Trifolium fragiferum (Fabaceae)
Strawberry clover

Origin: Europe, Asia Minor, North Africa, Canary Isles and Madeira; **Height of foliage**: 2 to 15 cm depending on cultivation conditions and degree of foot traffic; **Height when in flower**: 5 to 20 cm; **Spread**: 50 cm and more; **Position**: sun; **Hardiness**: –15 °C and below (the foliage may be superficially burnt by the cold when the temperature falls to –8 to –10 °C); **Drought resistance code**: 3.

A perennial with oval leaves divided into three leaflets, pale green in spring then dark green in summer. The plant spreads rapidly by its rhizomes and by its lateral stems which root on contact with the soil. It forms a magnificent carpet that withstands regular foot traffic. Its appearance and height

At the end of winter the foliage of *Trifolium fragiferum* becomes such an intense green that it looks almost artificial: bacterial activity in the soil sets off massive self-fertilization of the plant by means of the nitrogen-fixing nodules along its roots.

A wild lawn where *Trifolium fragiferum* and *Plantago coronopus* are dominant. This type of wild lawn requires little maintenance and withstands regular foot traffic.

The pink flowers of the strawberry clover are, with a little imagination, reminiscent of raspberries or strawberries.

depend on the degree of foot traffic. In areas that are walked on a lot, the leaves are small and the plant forms a fine, flat, ground-hugging carpet all year round. In areas that are not much frequented, the leaves are larger and the height of the vegetation follows a seasonal cycle: in autumn and winter the carpet remains low, while from February onwards the foliage takes on an amazing bright green that looks almost artificial as bacterial activity in the soil triggers a massive self-fertilization through the nitrogen-fixing nodules on its roots (see page 119); in spring the vegetation grows in a spectacular manner and rapidly becomes thicker, reaching a height of 15 to 20 cm when the plant comes into flower; finally, after flowering, the tall growth becomes floppy and partially dries out. When one wants a regular-looking carpet, there are thus two methods: one can either plant *Trifolium fragiferum* in an area

that is widely used so that the regular foot traffic keeps it low and compact throughout the year, or one can mow it regularly from March to June to keep the carpet low. In this case it is not necessary to mow during the rest of the year as the great growth spurt is a purely springtime phenomenon. A small manual lawn mower with a spiral blade, without a box to collect the cuttings, is perfectly suitable for this type of mowing.

The strawberry clover flowers at the end of spring, attracting numerous bees which come to make the most of the abundant nectar. The pink, or sometimes white, flowers are grouped in oval flower heads, recalling the shape of a raspberry or strawberry, hence the name of the plant (although the analogy is rather unconvincing, poor Linnaeus having apparently run out of imagination when he named this clover). When they fade, the flowers are replaced by light cream-coloured

seedheads with a curious membranous texture.

The strawberry clover is unfussy about soil type. It is a tough and adaptable plant which is easy to grow. In our experience, it is one of the best choices if one wants a single-species carpet that grows fast. In zones of the garden that are not irrigated it loses some of its leaves during summer. If it is to maintain good foliage all year round it requires thoroughly deep watering about once a fortnight in summer. The more the carpet is walked on, the smaller the leaf surfaces, limiting water loss. Too frequent watering is not beneficial: when conditions are hot and humid the clover is vulnerable to various cryptogamic diseases, rust or *Oidium*, which do not harm the plant much but mar its appearance. If in our garden *Trifolium fragiferum* happens to suffer a brief attack of rust or *Oidium*, for example during a warm and damp spring, we mow it flat to allow its vegetation to regenerate.

The strawberry clover can be planted in a mixture of other vigorously growing carpeting plants. It could be planted together with *Phyla canescens* for example; the handsome winter foliage of the clover would mask the foliage of the *Phyla* when it becomes less attractive in winter. The strawberry clover can also be planted with the hybrid Bermuda grass, *Cynodon* 'Santa Ana'. Like all grasses, *Cynodon* is greedy for nitrogen: the clover serves as a fertilizing plant, reinforcing the colonizing power of the carpet of *Cynodon*. When *Trifolium* and *Cynodon* are grown in association, the two plants mutually balance one another: the clover strengthens the *Cynodon* and the *Cynodon* in turn, by using some of the nitrogen fixed by the clover, reduces the latter's spring growth, with the result that it needs to be mown less frequently. Finally, the strawberry clover can form the basis of a wild lawn that is home to many species such as *Achillea millefolium*, *Bellis perennis*, *Plantago coronopus*, *Prunella vulgaris* and *Sanguisorba minor*. The planting density of 4 per square metre applies to a single-species carpet.

Propagation by cuttings in autumn, winter or spring. In our experience, sowing directly in the ground gives disappointing results when one wants to create a single-species patch since germination is slow and uneven. However, if one is making a wild lawn that includes many "weeds", sowing directly in situ is practicable.

• **Trifolium repens** is the common lawn clover or white clover. It can be distinguished from the strawberry clover by its heart-shaped leaflets, its larger leaves and flowers, and its markedly taller vegetation, requiring more frequent mowing. It is also greedier of water in summer. Its white flowers are a very good source of honey. It is one of the main constituents of the "ecological lawns" that are being more and more widely planted in North America as an alternative to lawns consisting only of grasses. Micheline Lévesque's book, *L'Écopelouse. Pour une pelouse vraiment écologique*, published in Quebec, gives some idea of the extent of the anti-lawn movement spreading through North America (see the bibliography). Ecolawn supporters plant this clover together with other lawn "weeds" to create lawns that do not require either fertilizers or pesticides. The climate of Quebec

The white flowers of *Trifolium repens* decorate a path mown in a wild lawn at the Royal Botanic Gardens, Kew.

allows this type of natural lawn to remain perfectly green in summer, so that the only maintenance needed is an occasional mowing to keep it short enough to be walked on. In mediterranean-climate regions, by contrast, there are various options for maintaining a lawn based on white clover: one may let it follow its natural cycle and dry out almost completely in summer, regenerating naturally with the first autumn rains; one may irrigate it once or twice a month to keep it more or less green, accepting that some of the vegetation will lose its leaves in summer; or, finally, one may water it deeply about once a week, which will enable one to have a green and dense lawn throughout the whole summer.

Seed mixtures for wild lawns are increasingly available on the market. They often include a small percentage of grasses that germinate rapidly, such as English rye grass and sheep's fescue. The purpose of these grasses is to provide a preliminary groundcover until the other slower-growing species become established. Depending on the watering regime adopted, these grasses may continue to form part of the wild lawn in the medium term, or may disappear completely after the first summer. *Trifolium repens* is unfussy about soil type. Origin: Europe, Asia, North Africa; Hardiness: −15 °C and below. Drought resistance code: 1. Planting density when pot-grown plants are used: 4 per square metre. Sowing density of a clover-based wild lawn: 15 grams per square metre.

Propagation by seed sown directly in the ground in early autumn or late winter.

• **Verbena rigida** is a perennial with rough-textured toothed leaves that are deciduous in winter. It spreads by means of its rhizomes and forms a broad, vigorous groundcover, Its very abundant mauve flowers appear from May to July. The cultivar 'Lilacina' has pretty, luminous pale mauve flowers. In our garden we have had fun putting in a few plants of *Verbena rigida* 'Lilacina' at the edge of a lawn composed of *Zoysia tenuifolia* and *Achillea coarctata*, and the result is spectacular every spring: the *Zoysia* is thickly studded with yellow and mauve flowers, especially at the edges which are not much walked on, where it is less dominant. Origin: Southern Brazil, Argentina. Hardiness: −10 to −12 °C. Drought resistance code: 3. Planting density: 2 or 3 per square metre.

• **Veronica polifolia** spreads slowly by means of its lateral stems that root on contact with the soil. The bright blue flowers, which appear in April-May, are set off by the velvety, grey, soft-looking foliage. *Veronica polifolia* can be used in a gravel garden together with other grey- or silver-leaved plants such as *Artemisia pedemontana*, *Cerastium candidissimum* and *Teucrium aureum*. It requires perfectly drained soil. Origin: Turkey, Lebanon, Israel. Hardiness: −12 to −15 °C. Drought resistance code: 4. Planting density: 9 per square metre.

Veronica polifolia forms a small cushion covered in bright blue flowers in April-May.

The greater periwinkle, *Vinca major*, is an invasive groundcover that thrives in shade or semi-shade.

• **Viburnum tinus**, laurustinus, is a pioneer plant which self-seeds freely at the foot of trees, shrubs and sub-shrubs in the wild parts of the garden, so much so in fact that it is often seen as an invasive plant. It is spread by birds which eat its berries then excrete the seeds as they perch on branches. In our garden we have observed that laurustinus is immune to the anti-germination properties (allelopathy) of Mediterranean shrubs like rosemary, cistus or *Phlomis*: it is one of the few species that can self-seed easily in a bed densely planted with these shrubs, spurring the wild garden's evolutionary passage towards a pre-forest stage. The white flowers appear in winter and early spring. Their pollen is an important source of food for pollinators and beneficial insects such as hoverflies. Origin: Mediterranean Basin. Hardiness: −12 to −15 °C. Drought resistance code: 3. Planting density: 1 per square metre.

• **Vinca major**, the greater periwinkle, puts out long stolons that tend to be invasive. It forms a thick carpet, very ornamental when the plant flowers in spring. This is a useful plant for colonizing large shady or semi-shaded areas, for example on inaccessible slopes. Origin: Western Mediterranean Basin. Hardiness: −15 °C and below. Drought resistance code: 2.5. Planting density: 4 per square metre.

• **Vinca minor**, the lesser periwinkle, is an unbeatable groundcover for shade. The plant spreads by means of its lateral stems which root on contact with the soil. The flowers may be mauve, violet-blue or white depending on the variety. In our garden we grow the cultivar 'La Grave', whose deep violet-blue flowers are especially beautiful. The plant spreads slowly during the first years but in time forms an even groundcover whose dense vegetation limits competition from weeds effectively. In the driest years the foliage dies back and looks sad at the end of summer, but the plant refurbishes quickly thanks to the new shoots which appear with the first autumn rains. To maintain good foliage in summer, the plant can be watered about once a fortnight during the hot period. A striking effect can be achieved by planting the lesser periwinkle together with common ivy (*Hedera helix*) in a shady site that is occasionally mown. This gives a very low-growing groundcover that withstands a moderate amount of foot traffic and in which the delicate flowers of the periwinkle decorate the sombre carpet of ivy in March-April. This mixed carpet could serve as the basis for a planting including taller shade-loving plants, such as *Acanthus mollis* or *Ampelodesmos mauritanicus*. The lesser periwinkle is unfussy as regards soil type. However, it grows faster during the first years in a friable moist soil that has been decompacted to a good depth. Origin: Europe, Southern Russia, the Caucasus. Hardiness: −15 °C and below. Drought resistance code: 3. Planting density: 9 per square metre.

Viola hederacea (Violaceae)

Origin: South-East Australia, Tasmania; **Height of foliage**: 2 to 10 cm depending on cultivation conditions and degree of foot traffic; **Height when in flower**: 10 to 15 cm; **Spread**: 40 cm or more; **Position**: shade or semi-shade; **Hardiness**: −6 to −8 °C; **Drought resistance code**: 1.

A perennial with light green evergreen leaves which makes a good groundcover in mild climates. The plant spreads laterally by means of its rhizomes and its stolons which root from each node. It forms a small carpet that withstands a moderate amount of foot traffic and thrives in shade or semi-shade. The small white flowers with pale mauve throats are perched on fine pedicels. They appear at the beginning of summer and then again in autumn. The plant may sometimes flower all summer long if conditions are sufficiently moist. In periods of drought it becomes dormant and loses its leaves in summer, after which new growth from the rhizomes occurs with the first autumn rains. A more or less weekly watering allows the plant to remain green throughout the year. In Australia, Israel and California, this violet is often used as a single-species carpet to replace lawn in shady situations. Having tried it out in our garden, we believe that the best way to use this pretty plant is probably in mixed plantings. One could make interesting flowering carpets capable of withstanding moderate foot traffic by planting it together with other carpeting plants that like shade, such as *Dichondra repens* or *Glechoma hederacea*. On large areas the mixed carpet could be punctuated by taller perennials such as *Geranium* 'Rambling Robin', *Ajuga reptans*, *Viola odorata* or *Salvia spathacea*. *Viola hederacea* prefers light, well-drained soils. Planting density: 6 per square metre.
Propagation by division in autumn or by cuttings in late winter.

Zoysia tenuifolia (Poaceae)
Mascarene grass

Origin: Mascarene archipelago; **Height**: 2 to 20 cm depending on cultivation conditions and intensity of foot traffic; **Spread**: 50 cm or more, but growth is very slow during the first year; **Position**: sun; **Hardiness**: –12 to –15 °C; **Drought resistance code**: 1.

Zoysia tenuifolia is a very narrow-leaved grass which forms a remarkably thick and soft carpet. It can withstand heavy foot traffic and does not need any mowing in the parts most frequently walked on. By contrast, in the parts that are not much walked on it gradually grows taller and requires an occasional mowing. However, its very thick vegetation makes it hard to mow and the best results are obtained using a powerful professional lawn mower with a spiral blade, of the kind that gardeners do not generally possess. In our experience, *Zoysia tenuifolia* is thus a lawn which should be kept for areas that are regularly walked on, where it requires no mowing. When larger areas are to be covered, *Cynodon* 'Santa Ana' is more suitable: it withstands heavy foot traffic equally well, grows markedly faster, resists drought better and can be mown easily with a normal lawn mower. Nevertheless, for small areas its unique humpy appearance makes *Zoysia tenuifolia* irreplaceable. In spite of its slightly prickly foliage, it wins the vote of children who play on its supple carpet as on a judo mat.

Zoysia tenuifolia is a warm-season or macrothermic grass (see page 41): it turns completely yellow during its period of winter dormancy. In our garden *Zoysia* generally yellows between December and early May.

Although its relatively good resistance to cold would in theory allow *Zoysia* to be planted in regions with harsh winters, the length of its winter dormancy rules it out in non-mediterranean zones.

Zoysia tenuifolia produces a small amount of seed, whose germination is slow and chancy. It spreads above all by its rhizomes, which gradually colonize all available space. Since it is not possible to sow it, young plants raised from cuttings are generally used in gardens. The slow growth of *Zoysia tenuifolia* during the first year means that it requires scrupulous maintenance to prevent it from being swamped by weeds while it is becoming established. Alternatively, it is possible to plant *Zoysia* together with fast-growing perennial groundcovers, whose job it is to provide a preliminary cover, and which will be progressively replaced by the very dense vegetation of the *Zoysia*. One could, for example, mix *Zoysia* with different species of rhizomatous achilleas, such as *Achillea crithmifolia* or *Achillea coarctata*. In our garden we have used a *Zoysia tenuifolia*-*Achillea coarctata* mixture (8 pots of *Zoysia* to 1 pot of *Achillea coarctata*) to create the small patch of lawn that abuts our terrace. The result of this experimental planting exceeded our expectations: from the end of the first year the soil was entirely covered by the mixture of the two plants living successfully side by side, with the achillea at the beginning clearly dominant. For a few years the achillea flowered abundantly through the carpet of *Zoysia*, forming an amazing and very ornamental flowering lawn. Over time the *Zoysia* got the upper hand, gently driving out the achillea which now exists only on the margins where the grass is less dense.

Zoysia tenuifolia withstands salt spray and can be used as a front-line plant beside the sea. It is unfussy about soil type. It grows more rapidly during the first year in a friable, well-drained and thoroughly decompacted soil. In the Montpellier region, *Zoysia tenuifolia* needs a deep watering about once every eight or ten days in order to keep its foliage deep green in summer. Planting density: 9 per square metre.

Propagation by cuttings in spring. Although fairly slow, this method of propagation is easy to carry out; you can produce enough plants to fill a small number of pots every year and then plant the selected area in successive sections. It is also possible to source Zoysia *in the form of turf squares, produced by lawn companies in Italy, Spain and Portugal.*

• **Zoysia japonica** can be distinguished by its broad leaves and rapid growth. During its dormant period in winter the leaves become yellow-brown. It tolerates both salt and high temperatures well. It is relatively greedy of water and requires regular mowing, both of which lessen its advantages over a conventional lawn. Origin: Japan. Hardiness: –12 to –15 °C. Drought resistance code: 1. Planting density: 4 per square metre if pot-grown plants are used, but this grass is generally established from seed.

On a small area, in a part of the garden that receives occasional irrigation, *Zoysia tenuifolia* makes a striking humpy lawn which withstands intensive foot traffic. Here it s planted in combination with *Achillea coarctata*.

Zoysia tenuifolia is a warm-season grass that turns completely yellow during its winter dormancy. Here, the narrow leaves are delicately outlined with hoar frost which sparkles in the light of a February morning.

USEFUL ADDRESSES

The Mediterranean Garden Society
mediterraneangardensociety.org
An international forum devoted to
furthering knowledge and appreciation
of plants and gardens suited to the
mediterranean climate regions of the
world.

Mediterranean Plants and Gardens
medpag.org
Mediterranean Plants and Gardens
is an association for people with
particular interest in the flora and
gardens of Mediterranean climates.

GARDENS
United Kingdom
The Beth Chatto Gardens and Nursery
Elmstead Market
Colchester
Essex CO7 7DB
bethchatto.co.uk

The Savill Garden's Dry Garden
Wick Lane
Englefield Green
Surrey TW20 0UU
theroyallandscape.co.uk

Dry Garden, RHS Hyde Hall
Creephedge Lane
Rettendon
Chelmsford
Essex CM3 8ET
rhs.org.uk

The Desert Wash (Californian plants)
East Ruston Old Vicarage
East Ruston
Norwich
Norfolk NR12 9HN
e-ruston-oldvicaragegardens.co.uk

The Dry Garden, Cambridge
University Botanic Garden
1 Brookside
Cambridge CB2 1JE
botanic.cam.ac.uk

The Mediterranean Dry Garden,
Yorkshire Lavender Gardens
Terrington, York
North Yorkshire YO60 6PB
yorkshirelavender.com

Denmans Garden
Denmans Lane
Fontwell
West Sussex BN18 0SU
denmans-garden.co.uk

Mediterranean style gravel garden,
Knoll Gardens
Hampreston
Wimborne
Dorset BH21 7ND
knollgardens.co.uk

USA
Balboa Park
San Diego CA
balboapark.org/in-the-park/Gardens

San Diego Botanic Garden
Encinitas CA
sdbgarden.org

The Huntington
San Marino CA
huntington.org

Los Angeles County Arboretum and
Botanic Garden
Arcadia CA
arboretum.org

Rancho Santa Ana Botanic Garden
Claremont CA
rsabg.org

San Luis Obispo Botanical Garden
San Luis Obispo CA
slobg.org

University of California Santa Cruz
Arboretum,
Santa Cruz CA
arboretum.ucsc.edu

San Francisco Botanical Gardens
San Francisco CA
sfbotanicalgarden.org

University of California Botanic
Garden at Berkeley
Berkeley CA
botanicalgarden.berkeley.edu

The Ruth Bancroft Garden
Walnut Creek CA
ruthbancroftgarden.org

University of California Davis
Arboretum
Davis CA
arboretum.ucdavis.edu

List of Southern California Gardens:
bewaterwise.com/gardens2visit.html

NURSERIES

United Kingdom

The Beth Chatto Nursery
Elmstead Market
Colchester
Essex CC7 7DB
bethchatto.co.uk

Knoll Gardens
Stapehill Road
Hampreston
Wimborne BH21 7ND
knollgardens.co.uk

Dyson's Nurseries (salvia specialist)
Great Comp Garden
Comp Lane, Platt
Borough Green
Nr Sevenoaks
Kent TN15 8QS
dysonsalvias.com

Downderry Nursery (lavender and
rosemary specialist)
Pillar Box Lane
Hadlow
Tonbridge
Kent TN11 9SW
downderry-nursery.co.uk

Italy

Le Essenze di Lea (specialises in
Salvia and other Lamiaceae, oregano,
phlomis, rosemaries, thymes)
Loc. Martinoni 6
55011 Spianate (LU)
Italy
leessenzedilea.com

USA

Retail:

Annie's Annuals
740 Market Ave
Richmond CA 94801
anniesannuals.com

Australian Native Plants Nursery
Nye Road
Casitas Springs CA 93001
australianplants.com (by appointment)

California Flora Nursery
2990 Somers St
Fulton CA 95439
calfloranursery.com

Cedros Gardens
330 S Cedros Ave
Solana Beach CA 92075
cedrosgardens.com

Cistus Nursery
22711 NW Gillihan Rd
Portland OR 97231
cistus.com

Flora Grubb Gardens
1634 Jerrold Ave
San Francisco CA 94124
floragrubb.com

Mission Hills Nursery
1525 Fort Stockton Drive
San Diego CA 92103
missionhillsnursery.com

Seaside Gardens
3700 Via Real
Carpinteria CA 93013
seaside-gardens.com

Sierra Azul Nursery and Gardens
2660 East Lake Avenue
Watsonville CA 95076
sierraazul.com

Terra Sole Garden Center
5320 Overpass Rd
Santa Barbara CA 93111
terrasol-gardencenter.com

The Dry Garden
6556 Shattuck Ave
Oakland CA 94609
thedrygardennursery.com

Xera Plants
1114 SE Clay St
Portland OR 97214
xeraplants.com

Mail Order Only:
High Country Gardens
highcountrygardens.com

Larner Seeds
larnerseeds.com

Wholesale:
Monterey Bay Nursery
montereybaynursery.com

Native Sons
nativeson.com

San Marcos Growers
smgrowers.com

Suncrest Nurseries
suncrestnurseries.com

Australia

Lambley Nursery and Gardens
"Burnside"
395 Lesters Rd
Ascot, Victoria 3364
lambley.com.au

SEED SUPPLIERS

International

B & T World Seeds
Paguignan
34210 Aigues-Vives
France
b-and-t-world-seeds.com

Specialist seed merchants offering seed mixtures for mediterranean flowering meadows
France

Nova-Flore
ZA des Fontaines
49330 Champigné
France
novaflore.com

Phytosem
ZI Plaine de Lachaup
Châteauvieux
France
phytosem.com

Supplier of bulbs for wild lawns
France

Bulb'Argence
Mas d'Argence
30300 Fourques
France
bulbargence.com

GARDENERS AND LANDSCAPE DESIGNERS IN FRANCE

This list is of course not exhaustive, since many professionals have for the last few years been turning towards the creation of gardens that require less water and less maintenance. I mention here only a brief selection of landscape architects who have been specializing in lawn alternatives for many years.

ADELFO
Jean-Baptiste Pasquet
Le Village
26160 Manas
France
piscines-jardins-naturels.com

Erik Borja
Domaine des Clairmonts
26600 Beaumont-Monteux
France
erikborja.fr

Bruno Demoustier
Pépinière Casa Fiurita
Route de Bastia
20220 L'Ile-Rousse
France
Tel. : 04 95 60 23 81

Florence Hausard
3, place César-Ossola
06130 Grasse
France
Tel. : 04 93 36 96 07

Jardin Gecko
Jean-Jacques Derboux
Route de Sainte-Croix
34820 Assas
France
jardingecko.com

Mouvements et Paysages
Jean-Laurent Felizia
Chemin Val-des-Rêves-d'Ors
Traverse de la Croix-des-Iles
83980 Le Lavandou
France
mouvementsetpaysages.fr

Scape SARL
Helen and James Basson
Le Mas de la Fée
Chemin du Terray
06620 Le Bar-sur-Loup
France
scapedesign.com

USEFUL CONVERSIONS

To Convert Temperature
°C = 5/9 × (°F−32)
°F = (9/5 × °C) + 32

To Convert Length	*Multiply by*
Kilometres to miles	0.62
Metres to yards	1.09
Metres to feet	3.28
Centimetres to inches	0.39
Millimetres to inches	0.04

To Convert Area	*Multiply by*
Square centimeters to square inches	0.155
Square metres to square feet	10.8
Square metres to square yards	1.2
Hectares to acres	2.5
Square kilometres to square miles	0.386

To Convert Weight	*Multiply by*
Grams to ounces	0.035
Kilograms to pounds	2.20

BIBLIOGRAPHY

Borman. F. H., Balmori D. & Geballe G. T., *Redesigning the American Lawn. A Search for Environmental Harmony*, Yale University Press 2001.

Collectif Les Ecologistes de l'Euzière, *Les Salades sauvages. L'Ensalada champanèla*, Les Ecologistes de l'Euzière, 2003.

Daniels S., *The Wild Lawn Handbook, Alternatives to the Traditional Front Lawn*, Macmillan, 1995.

Filippi O., *The Dry Gardening Handbook : Plants and Practices for a Changing Climate*, Thames and Hudson, 2008.

Hobhouse P., *Gardening Through the Ages, An Illustrated History of Plants and Their Influence on Garden Styles – from Ancient Egypt to the Present Day*, Simon & Schuster, 1992.

Jenkins V. S., *The Lawn, A History of an American Obsession*, Smithsonian Books, 1994.

Jones L., *Serre de la Madone*, Actes Sud/Dexia éditions, 2002.

Landsberg S., *The Medieval Garden*, The British Museum Press, 1995.

Lévesque M., *L'Ecopelouse. Pour une pelouse vraiment écologique*, Bertrand Dumond. 2008.

Lloyd C. & Hunningher E., *Meadows*, Timber Press, 2004.

Oudolf P. & Kingsbury N., *Planting Design : Gardens in Time and Space*, Timber Press, 2005

Prévôt P., *Histoire des jardins*, éditions du Sud-Ouest, 2006.

Rackham O. & Moody J., *The Making of the Cretan Landscape*, Manchester University Press, 1996.

Sette R. & Pavia F., *Calades. Les sols de pierre*, Le Bec en l'air, 2008.

Steinberg T., *American Green, The Obsessive Quest for the Perfect Lawn*, W. W. Norton & Company Ltd., 2006.

A PROTOCOL FOR CATEGORIZING INVASIVE GROUNDCOVER PLANTS

We propose a protocol to help decide on the categorization of groundcover plants considered invasive, which recommends restrictions for their use in gardens and public spaces.

This protocol is encapsulated by the following diagram, after Filippi & Aronson, 2010[1]:

EVALUATING AN INVASIVE GROUNDCOVER PLANT

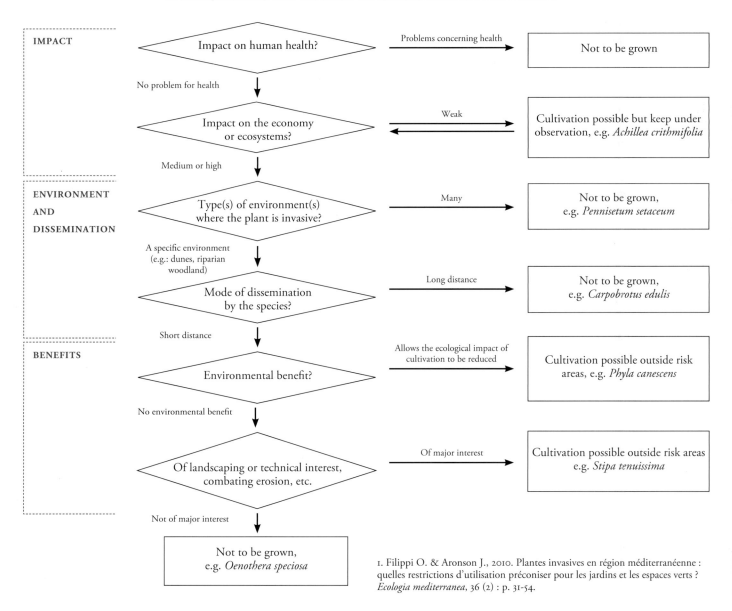

1. Filippi O. & Aronson J., 2010. Plantes invasives en région méditerranéenne : quelles restrictions d'utilisation préconiser pour les jardins et les espaces verts ? *Ecologia mediterranea*, 36 (2) : p. 31-54.

EXAMPLES OF THE CATEGORIZATION OF INVASIVE GROUNDCOVER PLANTS

The three lists below illustrate the use of the protocol to assist in decision making: they give a categorization for a selection of groundcover plants applicable to the gardens of South-West Europe. These plants, some of which are very common in gardens, are taken from the DAISIE database (see europe-alien.org), which lists exotic plants considered to be potentially invasive by different conservation agencies in Italy, Spain, Portugal and France.

1. Examples of groundcover plants to be avoided in all gardens, since they can easily escape from the garden (due to their modes of dissemination over a distance) and spread to an environment or environments where they have a negative impact:

Baccharis halimifolia
Carpobrotus sp.
Cortaderia selloana
Oenothera speciosa
Oxalis pes-caprae
Paspalum vaginatum
Pennisetum clandestinum
Pennisetum setaceum
Solanum elaeagrifolium

2. Examples of groundcover plants to be avoided in gardens that are situated close to various high-risk zones, but which can be grown outside these areas since their mode of dissemination does not allow them to spread far:

SPECIES	ENVIRONMENT NEAR WHICH CULTIVATION SHOULD BE AVOIDED
Phyla canescens	over-grazed salt meadows subject to temporary flooding
Stenotaphrum secundatum (sterile variety)	humid zones near the coast
Stipa tenuissima	over-grazed steppes

3. Examples of groundcover plants considered to be potentially invasive but which can be grown in gardens without any particular restrictions. These plants do not have any negative impacts on biodiversity, the functioning of ecosystems, economic activities or human health.

Acanthus mollis
Achillea crithmifolia
Artemisia pontica
Capparis spinosa
Centaurea cyanus
Cerastium tomentosum
Ceratostigma plumbaginoides
Crepis sancta
Cymbalaria muralis
Delosperma cooperi
Dichondra repens
Erigeron karvinskianus
Erysimum × cheiri
Eschscholzia californica
Gazania rigens
Helichrysum orientale
Iris × germanica
Iris unguicularis
Jasminum nudiflorum
Medicago arborea
Medicago sativa
Origanum majorana
Rhus coriaria
Salvia fruticosa
Salvia sclarea
Santolina chamaecyparissus
Senecio cineraria
Soleirolia soleirolii
Sternbergia lutea
Trachelium caeruleum

INDEX OF PLANT NAMES

Common name entries refer the reader to the botanical name. Where the English common name is very close to the botanical name (for example thyme/*Thymus*), the common name is not listed and the reader should refer directly to the botanical name.

Page numbers in bold text refer to detailed descriptions of plants.

Page numbers in italics refer to plant names mentioned in the captions to illustrations.

Calendula officinalis 16, 153
California poppy, see *Eschscholzia californica*
Campanula portenschlagiana 91
Campion, see *Silene*
Capparis spinosa 164, 233
Caper, see *Capparis spinosa*
Carex halleriana 57, 59, 61, 91, 176, **177**, 191, 202, 220
Carpobrotus acinaciformis 159
Carpobrotus edulis 159, 232
Carpobrotus sp. *160, 160, 200,* 233
Carrot, wild, see *Daucus carota*
Catananche caerulea 115
Centaurea bella *33,* 55, *56,* 56, 61, *74,* 77, 91, 134, *170, 175,* **177**, *177, 186,* 199, *203, 205, 211, 214, 216,* 218
Centaurea cyanus 115, 153, 164, 233
Centaurea scabiosa 213
Centranthus ruber *85,* 87, 91, *101,* 101, 102, 105, *169,* **177**, *183,* 217
Cephalaria leucantha 115
Cerastium candidissimum 37, 80, 83, 91, 174, **178**, *178,* 198, *198,* 202, 211, *225*
Cerastium tomentosum 233
Ceratostigma plumbaginoides 83, 91, **178**, 233
Chamaemelum nobile 53, 56, 58, 61, 77, 91, **178**, *178*
Cheiranthus cheiri, see *Erysimum* × *cheiri*
Chicory, see *Cichorium intybus*
Choisya 'Aztec Pearl' 99
Chrysanthemum coronarium, see *Glebionis coronaria*
Chrysanthemum segetum 115
Cichorium intybus 111, *111,* 115, 123, *123,* 150, 153, 197
Cistus albidus 105, 179, 180
Cistus creticus 105, 180
Cistus creticus 'Calcosalto' 83, 91, **179-180**, *179*
Cistus laurifolius 83, 179
Cistus monspeliensis 86, 105, 180
Cistus salviifolius 'Bonifacio' 91
Cistus × *argenteus* 'Blushing Peggy Sammons' 93
Cistus × *florentinus* 'Tramontane' 83, 99, *119,* **178-179**, *178*
Cistus × *ledon* 99, **179**, 201
Cistus × *pauranthus* 'Natacha' 83, 99, **179**, *179,* 201, 213
Cistus × *pulverulentus* 99, **179**, *179,* 207, *217*
Cistus × *purpureus* 99, 180
Cistus × *skanbergii* 59, 180, 202
Cistus × *tardiflorens* *96,* 99, **179-180**, 194, 201
Cistus × *ultraviolaceus* 180, *181*
Cistus × *verguinii* 208
Cistus × *verguinii* 'Paul Pècherat' 99, 180

Clary sage, see *Salvia sclarea*
Clematis cirrhosa 88, 91, **180**, 192
Clematis flammula 88, 91, *105, 105,* **180**
Clinopodium nepeta subsp. *glandulosum,* see *Calamintha nepeta*
Clover, common lawn, see *Trifolium repens*
Clover, strawberry, see *Trifolium fragiferum*
Cneorum tricoccon 80
Colchicum lusitanum 59, 72, 77, 181, 195
Coleonema album 185
Consolida regalis 115
Convolvulus althaeoides 155, *156*
Convolvulus arvensis 153
Convolvulus cneorum 83, 87, *180,* **181**
Convolvulus sabatius 91, **180**, *180*
Corn cockle, see *Agrostemma githago*
Cornflower, see *Centaurea cyanus*
Coronilla valentina subsp. *glauca* 102, *104,* 105, 176, 183, 197, 209
Coronilla valentina subsp. *glauca* 'Citrina' 209
Coronilla minima 83, 91, 119, **181**, *181*
Cortaderia selloana *159,* 233
Cotula lineariloba 57, 59, 61, 91, **181**, *181*
Crepis sancta 65, 66, 69, *197, 197,* 233
Crepis vesicaria subsp. *taraxacifolia* 153
Crithmum maritimum 200
Crocus goulimyi 25, 59, 71, 77, **181**
Crocus sativus 59, 77, 181
Crocus speciosus 197
Crocus tommasinianus 69, 197
Cyclamen persicum 59
Cyclamen hederifolium 83, 91, **181**
Cymbalaria muralis 87, 91, **181-182**, *182,* 233
Cynodon dactylon 182
Cynodon 'Santa Ana' 41, 43, 44-45, *44,* 46-47, *47,* 58, 89, 91, 138, 142, *142,* 168, **182**, *182,* 225, 227

Dandelion, see *Taraxacum officinale*
Daisy, see *Bellis perennis*
Daffodil, see *Narcissus*
Daucus carota *107,* 111, 115, 123, *123,* 150, 152-3
Delosperma cooperi 83, 91, 183, 233
Dichondra argentea 57, 61, 91, **183**, *183*
Dichondra repens (syn. *Dichondra micrantha*) 53, 58, 61, 134, 135, **182-183**, *183,* 189, 199, 216, 226, 233
Dimorphotheca caulescens **183**
Dittany, see *Origanum dictamnus*

Dittrichia viscosa 105, 153
Dorycnium hirsutum 91, *102*, 102, 105, *169*, 176, 183, *183*, 207
Dorycnium pentaphyllum 105, 119, *119*, *175*, **183**
Drooping brome, see *Bromus tectorum*
Drosanthemum hispidum 83, 91, **183**, *183*, 214
Dymondia margaretae (syn. *Dymondia repens*) 53, 77, 91, **183-184**, *184*

Echium vulgare 115, 153
Epilobium canum 217
Epilobium canum 'Catalina' 195
Epilobium canum 'Western Hills' 98, 99
Eremurus × *isabellinus* 'Pinokkio' *102*
Erysimum × *cheiri* 91, 172, 233
Erica manipuliflora 99, **184**, *184*, 217
Erigeron canadensis 153
Erigeron karvinskianus 77, 86, 87, 91, 105, 153, *161*, **184**, *184*, 185, 198, 233
Erodium trifolium 77, 91, *178*, **184-185**, *185*, 187
Eschscholzia californica 105, 115, *159*, **185**, 192, 214, 233
Euphorbia ceratocarpa 99, **186**, *186*, 208
Euphorbia characias 102, 105, 176, 183, **186-187**, 207
Euphorbia characias subsp. *wulfenii* 83, *102*, 175, 187, *187*, 217, *218*, 219
Euphorbia 'Copton Ash' 83, **186**
Euphorbia cyparissias 57, *85*, 91, 103, *104*, 105, 153, 174, *174*, **187**, *218*
Euphorbia dendroides 99, **187**, *187*, 218-219, *219*
Euphorbia myrsinites 83, *85*, 87, 91, *101*, 105, 185, **187**, *205*, 223
Euphorbia rigida 83, *101*, 105, *145*, *167*, 175, *175*, **185-186**, *185*, *186*, 187, *187*, 189, 192
Euphorbia spinosa 83, **187**, *201*

False Kikuyu grass, see *Stenotaphrum secundatum*
Fennel, see *Foeniculum*
Foeniculum vulgare 101, 104, 105, 111, 115, 152, 197
Frankenia laevis 37, 46, 49, 52, *52*, 53, *55*, *56*, 57, 61, *61*, 67, 128, *128*, 148, 152, 168, **187-188**, *187*, 198, *198*, 204

Galium verum 115
Gaura lindheimeri *101*, 105, 217
Gazania rigens 233
Genista aetnensis *114*, 115
Geranium macrorrhizum 58, 91, 99, **188**, 211
Geranium 'Rambling Robin' 99, **188**, *188*, 226
Geranium sanguineum 33, 77, 91, *183*, 185, **188**, *188*, 189, 198
Geranium × *cantabrigiense* 77, 188

Geranium × *cantabrigiense* 'Biokovo' **188**
Geranium × *cantabrigiense* 'Karmina' 188
Germander, see *Teucrium*
Germander, wall, see *Teucrium chamaedrys*
Glaucium flavum *85*, 91, 105, 110, 115, 187, **188-189**, *189*, 211, 214
Glebionis coronaria 115, *108*
Glechoma hederacea 58, 61, 69, 122, 183, **189**, *189*, 199, 211, 226
Globularia alypum 28, 81, 83, 91, *119*, **189**
Goniolimon speciosum 77, 91, 105, 187, **189**, *199*, 211, 214, 219
Grape hyacinth, see *Muscari*
Grape hyacinth, tasselled, see *Leopoldia comosa*
Ground-ivy, see *Glechoma hederacea*

Halimione portulacoides 122-123, **189-90**
Hartwort, Mediterranean, see *Tordylium apulum*
Hawksbeard, see *Crepis sancta*
Hedera helix 25, 99, 189, **190**, 226
Helianthemum alypoides 187
Helianthemum caput-felis 175
Helichrysum italicum 87
Helichrysum italicum subsp. *serotinum* 91
Helichrysum orientale 28, 83, 91, **190**, *190*, 200, 215, *216*, 233
Helichrysum stoechas 212
Helleborus argutifolius 189
Helleborus lividus subsp. *corsicus*, see *Helleborus argutifolius*
Helminthotheca echioides 149, 153
Herniaria glabra 53, 59, 61, 87, 91, **190**
Hertia cheirifolia 83, 91, **190**
Hieracium pilosella, see *Pilosella officinarum*
Hoary cress, see *Lepidium draba*
Honeysuckle, see *Lonicera*
Hordeum murinum 27
Horned poppy, see *Glaucium flavum*
Hottentot fig, see *Carpobrotus edulis*
Houseleek, see *Sempervivum*
Hyparrhenia hirta 138, **190**
Hypericum aegypticum 91
Hypericum balearicum 99, *146*, 175, 185, **190**, 201
Hypericum empetrifolium 80, 83, 194
Hypericum olympicum 'Citrinum' 83, 91, **191**, *191*
Hypericum perforatum 115

Ipheion uniflorum 191, 197
Ipheion uniflorum 'Rolf Fiedler' 59, *59*, 91, **191**, *191*
Iris, Algerian, see *Iris unguicularis*
Iris, bearded, see *Iris* × *germanica*

Rosmarinus officinalis 'Cap Pertusato' 206, **208**
Rosmarinus officinalis 'Corsican Blue' **208**
Rosmarinus officinalis 'Joyce de Baggio' 206, **208**
Rosmarinus officinalis 'Montagnette' 91, 206, **209**, *209*
Rosmarinus officinalis 'Punta di Canelle' 206, **208**
Rosmarinus officinalis 'Rose de Corse' **208**
Rosmarinus officinalis 'Santa Barbara Blue' 206, **208**
Rosmarinus officinalis 'Sappho' 187, **208-209**, 218
Rosmarinus officinalis 'Sierra de Cazorla' 206, **209**
Rosmarinus officinalis 'Spice Islands' 99, 197, 206, *208*, **209**
Rosmarinus officinalis 'Ulysse' 206
Rosmarinus officinalis 'Vicomte de Noailles' **209**
Rosmarinus × mendizabalii 80, 83, 206, **209**
Rosmarinus × noeanus 83, 206, **209**
Rumex acetosella 115
Rue, see Ruta graveolens
Ruta graveolens 87, 91

Saffron, see Crocus sativus
Salad burnet, see Sanguisorba minor
Salvia 'Allen Chickering' 156
Salvia 'Bee's Bliss' 83, 91, **209**, *209*, 210
Salvia candelabrum 194, 210
Salvia chamaedryoides 83, 168, 195, 217, *219*
Salvia clevelandii 83, 87, 91, 194, 223
Salvia dominica 91
Salvia fruticosa 83, 99, **210**, *210*, 213, *218*, 233
Salvia greggii 217
Salvia interrupta 83, 100, 194, **210**, *210*
Salvia lavandulifolia 83, 91, 211
Salvia lavandulifolia subsp. blancoana 41, 181, *186*, 210
Salvia lavandulifolia subsp. oxyodon 193, 202
Salvia leucophylla 26
Salvia microphylla 99, 217
Salvia multicaulis 77, *134*, **210**, *210*
Salvia officinalis 25, 27, 147, *148*, 210
Salvia pomifera 83, 91, 97, 210
Salvia sclarea 91, 102, 105, 115, 164, 207, 233
Salvia spathacea 58, 91, 189, **211**, *211*, 226
Salvia verbenaca 57, 58, 77, 191, 202, **211**, *211*, 214
Samphire, see Crithmum maritimum
Sanguisorba minor 18, 66, 69, 91, 115, 123, **211**, 225
Santolina benthamiana 175, 186, 212
Santolina chamaecyparissus 99, 164, 212, 233
Santolina magonica 28, 83, 91, 99, *120*, **212**, *212*, 215
Santolina insularis 83, 91
Santolina rosmarinifolia 213

Santolina viridis 91
Santolina viridis 'Primrose Gem' 83, 86, *179*, 212, 213
Santolina × lindavica 83, 99, *105*, *175*, *186*, *193*, 194, 201, 212
Sarcopoterium spinosum 25, 25, 26, 99, 207, **212**, *212*, 213, 220, 220
Satureja thymbra 210
Sages, see Salvia
Scabiosa argentea 77, 91, 211, **212**, 214
Scabiosa cretica 83, 85, *179*, 202, **213**, *213*, 223
Scabiosa hymettia 83, 91
Scabiosa minoana 83, 156, *175*, *205*, **213**, *213*
Sea purslane, see Halimione portulacoides
Securigera varia *105*, **213**, *213*
Sedum album 88, 191, **213**, *214*
Sedum album 'Coral Carpet' **213**
Sedum gypsicola 191, **214-215**, *215*
Sedum ochroleucum 192, **214-215**, *215*
Sedum sediforme 57, 191, **215**, *215*
Sedum sp. *58*, 91, 214
Self-heal, see Prunella vulgaris
Sempervivum arachnoideum 215
Sempervivum calcaratum 215
Sempervivum sp. 87, 91
Sempervivum tectorum 91, 215
Senecio cineraria 233
Senecio inaequidens 151, 153, *162*
Senecio viravira 83, *133*
Shrubby hare's ear, see Bupleurum fruticosum
Sideritis cypria 83, 195
Silene ucrainica **215**, *215*
Silene vulgaris 110, 115
Sinapis alba 66, 115, 153
Sixalix atropurpurea subsp. maritima 115, *145*, 153
Smooth golden fleece, see Urospermum dalechampii
Snapdragon, see Antirrhinum
Solanum elaeagnifolium 233
Soleirolia soleirolii 58, *58*, *59*, 61, *87*, 91, 199, **215-216**, 233
Sonchus sp. 153
Spartium junceum 105
Spring cinquefoil, see Potentilla neumanniana
St John's wort, Cretan, see Hypericum empetrifolium
Stachys byzantina 79, 83, 91, **216**, *216*
Stachys cretica 83, *175*, 195, 223
Star-of-Bethlehem, see Ornithogalum umbellatum
Stenotaphrum secundatum 41, *42*, 43, 44, 45, 46, *47*, 164-165, **216**, 233
Sternbergia lutea 59, *72*, 77, 181, *195*, 214, 233

Sticky fleabane, see *Dittrichia viscosa*
Stipa barbata *30, 31, 71, 77,* **217**, *217*
Stipa calamagrostis *156, 195,* **216-217**, *217*
Stipa gigantea 202
Stipa juncea *77,* **217**
Stipa pennata *77, 115, 217, 218*
Stipa tenuissima *99, 102, 105, 214,* **217-218**, *218, 232, 233*
Stonecrop, Mediterranean, see *Sedum sediforme*
Stonecrop, white, see *Sedum album*

Tanacetum densum *11, 41, 55, 56, 56, 57, 57, 61, 74, 77, 79, 91,*
134, 173-174, 175, 177, 186, 203, 205, 210, **218**, *219*
Taraxacum officinale *17, 21, 22, 55, 64, 64, 65, 66, 67, 69, 113,*
150, 152, 152, 153, 197, 205
Teucrium aureum *77, 91, 196, 219, 225*
Teucrium chamaedrys *57, 58, 77, 176, 191, 219, 220*
Teucrium cossonii *81, 83, 91, 193, 202, 219, 220*
Teucrium divaricatum *83, 219*
Teucrium flavum *91, 104, 105, 176,* **218**, *219*
Teucrium fruticans *95, 99, 172, 197, 208*
Teucrium fruticans 'Agadir' **218-219**, *219*
Teucrium fruticans 'Ouarzazate' *187*
Teucrium lusitanicum *83, 91, 219, 223*
Teucrium luteum *77*
Teucrium marum *57, 83, 86, 87, 91, 218,* **219-220**, *220, 221*
Teucrium montanum *77, 83, 219*
Teucrium × lucidrys *57, 99, 220*
Throatwort, see *Trachelium caeruleum*
Thymbra capitata *25, 83, 210, 215,* **220-221**, *220*
Thymus camphoratus *57, 83, 191,* **223**
Thymus capitatus, see *Thymbra capitata*
Thymus ciliatus *33, 49, 49, 50, 52, 53, 55, 55, 56, 56, 57, 58, 61,*
77, 86, 87, 87, 91, 127, 134, 135, 143, 177, 188, 198, 199, 203,
221, *221*
Thymus glabrescens subsp. *urumovii*, see *Thymus hirsutus*
Thymus herba-barona *53, 56, 58, 61, 77, 188,* **221**
Thymus hirsutus *49, 52, 53, 53, 55, 56, 58, 60, 61, 87, 87, 88, 91,*
188, 197, 203, 215, **221-222**, *221, 222,*
Thymus leucotrichus subsp. *neiceffii* *53, 56, 61, 77, 222*
Thymus mastichina *83, 91,* **223**, *223*
Thymus pannonicus *221, 222*
Thymus praecox *26, 49, 51, 52, 56, 57, 61, 77, 190, 196, 204,*
221, 222, 222
Thymus praecox subsp. *polytrichus* *56, 61, 77, 221,* **222**, *223*
Thymus serpyllum 'Album' *222*
Thymus serpyllum 'Elfin' *49, 53, 59, 61, 87, 87, 88, 91, 130, 190,*
222
Thymus serpyllum 'Lemon Curd' *56, 61, 91, 221, 222*

Thymus vulgaris *57, 58, 83, 176, 202,* **223**
Tordylium apulum *66*
Tordylium maximum *115*
Torilis arvensis *115, 151, 153*
Trachelium caeruleum *91, 233*
Trifolium fragiferum *47, 51, 53, 58, 61, 66, 69, 89, 90, 91, 119,*
128, 138, 153, 155, 168, 182, 196, 203, 204, 211, **224-225**, *224,*
225
Trifolium incarnatum *115*
Trifolium pratense *69, 115*
Trifolium purpureum *115*
Trifolium repens *69, 153,* **225**, *225*
Tripleurospermum inodorum *115, 153*
Tristagma peregrinans 'Rolf Fiedler', see *Ipheion uniflorum*
'Rolf Fiedler'

Urospermum dalechampii *65, 66, 69, 153*

Valerian, see *Centranthus ruber*
Verbascum blattaria *115*
Verbascum phlomoides *115*
Verbascum sinuatum *105, 115*
Verbascum thapsus *115, 153*
Verbena bonariensis *202*
Verbena rigida *46, 83,* **225**
Verbena rigida 'Lilacina' *47, 225*
Veronica filiformis *69*
Veronica polifolia *83, 91, 191, 223,* **225**, *226*
Vetch, see *Vicia cracca*
Viburnum tinus *97, 99, 104, 105, 176, 204,* **226**
Vicia cracca *115*
Vinca major *99,* **226**, *226*
Vinca minor *211,* **226**
Vinca minor 'La Grave' *226*
Viola hederacea *58, 61, 183, 189,* **226**
Viola odorata *226*
Violet, see *Viola odorata*
Virgin's Bower, see *Clematis flammula*

Wall barley, see *Hordeum murinum*
Wallflower, see *Erysimum × cheiri*
Wormseed, see *Ambrosia artemisiifoia*

Yarrow, see *Achillea*

Zoysia japonica **227**
Zoysia tenuifolia *36, 37, 41, 41, 42, 43, 44, 45, 46, 46, 47, 87,*
91, 136, 136, 137, 140, 142, 225, **227**, *227*